KEY TO
INTRODUCTORY HEBREW GRAMMAR

KEY

TO THE EXERCISES IN

THE LATE PROFESSOR A. B. DAVIDSON'S REVISED

INTRODUCTORY HEBREW GRAMMAR

WITH EXPLANATORY NOTES

BY

JOHN EDGAR McFADYEN

B.A.(OXON.), M.A., D.D.

PROFESSOR OF OLD TESTAMENT LANGUAGE, LITERATURE, AND THEOLOGY
UNITED FREE CHURCH COLLEGE, GLASGOW

AUTHOR OF
"THE USE OF THE OLD TESTAMENT"
"THE INTEREST OF THE BIBLE" ETC.

EDINBURGH : T. & T. CLARK, 38 GEORGE STREET

1924

PRINTED IN GREAT BRITAIN BY
MORRISON AND GIBB LIMITED
FOR
T. & T. CLARK, EDINBURGH
LONDON: SIMPKIN, MARSHALL, HAMILTON, KENT, AND CO. LIMITED
NEW YORK: CHARLES SCRIBNER'S SONS

PREFACE.

OPINIONS differ widely with regard to the wisdom and expediency of publishing a Key. Students have their own reasons for welcoming such things, but the first instinct of teachers may well be to protest. They may be honestly afraid that their students will too readily succumb to the temptation to resort to this perilous aid, before they have exercised their own minds to the proper degree upon the often irksome task of translation. It was probably for this reason that the late Professor A. B. Davidson steadily resisted repeated requests to publish a Key to his popular *Hebrew Grammar*.

There is much, however, to be said on the other side. The interests of students in Universities and Theological Colleges are not the only interests to be considered. It is within my knowledge that there are men working in loneliness in many parts of the land—some painfully endeavouring to recapture whatever Hebrew they once knew, others facing the language for the first time with no teacher and no means of readily ascertaining whether the translations which they have so laboriously excogitated are accurate or faulty. To such men a Key, especially if it discussed and explained the difficulties encountered could hardly fail to be a boon.

But even College students may profit from the con-
scientious use of such a help. A friend to whom I showed
the manuscript asked, " But how will you keep it from your
students? " I replied that, so far from desiring to keep it
from them, it would be my hope that they would diligently
use it. One may be permitted to believe that a person
who is old enough to learn Hebrew may be trusted to
bring to his task some measure of conscience and of self-
respect. It is obvious that he must begin by doing his
own work as doggedly and honestly as if the Key were not
in existence. He must make his own experiments and
mistakes, for it is chiefly in this way that he learns where
the difficulties lie, and what to look out for in grammatical
form, syntax and idiom when he reads the literature itself.
Then, having done his best, let him turn to the Key and
carefully compare with it his own translation, resolutely
declining to pass on until he clearly understands the
differences, if there be any.

A bare translation, however, unaccompanied by explanations, would leave the student at many points
unsatisfied. I have therefore appended to each Exercise
a series of Notes that deal with the difficulties, explaining
how the forms are arrived at, emphasizing—sometimes with
deliberate reiteration—the principles on which they rest,
and showing what is erroneous in forms which may appear
plausible. With the Notes I have also interwoven copious
illustrations, drawn from the Old Testament itself, of the
various grammatical and syntactical phenomena as they
emerge; so that any one who resolutely works his way
through these and faithfully consults all the references to

the *Grammar* should, if he takes the trouble to extend his vocabulary, be at the end in a position not only to write tolerable Hebrew prose, but—what is of more importance —to read with comparative ease, and with a real appreciation of the subtler shades of meaning, practically all the prose and much of the poetry of the Old Testament.

The serious student should, however, in addition possess and work through Davidson's *Hebrew Syntax* (T. & T. Clark), which is an invaluable presentation of the main syntactical facts; and as his curiosity in connexion with the verb advances, he ought to supplement this with Driver's *Hebrew Tenses* (Clarendon Press, Oxford). The most satisfactory and illuminating discipline of all is to work thoroughly through some book of the Old Testament whose grammatical and syntactical usages have been carefully discussed by a competent Semitic scholar. Among such books may be warmly recommended Driver's *Notes on the Hebrew Text of the Books of Samuel* (Clarendon Press, Oxford), C. F. Burney's *Notes on the Hebrew Text of the Books of Kings* (Clarendon Press, Oxford), Spurrell's *Notes on the Hebrew Text of the Book of Genesis* (Clarendon Press, Oxford), and T. H. Robinson's *The Book of Amos, Hebrew Text* (S.P.C.K.). The beginner, especially if he has no tutor, would do well to go carefully through the Rev. Duncan Cameron's *First Hebrew Reader* (T. & T. Clark), which is a very helpful inductive study of the Hebrew text of the Book of Jonah. For fuller explanations of ordinary forms than are to be found in the shorter *Grammars*, and for adequate discussion of the rarer forms, Cowley's translation of *Gesenius' Hebrew Grammar, as edited and enlarged by the late E. Kautzsch* (Clarendon Press, Oxford), will always be consulted with profit.

The judicious use of the Key by students will, it is hoped, leave the teacher of the Old Testament more free to devote himself to his proper task of initiating them into the meaning and range of that great literature, with its multitude of religious, historical, literary and critical problems. As things are, he is tempted, and almost obliged, to devote a disproportionate amount of effort to the purely linguistic aspect of his work, and to leave too little time for his larger task of interpreting the literature in a way which will quicken the minds of his students and react fruitfully upon the practical work of their later ministry, of which preaching constitutes so large a part. If, by the help of the Key, students can be brought to do most of the linguistic work for themselves, the teacher is to that extent relieved for other and more important tasks; and if he has any doubt of the fidelity of their work or the accuracy of their knowledge, he can put these to an occasional test by devising for translation supplementary sentences of his own.

The Notes should be gone over very carefully at least twice, as, in the nature of the case, some of the earlier illustrations found there can hardly be fully intelligible until the later sections are mastered. On a second reading, however, the whole should be luminous; and this will have the further advantage of furnishing the student with an opportunity of testing the accuracy of his knowledge of the Grammar as a whole. Whatever value the Key may possess will be doubled to the student who will take the additional trouble of translating the Hebrew sections of it back into English and the English into Hebrew. On pages 137–145 are Indices, which will enable him to find with ease any Note he may desire to consult.

I desire to express my very deep sense of obligation to the Rev. Duncan Cameron, B.D., Director of Religious Instruction, Provincial Training College, Edinburgh, and Assistant to the Professor of Hebrew, Edinburgh University, for his great kindness in helping me with the proof-sheets. He has read them with extraordinary care, and out of his wide and intimate knowledge of the language and his large and successful experience in teaching, he has enriched the Notes at many points and in many ways with very valuable suggestions, most of which I have incorporated and all of which I herewith gratefully acknowledge.

ROBIN HOOD'S BAY,
YORKSHIRE, 28th August 1924.

REFERENCES AND ABBREVIATIONS.

(*a*) Where the sign § appears alone, the reference is to the
paragraph in the Grammar (Twenty-second Edition,
et seq.) indicated by the number that follows.

(*b*) The letters A and B (occasionally also C, and twice D)
indicate the different sections set for translation
within the same paragraph of the Grammar. They
are used throughout the Key simply to facilitate
reference in the Notes to earlier (or later) Notes
where the same or similar phenomena are discussed.

(*c*) *Syntax*, by itself, stands for A. B. Davidson's *Hebrew
Syntax* (T. & T. Clark).

(*d*) G.K. stands for Cowley's translation of *Gesenius-
Kautzsch's Hebrew Grammar* (Clarendon Press,
Oxford).

(*e*) *BDB* stands for Brown, Driver and Briggs, *A Hebrew
and English Lexicon of the Old Testament* (Clarendon
Press, Oxford).

KEY TO
INTRODUCTORY HEBREW GRAMMAR.

§ 1.

A.

b y th,[1] d bh r, y r dh, y r kh, g n bh, z q n, y m ṭ, ṭʿm, mʿṭ, ʿç h,
h ḥ sh kh, q ç ph,[2] m gh n, m y m, r ç ḥ, k nʿn, ʾth h, ʾz n.

[1] The transliteration byθ, dβr, yrδ, yrχ, etc., would be better, because
less ambiguous, as *th* might, in certain circumstances, represent תה (e.g.
tʿhôm תהום *the deep*: for ו=ô see § 2. 3 c) ; but the system adopted has
the advantage of avoiding Greek letters.

[2] The next word (which should appear as כפים and be transliterated
k pp y m) may here be passed over, as it cannot be understood till we
reach § 7. 4 (cf. § 43).

B.

יב, ב, ל, לם, מל, סט, סט, שן, לך, גד, דג, קום, רץ, כף, צו, הם,
מס, מט, עץ, רע, אם, יין, נגן, מים, עופף, חמס, ציץ, תמם:

[1] So, rather than בה, for the reason given in the preceding note.
But *bh*, if a vowel came between the *b* and the *h*, would have to be
בה, as in בהן *bōhen*, thumb.

§ 2.

A.

mâ, mê *or* mî, mêmê *or* mêmî *or* mîmê *or* mîmî, lê *or* lî, lô
or lû, lên *or* lîn, lôn *or* lûn, shêrô *or* shîrô *or* shêrû *or* shîrû,
qômâ *or* qûmâ, lôlê *or* lûlê *or* lôlî *or* lûlî, shêrôth *or* shîrôth
or shêrûth *or* shîrûth, hênêq *or* hênîq *or* hînêq *or* hînîq,
hôshêʿâ *or* hûshêʿâ *or* hôshîʿâ *or* hûshîʿâ, ṣôṣêm *or* ṣûṣêm *or*

ṣôṣîm *or* ṣûṣîm, hôrêthê *or* hôrîthê *or* hôrêthî *or* hôrîthî *or any one of these four forms with* hû *in the first syllable instead of* hô, qôl *or* qûl, qôlôthênô *or* qôlôthînô *or* qôlôthênû *or* qôlôthînû *or any one of these four forms with* û *in either or both of the first two syllables instead of* ô, ʿôph *or* ʿûph, hôbhêshô *or* hôbhîshô *or* hôbhêshû *or* hôbhîshû *or any one of these four forms with* hû *in the first syllable instead of* hô, hêlêlê *or* hêlîlê *or* hêlêlî *or* hêlîlî *or any one of these four forms with* hî *in the first syllable instead of* hê, hôlêkhô *or* hôlîkhô *or* hôlêkhû *or* hôlîkhû *or any one of these four forms with* hû *in the first syllable instead of* hô, nâ.

All the alternative forms given above are theoretically possible, but in point of fact the actual forms are seldom more than two (*e.g.* mê, *the waters of*, § 17, and mî, *who?* § 13. 3, are real words) and usually only one, *e.g.* hêlîlî, *howl*, 2nd sing. fem. imperative. It would serve no good purpose, however, at this stage to indicate the forms in actual use and to rule out the others, as the reasons for this can only be understood as our knowledge of the language advances. Naturally the transliterated words in the rest of the Exercise, as printed in the Grammar, are real Hebrew words.

Note that the vowels in the above Exercise are all marked with the circumflex accent. This is because they are consonantally represented, and they are so represented because they are pure or naturally long vowels, and therefore unchangeable. To mark them with a horizontal stroke above (e.g. *ā*) instead of with a circumflex accent (*â*) would imply that they were merely tone-long vowels, in which case they would not have had consonantal representation.

B.

קוּם, קוֹם, שִׁיר, שִׁירִים, סוּס, סוּסוֹתֵינוּ, קוּץ, לִי, לוֹ, לוּ, מִי,
מֵשִׁיב¹, מוּת, הֵילִיל, חוּל, חִילָה, הוֹצִיא, צִיף, מֵיקִיץ², טוּבִי,
נִירִי, הוֹשִׁיבוּ, הוֹלִיכוּ, לוּלִי, מֵינִיקוֹתֵינוּ:

¹ This transliterates *mêshîbh* which, however, has been inadvertently retained from former editions (as no such word exists) and should be replaced either by *môshîbh* מוֹשִׁיב (Hiph. ptc. of יָשַׁב, § 39. 2) or by *mêshîbh* מֵשִׁיב (Hiph. ptc. of שׁוּב, § 40. 3 a).

² This word, like that in Note 1, should really appear as *mêqîç*, and be transliterated by מֵקִיץ, as the first vowel is only tone-long (*Grammar*, p. 152, 2 (7), and § 40. 3 a).

§ 3.

A.

yādh, gêr, ḥēn, ḥōq, gam, ʿal, sûm, ʾim, ʾaph, ʿᵃbhōdh, bᵉkhâ, dōbh, çar, çârâ, ʿîr, ʾᵉkhōl, ḥᵃzaq, ʾᵃsher, rᵉphōs, shôphēṭ, qûm, rāç, rûç, hᵃgham, wāw, dᵉbhar, ʾᵉmeth.

The short vowels are left unmarked in transliteration ; the naturally long vowels, which are consonantally represented, have the circumflex accent ; the merely tone-long vowels are marked by a horizontal stroke above them. In one of the above words (נֵר) a vowel that etymology shows to be naturally long (hence *ê*) would be almost inevitably mistaken for a tone-long vowel (*ē*), the more so, as it has no consonantal representation (it is not נִיר).[1] Again there is nothing to indicate that in צָרָה the first vowel is unchangeably long (*â*, not *ā*). These difficulties will be cleared up later (נֵר in § 41. 1 a, and צָרָה in § 43. 2) and need not now detain us.

The *ô* in *shôphēṭ* (which is the regular form of the active participle) is unchangeably long. It is written sometimes with, and sometimes without, consonantal representation : cf. § 21. 3. It has to be remembered that the naturally long vowel, while it very frequently has consonantal representation, does not have it invariably or inevitably. When, therefore, the vocalic consonant is omitted, only a knowledge of forms, to be acquired later, enables us to decide whether the vowel in question is pure long or tone-long.

---

[1] This form only appears once—in 2 Chr. 2¹⁶.

B.

גַּם, בּוֹר, בּוֹשׁ, שׁוּב, שִׁיר, שׁוֹר, שָׁם, חֹק, אִם, עָם, כֹּל, קוֹל, עָם, הַר, רֹב, רוּץ, הָרַג, צֵל, חֵיק, מָשָׁל, מְשָׁל, קוֹטֵל, שָׁלוֹם, יָרוּץ, קוֹמַם, פְּעָלוֹ, אָסֹף, הֶחֱזִיק:

In the above transliterations the vowel with circumflex accent, as indicating an unchangeably long vowel, has been invariably represented by the appropriate vocalic consonant. In actual Hebrew usage, however, as has been said above, this is not invariable. But it is well for beginners to mark in this way the distinction between a pure or naturally long (and therefore unchangeable) vowel, and a tone-long vowel. The latter does not deserve or receive consonantal representation.

§ 4.

קוּם, קוֹם, שִׁיר, שִׁירִים, סוּס, סוּסוֹתֵינוּ, קוֹץ, לִי, לוֹ, לוּ, מֵי,
¹מֵישִׁיב, מוֹת, הֵילִיל, חוּל, חִילָה, הוֹצִיא, צִיף, ²מֵיקִיץ, טוֹבֵי,
נִירִי, הוֹשִׁיבוּ, הוֹלִיכוּ, לוּלֵי, מֵינִיקוֹתֵינוּ :

¹ See Note 1 of § 2 B. The actual word is מֵשִׁיב (*mēshîbh*).
² See Note 2 of § 2 B. The actual word is מֵקִיץ (*mēqîç*).

§ 5.

A.

In the following transliterations vocal sh^ewa has been counted as a syllable.

’^e-lô-hîm, h̯°-lî, h̯ª-môr, ’ª-rî, mer-ḥāq, hª-lā-hēn, nish-q^e-lû, m^e-çaph-ç^e-phîm, qam-nû, q^e-çîr, lā-’ª-nā-shîm, hoq-t^e-lâ,¹ hiq-ṭîl, yapht.

¹ The first vowel of הַקְטְלָה, as it is the vowel of a short and un-accented syllable (the accented syllable here, as usually, is the *final* one), must be *short*, therefore o, not ā.

B.

קוֹטֵל, קָם, אֶכְתֹּב, מָקוֹם, וְלוֹ, מִזְמוֹר, קְטָלוֹ, שָׁמַיִם, קוּמוּ,
לְמִינֵהוּ, וּלְיָמִים, יֶרֶק, לִלְקֹט, לִמְלָכָה, לְשָׁלוֹם, שְׁמוֹנִים, שְׁנֵי,
מְקוֹמֵי, יוֹרְשִׁים, נִלְחַם, יִשְׂרָאֵל, שְׁמוֹ, נַעַר, הַמּוֹרִים, לְאָסֹף,
עֲמָלֵנוּ :

Here, as in § 3, the vowel with the circumflex accent, being un-changeably long, has uniformly received consonantal representation.

The word וּלְיָמִים *ûl^eyāmîm*, which seems to violate the rule that every Hebrew word or syllable must begin with a consonant, § 2. 3 a, is justified by the principle explained in § 15. 1 c, where it is shown that in certain circumstances the conjunction וְ (*and*) is pointed as וּ.

§ 6.

A.

לְבָבִי, מִדַּבָּרִים, זְקֵנִים, חֲדָשִׁים, כּוֹכָבִים, קְטָלוֹ, קְטַלְתֶּם,
קְטָלָנוּ, ¹קְטַלְנוּ, סְפָרִים, עֲנָבִים, צִדְקָתֵנוּ, דְּבָרֶיהָ, גְּדוֹלִים,
הַקִּימוֹתֶם, ¹שָׁמַיִם, חָכְמָה, אֲלָפִים, תָּשׁוּב, יָקִים :

¹ Notice, in connection with the words קְטַלְנוּ and שָׁמַיִם, why the
sheʷa cannot stand as the vowel of the first syllable. The rule is *not*
that the sheʷa is the proper vowel in the open syllable two places from
the *end* of the word, but two places from the *tone*, § 6. 2 (c) i. In
these words, however, it is indicated that the tone falls on the *penult*.
The vowel of the first syllable is therefore in the *pre*-tone ; and the rule
—which it is of fundamental importance to observe carefully—applies,
that the pretonic vowel, if open, is *long*, § 6. 2 b, and therefore in both
cases ָ , not ְ .

§ 7.

גַּם, כֹּל, דָּם, אֵת, בֵּן, מוֹת, פַּת, כַּף, כְּלֶב, תִּכְתֹּב, כָּתַבְתָּ,
בְּכוּ, לְבַד, דָּבָר, ¹בְּלֶכְתְּךָ, מִשְׁפָּט, מִדַבָּר, בָּתוֹךְ, מַלְכִּי, יַבְדֵּל,
כּוֹכָבִים, כְּבַדְתֶּם, תִּכְבְּדִי, ¹כַּסְפָּה, ¹חֶלְקָה, מִדַּבְּרֵיכֶם, ²לָרֶדֶת,
יֵרְבְּ, ³יֵבְךְ, גְּדוֹלִים, וְתָגֶל :

¹ See *Grammar*, p. 12, footnote 2.
² The accent in רֶדֶת is on the penult ; hence the vowel of the first
syllable, which is pre-tonic and open, is long. See Note 1 of Exercise
6 A.
³ Note that when, as here, final *kaph* with *sheʷa* (§ 3. 4 a) is not preceded by a vowel, it takes *daghesh lene*, just as ב would do (see preceding
word יֵרְבְּ).

²מְבַקְשִׁים, חַלּוֹן, הַמַּיִם, ²וַיִּנָּגְפוּ, לְמַדֶּת, דִּבֶּר, מִדַבָּר, סָפְדוּ,
מִסְפֵּד, בְּכַסְפְּכֶם, שָׁבַת, מִבְּנֵי, צִפּוֹר, יְכַתֵּב, בְּקָצְרְכֶם, בַּדָּם,
בּוֹדֵד, יִתְּנוּ, לְבַדּוֹ :

¹ The custom, however, is to omit the *daghesh forte* from the ק in
this and similar words, when written to a *sheʷa*, § 7. 5.
² The strict transliteration would be *way-yin-nā-ghᵉ-phû*. It could

not be read as *way-yin-nogh-pû*, for the ֶ, if read as a *short* vowel (*o*), would imply that the syllable was *closed*, and this would necessitate the insertion of a *daghesh lene* in the פ at the beginning of the next syllable. As there is no *daghesh lene*, the *sh^ewa* must be vocal : consequently נֶגְ must not be read as a closed syllable (*nogh*), but as *nă-gh^e*.

§ 8.

בֶּאֱמֹר, אֲבַדְתֶּם, אֱמֹר, יִשְׁחָטוּ, חֲזַק, שָׁלֹוחַ, הִשְׁלִיחַ, שָׁמֹעַ, שֹׁמֵעַ, רֶגַע, יֶהְפֵּךְ, בְּרַד, שָׁרִים, ¹הֶחֱזִיק, טַעֲמוּ, כֶּאֱמֶת, נֶאֱמַר, לֶחֳלִי, לַאֲרִי, בַּחֲמֹר, מָעֳמָד, יַעֲמֹד, ²יַעַמְדוּ:

¹ Usually, however, ח (at the end of a syllable) takes the simple, silent sh^ewa rather than the composite.

² Both sh^ewas in יַעַמְדוּ are sounded—the first, obviously, as it is composite (=ᵃ), and the second no less obviously ; for if it were silent, the ד would require a daghesh (דּ), § 7. 2 b. But two sounded sh^ewas must not come together, § 6. 2 d ; the first must be raised to a full vowel. Under a guttural, the full vowel will naturally be the one corresponding to the composite *sh^ewa*, § 6. 2 (d) ii. In other words, ֲ here will be replaced by ַ, and the result will be יַעַמְדוּ.

§ 9.

q^erû'âw, 'al, lô', ûbhêthô, nôl^edhû,¹ yîṭabh, ç^ebhā'ôth, bā'û, bārā', b^erē'shîth, 'er'ê² liqra'th,³ yishmā'ēl,⁴ mâthayim,⁵ sā'ûnî, sh^elômô,⁶ b^eyāmâw, tighlênâ,⁷ yaqnî'ûhû,⁶ millêthîw,⁸ kāṣûy, shālēw, gôy, qaw, 'ᵃdhônāy,⁶ râshîm,⁹ bo'shô,¹⁰ k^elāyôth, lûlê, qônê.¹¹

¹ The absence of the daghesh from ד shows that the preceding sh^ewa must be sounded, § 7. 2 b.

² This transliteration cannot be fully understood till we reach § 44, and the student need not perplex himself with it at this stage. Suffice it here to see that the ה is not a genuine letter of the root (which appears in the Dictionary as רָאָה), but a mere vowel sign, here representing, as it occasionally does, a long *e* (*Grammar*, p. 12, footnote 1). For ֶ as a long vowel, see *Grammar*, p. 25, small print in middle of page. The ה, which came to be wrongly regarded as part of the root, should not be transliterated, as it is not consonantal.

Much could be said for the transliteration, adopted by some German scholars, of ֳ by *ä* (here *'er'å̆*). This would enable us to distinguish between הָ ֳ (or יָ ֳ)=*å̆*, and הָ ֵ (or יָ ֵ)=*ê*, and so to avoid confusion. The form הָ ֳ is not common. This form, and הָ ֵ (see the last word of the Exercise) are chiefly found in verbs which have ה for their last letter, § 44. 1, and in nouns derived from them, § 45. 3.

³ The sh^ewa is silent, for a reason to be explained later, § 21. 2 (a) ii.

⁴ This proper name (Ishmael) is strictly a sentence of two words (יִשְׁמַע אֵל = *God hears*) in which the א has obviously (§ 5. 5) consonantal value. But when treated as a single word, the last syllable begins with ע, and the א, which has no longer consonantal value, may be omitted in transliteration.

⁵ The א here has no consonantal value, though it obviously has in the sing. of the word (מֵאָה) of which this is the dual (*Grammar*, p. 165, no. 200).

⁶ The first *o* in שְׁלֹמֹה, the *o* in אֲדֹנָי, and the *u* under the א in יַקְנִיאֵהוּ are all, for satisfactory philological reasons, naturally long, though they do not happen to be here represented by the consonantal *waw* (שְׁלֹמֹה never seems to be so represented). Hence *ô* and *û* rather than *ō* and *ū*.

The second *o* in שְׁלֹמֹה is represented by ה. This is rare (*Grammar*, p. 12, footnote 1).

⁷ For יָ ֳ = *ê* (or *å̆*), see Note 2, esp. last paragraph : also *Grammar*, p. 25, small print in middle of page.

⁸ The א (though part of the root) has *here* no consonantal value. If it were treated consonantally (*mille'thîw*) we should have the anomaly of a long vowel in a closed unaccented syllable (the accent falls on the last syllable). The *çere*, which may seem strange accompanying the א, will be understood when we reach § 38. 1 (3) a.

⁹ See Note 5 : also *Grammar*, p. 137, line 8.

¹⁰ The ֳ is *o*, not *å̆*, as it is the vowel of the short unaccented syllable.

¹¹ Here, as in אֲרָאֶ above, the ה should not be transliterated, as it has no consonantal value (see Note 2).

§ 11.

A.

1. The night and the day.   2. The man and the woman. 3. The great darkness.   4. The firmament is high.   5. The

silver is good.   6. The evening and the morning.   7. The darkness is great upon the waters.

The man is good.   8 טוֹב הָאִישׁ׃

The great day.   9 הַיּוֹם הַגָּדוֹל׃

B.

‏1 הַיּוֹם׃ 2 הַבֹּקֶר׃ 3 הַלַּיְלָה׃ 4 הָאוֹר טוֹב or טוֹב הָאוֹר׃

‏5 הָאוֹר הַטּוֹב׃ 6 [1]הָרָקִיעַ הָרָם׃ 7 הָאִישׁ [2]וְהָאִשָּׁה׃ 8 גָּדוֹל

‏[3]הַחֹשֶׁךְ or הַחֹשֶׁךְ גָּדוֹל׃ 9 הָאִישׁ הַטּוֹב׃ 10 יוֹם גָּדוֹל׃

‏11 טוֹב [4]הַזָּהָב or הַזָּהָב טוֹב׃ 12 הֶעָפָר [5]עַל־הַמַּיִם׃

[1] At this early stage it might seem superfluous to insert the *methegh* (§ 10. 2 a), as a knowledge of the grammar is so much more important than a knowledge of the accents. But in reality it is well worth while to accustom ourselves, from the beginning, to insert this accent, at the points where it would appear in the printed text. For, besides helping us to appreciate the rhythm of the language, it compels us to ask ourselves where the accent falls, and to note, as we learn the vocabulary, any cases which do not conform to the general rule that the accent is on the last syllable, § 5. 1 a. Without accurate knowledge of the syllable on which the accent falls, it is impossible to write Hebrew accurately. Read § 5. 1 and § 10. 2 a carefully.

[2] Note that the word for *woman* is not אִישָׁה but אִשָּׁה, the double שׁ representing a lost *n* (see p. 153). אִישָׁהּ with the point called *mappîq* in the ה (§ 7. 8) would mean *her husband* (§ 19. 2, p. 68).

Note again the *methegh* in the *open* syllable *two* places from the tone.

[3] We do not here write הַחֹשֶׁךְ. The accent falls on the *first* syllable of חֹשֶׁךְ (*hō*)—words of this kind, which seem to be an exception to the general rule of the accent, § 5. 1 a, will be clearly understood when we reach § 29 ; therefore, though the syllable with the article (הַ) is open, it does *not* take the methegh, as it does not stand *two* places from the tone, but in the *pre-tone*, and the vowel in the pre-tone is in no danger of being "hurried over," § 6. 2 a; *Grammar*, p. 39, lines 4 and 5.

[4] Here again we do not write הַזָּהָב, for the vowel of the first syllable, which is a *closed* syllable, is obviously in no danger of being "hurried over."

[5] The perpendicular stroke accompanying the ָ in מִיַם could not be the *methegh*, as this is the accent for the vowel of the open syllable *two places from the tone*. The stroke here accompanies the vowel of the *tone itself*, מַיִם being accented on the penult, *máyim*. It is an accent

which regularly appears at the end of a verse, and indicates pause : if the accented vowel at the end happens to be short, it becomes in this position long, § 10. 4 a ; *i.e.* ˍ becomes ˍ. The sign is known as *ṣillûq* (*Grammar*, p. 71, footnote 1, and p. 230, 2 a), and it is inserted throughout the Exercises *in places where the vowel is in this way affected*. Thus we do not trouble to write מִדְבָּר (with *ṣillûq*) at the end of a sentence (though it would so appear in the printed editions), because the vowel is not affected ; but we do write מָיִם, because, in any other place than pause, this would be written מַיִם.

There is never any possible confusion between *methegh* and *ṣillûq*, the latter always being on the tone, the former two places from the tone. In הָאָרֶץ (at the end) the ˌ must be *ṣillûq* ; הָאָרֶץ would be impossible, as *methegh* could not stand in the pre-tone. In הָאָדָם the stroke under the ה is *methegh*, and that under the ד is *ṣillûq*.

§ 12.

A.

1. The palace is lofty. 2. The mountain is very high. 3. The evening is good. 4. Thou art God.[1] 5. Thou art the woman. 6. The sword is on the dust. 7. The good servant. 8. A tall and great people. 9. The people are very powerful. 10. The hand and the eye. 11. The heavens and the earth. 12. The powerful and great[2] people. 13. I am the wise man.

The man is wise	חֲכַם הָאִישׁ׃	14
The sore disease	[3]הֳחֳלִי [4]הָרָע׃	15

[1] The article before אלהים suggests *the one true God*; the contest on Carmel between Yahweh and the Phœnician Baal ends with the triumphant words יְהוָה הוּא הָאֱלֹהִים " *Yahweh is* (the true) *God*" (1 Kings 18[39] : cf. 2 Chr. 33[13]). But when the article is omitted the word has, in general, just the same meaning ; in this case, however, it is regarded as practically a proper name.

[2] Notice that the article is repeated in Hebrew before the second adjective.

[3] Notice the *methegh* in the syllable second from the tone, the composite shᵉwa, which is vocal, counting as a syllable, § 10. 2 b and c.

[4] As this is not a sentence, but only a phrase, it is hardly worth while giving עַר, though final, the pausal vowel and accent עָר. In the sub-

sequent Exercises this practice will be maintained in the case of phrases as distinct from sentences.

It is only fair, however, to point out that, even when not pausal, הרע is very frequently pointed הָרָע ; *e.g.* Exod. 33⁴ *and the people heard* אֶת־הַדָּבָר הָרָע הַזֶּה *this word*: cf. Deut. 13¹² (though the same phrase is written in Deut. 17⁵ with הָרָע).

B.

הָעַיִן ‏1 : הַיָּד ‏2 : הָהָר רָם מְאֹד הוּא ‏1 3 : הֶעָפָר עַל־
הַמַּיִם הוּא ‏5 : אֲנִי הָאִישׁ ‏6 : אֲנַחְנוּ הָעָם ‏7 2 הַחֶרֶב :
הָאִישׁ הַטּוֹב הוּא הָאִישׁ הֶחָכָם ‏9 : הָעָם הַטּוֹב וְהֶעָצוּם ‏8 :
הַבֹּקֶר וְהָעֶרֶב הֵם הַיּוֹם ‏11 : הַחֹשֶׁךְ הוּא ‏3 הַלַּיְלָה ‏10 :
הָהָר הַגָּדוֹל וְהָרָם ‏13 : 4 הַחֹשֶׁךְ גָּדוֹל מְאֹד עַל־הָאָרֶץ ‏12
וְעַל־הַשָּׁמָיִם ‏14 : אַתָּה הָאִישׁ ‏15 : הֵם ‏5 הַשָּׁמַיִם ‏16 : הָאֶבֶן :

¹ Or simply רם מאד ההר.

² No *methegh* with the *a*, as it stands *immediately* before the tone (חֶרֶב *ḥérebh*).

³ *Pathaḥ* under the first ל lengthened to *qameç* in pause, § 10. 4 a.

⁴ For the omission of הוּא cf. the similar sentence in Exod. 11³ הָאִישׁ מֹשֶׁה גָּדוֹל מְאֹד בְּאֶרֶץ מִצְרַיִם *the man Moses was very great in the land of Egypt.* So 1 Kings 1⁴ וְהַנַּעֲרָה יָפָה עַד־מְאֹד *and the maid was very fair.*

⁵ No *methegh* with the vowel *a*, because, though the syllable is second from the tone, it is *shut*, § 10. 2 a.

§ 13.

A.

1. Who are ye? 2. This mountain is very high. 3. That night. 4. This is the day which God made.¹ 5. This powerful people. 6. This is the boy who heard the voice. 7. Who has borne these?² 8. The king sat upon the dust. 9. The man came,³ who had⁴ poured the water upon the ground. 10. How good is this day! 11. God

created the [5] heavens and the earth.   12. And one called [6]
to another and said, Holy is Yahweh.

The king took the sword   : לָקַח הַמֶּלֶךְ אֶת־הַחֶרֶב   13

This is the wise king   : זֶה הַמֶּלֶךְ הֶחָכָם   14

[1] Note that in the subordinate, as in the principal, clause, the verb
usually precedes the subject, § 13. 6.

[2] The question asked by Mother Zion, as she welcomes back from
exile, with wonder in her eyes, the multitude of her scattered children;
she hardly dares to believe they are really her own. Isa. 49²¹.

[3] בָּא means primarily *came in*, then (secondarily, though very
frequently) simply *came*.

[4] Hebrew has no plupf. The pf. does duty for both, § 46. I. 1 a 3.

[5] אֵת is more frequently written with the *maqqēph* (אֶת־), § 10. 3 b.
The un-hyphened form here, by slowing down the pace, imparts additional
impressiveness and dignity to the opening words of Genesis.
Note the repetition of אֵת (§ 13. 7 b) as well as of the article, with
both words.

[6] In strict grammar, this rather means, "and one *kept calling* . . .
and saying," etc. (Isa. 6³). With this idiom, however, the beginner need
not meantime trouble himself. The grammar involves the frequentative
idea, like the Latin or Greek impf. ; but, as the reason for this cannot be
understood till we reach § 23. 3 (cf. § 21. 3 b (*b*)), the above translation
may be accepted provisionally. Or more idiomatically "they called (*or
rather* kept calling) *to one another*." זֶה . . . זֶה is one of the Hebrew
devices for expressing the reciprocal pronoun.

B.

1 מִי אֵלֶּה : 2 מָה אַתֶּם : 3 מִי הָאִשָּׁה הַזֹּאת : 4 אֲנִי

הַמֶּלֶךְ הַגָּדוֹל אֲשֶׁר עַל־הָאָרֶץ : 5 הַיּוֹם הַגָּדוֹל הַהוּא :

6 זֶה רֹאשׁ טוֹב : 7 זֶה הָרֹאשׁ הַטּוֹב : 8 טוֹב הָרֹאשׁ הַזֶּה :

9 הָרֹאשׁ הַטּוֹב הַזֶּה : 10 זֶה הַיֶּלֶד הָרַע אֲשֶׁר שָׁפַךְ ¹אֶת־

הַמַּיִם עַל־הָאָרֶץ : 11 מֶה עָשָׂה הָאִישׁ : 12 מָה אֵלֶּה :

13 אֵלֶּה הַשָּׁמַיִם וְהָאָרֶץ אֲשֶׁר ²בָּרָא אֱלֹהִים ³הַיּוֹם :

14 הֶחָלִי הַגָּדוֹל ⁴וְהָרַע הַהוּא : 15 יָשַׁב עַל־הַמַּיִם ⁵הָהֵם :

16 מַה־גָּדוֹל הַהֵיכָל הַהוּא :

[1] It is well to accustom oneself, in composition, to use אֵת with the
definite accusative, as in prose it accompanies the accus. *very frequently*,

though not invariably : in poetry, however, it is commonly dispensed with.

² See Note 1 in section A of this Exercise.

³ In "this day," it is not necessary to express the *this* ; see § 11, line 7. Cf. Deut. 30¹¹·¹⁵·¹⁶ where in each case הַיּוֹם is equivalent to *this day*, and is so rendered in A.V. and R.V. Of course הַיּוֹם הַזֶּה is also correct, though not so common (cf. Josh. 3⁷).

⁴ Or הָרָע : see Note 4 (2nd paragraph) of Exercise 12 A.

⁵ Not הָהֵם : see § 13. 1, last line.

§ 14.

A.

1. God called the light day,¹ and the darkness he called night. 2. God rested on the seventh day from the work which he had made.² 3. The man ³ heard the voice in the garden. 4. The king ruled over the people. 5. The boy sat in this place. 6. Yahweh blotted out ⁴ everything which he had made, man and beast.⁵ 7. God made the man out of dust ⁶ from the ground. 8. God is in the temple.⁷

9   נָתַן אֶת־הַחֶרֶב לַמֶּלֶךְ :   He gave the sword to the king

10   כָּתַב הַיֶּלֶד בַּסֵּפֶר :   The boy wrote in the ⁸ book

¹ קָרָא=*call*, in all the chief senses of the English word—*to cry aloud, to summon*, and *to name* or *give a name to*. For the last sense, the usual construction is to put the name in the *accus.*, and to put the prepos. לְ before the person, place, or thing named. So here—"to (לְ) the light he *gave the name* day" (*acc.*). Cf. Gen. 35¹⁸ קָרָא־לוֹ בִנְיָמִין, to him he gave the name of Benjamin, i.e. *he called him Benjamin*.

² Note עָשָׂה ('āsâ) not עָשָׁה ('āshâ).

³ הָאָדָם is *the* man, *i.e.*, in the Genesis story, the first man. It was an easy step, by the omission of the article, to regard the word as a proper name and=Adam : cf. Gen. 4²⁵ 5¹. See Note 1 (on אֱלֹהִים), in Exercise 12 A.

⁴ The picturesque quality of this word (מחה) should be retained in the translation. It is more vivid than " destroy " : characteristically the former word belongs, as is here evident from the word יהוה, to the Yahwist source, and the latter to the priestly source (P).

⁵ Lit. " from man and unto (*lit.* as far as) beast "—a common idiom, equivalent to our " both . . . and." Note it for use in composition, and

cf. Gen. 19⁴ מִנַּעַר וְעַד־זָקֵן *both young and old.* עַד is frequently, but not necessarily, preceded by וְ.

⁶ *Man* and *dust* are in apposition. "When two nouns might form the subj. and pred. in a simple affirmation they become under a verb a double obj. acc. There are two cases : e.g. *man* is *dust* ;—he made *man* of *dust* (so-called acc. of *Material*) ; and, *the stones* are *an altar* (so-called acc. of *Product*). The nearer object is usually *definite*, and the more remote indefinite" (A. B. Davidson's *Hebrew Syntax*, § 76). In the translated sentence, *the man* is definite (it has the article and אֵת, § 13. 7 a), *dust* is indefinite (it is without the article). "He made *the man* (out of) *dust* from the ground." So Deut. 27⁶ (of) *whole stones* (אֲבָנִים indef. acc. without the article) shalt thou build *the altar* (אֶת־הַמִּזְבֵּחַ).

⁷ As the *palace* of God, considered as king, הֵיכָל is the *temple*.

⁸ By a curious idiom this may equally well mean "*a* book." In Hebrew an object is conceived as definite "not only because it is already known or has been mentioned before, but also because it is taken for a particular purpose, and so made definite in the speaker's or writer's mind" (Driver on Exod. 17¹⁴ כְּתֹב זֹאת בַּסֵּפֶר write this in *a* book, i.e. *the* book which is to be devoted to that purpose). Thus Amos 5¹⁹ "*as if a man did flee from a lion* (הָאֲרִי, *i.e.* the particular lion pursuing him at the time) *and a bear* (הַדֹּב) *met him.*" See Gesenius-Kautzsch, § 126 (*r, s*), Davidson's *Hebrew Syntax*, § 21 (*e*).

B.

1 לָאֲרִי : 2 נָתַן אֱלֹהִים אֶת־הָאִשָּׁה לָאִישׁ ¹לְאִשָּׁה :
3 בַּבֹּקֶר : 4 בַּשָּׁמַיִם הָאֵלֶּה : 5 בָּאָרֶץ : 6 בַּיּוֹם הַהוּא :
7 בְּהֵיכַל הָרָם : 8 קָרָא הָאֲרִי ²כַּחֲמוֹר : 9 קָרָא אֱלֹהִים
לָרָקִיעַ ³שָׁמַיִם וְלַיַּבָּשָׁה ⁴קָרָא ⁵אֶרֶץ : 10 עָפָר מִן־הָאֲדָמָה
הָאָדָם : 11 אָכַל מִן־הָעֵץ : 12 שָׁבַת הָעָם הֶחָכָם בַּיּוֹם
הַשְּׁבִיעִי : 13 לְעָפָר : 14 ⁶לֶחֳלִי : 15 בָּהָר הָרָם : 16 קָרָא
זֶה אֵלֶה ⁷וַיֹּאמֶר טוֹב יְהֹוָה :

¹ לְאִשָּׁה is the regular phrase in this connection—to give (נָתַן) or to take (לָקַח) *to wife*.

² In comparisons the definite article is usual—"the thing to which comparison is made naturally being known and distinct before the mind," *Syntax*, § 22 (e). *E.g.* in Isa. 1¹⁸ "If your sins be *like crimson* (כַּשָּׁנִים), they shall be white *like snow*" (כַּשֶּׁלֶג), *crimson* and *snow* have

both the article. It is *the* crimson and *the* snow familiar to everybody.
It would not be possible, however, to determine from the form כַּחֲמוֹר
alone, whether the article were inserted or not : it is either "like *an*
ass," § 8. 3 a, or "like *the* ass," § 11. b ; but Hebrew idiom decides in
favour of *the*.

[3] This is the pausal form of שָׁמַיִם. Besides the great pause at the
end indicated by *ṣillûq*, there are pauses within the verse ; and the
chief of these, usually about the middle, is indicated by the sign ˏ known
as *athnāḥ* (*Gram.*, p. 71, footnote 1). As this pause, like *ṣillûq*, has the
effect of raising short vowels to long ones, § 10. 4 a, it will be indicated
throughout the Exercises in cases where the vowel would be affected.

[4] For the moving back of the accent (קָרָא, instead of קָרָא) see § 10. 4
(c) iii.

[5] See § 10. 4 a. Cf. Jer. 22[29] אֶרֶץ אֶרֶץ אָרֶץ שִׁמְעִי דְּבַר־יְהוָֹה O land,
land, land, hear the word of Yahweh. (שִׁמְעִי, 2 sing. *fem.* imperative,
agr. with אֶרֶץ, *fem.*).

[6] Without the article. (With the article it would be לְחֳלִי : in pause
לָחֳלִי, § 10. 4 (c). Cf. Isa. 1[5] כָּל־רֹאשׁ לָחֳלִי *the whole head* (lit. all of the
head—poetic omission of the article) *is in a state of* (לְ) *sickness*, i.e. *is
sick*.

[7] Strictly speaking, for reasons which will be intelligible when we
reach § 23. 3, this would normally be וַיֹּאמֶר. But as the "calling" and
the "saying" are practically synonymous, the above translation is
defensible on the principle explained in § 23. 3 (7), and may meantime
be allowed to stand.

§ 15.

A.

1. Yahweh said to the woman. 2. Thou (*fem.*) hast
eaten of the tree. 3. In[1] God and Moses. 4. They cried[2]
to[3] God in the battle. 5. David and Jonathan. 6. A
lion and an ass. 7. Israel and Judah.

And on that day I wrote in the [4] book	8 וּבַיּוֹם הַהוּא כְּתַבְתִּי בַּסֵּפֶר׃
Moses and Miriam	9 מֹשֶׁה וּמִרְיָם׃
Day and night	10 יוֹם וָלַיְלָה׃

[1] Note that בְּ is the preposition commonly used in the phrase "to
believe in" or "trust in" (הֶאֱמִין בְּ) : cf. 2 Chr. 20[20] "believe *in* (בְּ)
Jahweh your God, believe *in* His prophets" ; and for the phrase in the

Exercise, cf. Exod. 14[31] "they believed *in* Yahweh and *in* Moses His servant." Note that Hebrew repeats the preposition.

[2] Normally the verb would come first, § 13. 6. When this is not the case, the reason sometimes is that special emphasis is intended to fall on the word or words that precede it. Here, *e.g.*, the meaning might be, "it was to *God* they cried," and not, say, to some idol. *E.g.* in Gen. 3[13] הַנָּחָשׁ הִשִּׁיאַנִי "*the serpent* beguiled me" ("the serpent" precedes "beguiled me"). This is = "it was the serpent that beguiled me"—*I* am not to blame. In other cases, however, the unusual order implies a turn of thought best represented by the English plupf. Cf. Gen. 6[8] וְנֹחַ מָצָא חֵן, which does not mean, "and Noah found favour," but (God had resolved to blot out the race) "but Noah *had found* favour." So the sentence in the Exercise might mean, "they *had cried* unto God in the battle." Only the context can enable us to decide as between the two possible meanings. See 1 Chr. 5[20]. This idiom should be noted.

[3] זעק is much more commonly used with אל.

[4] See Note 8 of § 14 A.

B.

1 אָמַרְתִּי לְאִישׁ : 2 שְׁבַתֶּנוּ בַּיּוֹם הַשְּׁבִיעִי : 3 וּמִן־הָעֵץ
אָכָלְנוּ : 4 מָחָה אֱלֹהִים מִן־הָאָרֶץ מֵאָדָם וְעַד־בְּהֵמָה :
5 עַם וָמֶלֶךְ : 6 אֵלִיָּהוּ [1]וֶאֱלִישָׁע : 7 מִי שָׁפַךְ אֶת־הַמַּיִם
עַל־הָאָרֶץ : 8 [2]שָׁמַעְתִּי אֶת־הַקּוֹל בַּגָּן : 9 אָמַרְתָּ קָדוֹשׁ
[3]יְהוָה : 10 [4]וְאֵלֶּה מִי אֵלֶּה : 11 יַבָּשָׁה וָמַיִם : 12 לַיְלָה
וָבֹקֶר : 13 לֹא חָכָם הָאָדָם כֵּאלֹהִים : 14 מָשַׁלְתָּ בָּעָם הַזֶּה :

[1] Not וֶאֱלִישָׁע. The elision of ֶיְ into .. occurs only with the word אֱלֹהִים and in the phrase לֵאמֹר, § 14. 1 c.

[2] Not, as might be supposed (§ 8. 2 a), שְׁמַעְתִּי. In verbs whose last radical is a guttural, the guttural in such a place is always written with the *silent* sh[e]wa ; the pronominal terminations consequently start a new syllable, and necessarily take the *daghesh* when they begin with ת. So שְׁמַעְתֶּם *ye have heard.* See *Grammar*, p. 218, column 1.

[3] The traditional pointing of יהוה, however erroneous (*Grammar*, p. 49, footnote), will be retained throughout the Exercises.

[4] Cf. Isa. 49[21] וְאֵלֶּה מִי גִדֵּל *and these—who brought* (them) *up?* This is not a case of a connexion of words expressing kindred or contrasted ideas, like those recorded in § 15. 1 d. Even, however, where there is no such connexion, וְ sometimes becomes וָ before the tone (though

chiefly at the end of a sentence or clause, *e.g.* Exod. 21¹² וָמֵת (for
וּמֵת) *and he shall die*). Consequently וָאֵלֶּה would be quite defensible
here : cf. Isa. 26¹⁹, where וָאָרֶץ appears at the very beginning of a
clause.

§ 16.

A.

1. The ox did not drink of the water, for it¹ was
bitter.² 2. These are the ill-favoured kine which the king
saw by³ the river.⁴ 3. Man has⁵ dominion over the
beasts⁶ and the fish. 4. Those are the princes and the
mighty men whom the king set over the people. 5. I said
to this people, righteous are ye. 6. These mountains are
very high. 7. I counted the stars. 8. How high those
palaces are ! The (two) hands. (Two)⁷ sides.

The king saw in a dream the ⎱ goodly kine by the river ⎰	9 רָאָה הַמֶּלֶךְ בַּחֲלוֹם אֶת־הַפָּרוֹת ⁸הַטּוֹבוֹת עַל־הַיְאֹר:
Yahweh remembers that we ⎱ are dust ⎰	¹⁰ ⁹זָכַר יְהוָֹה כִּי עָפָר אֲנָחְנוּ:

¹ מַיִם is plural ; hence "for *they* (הֵם) were bitter " (plur.).

² This order—מָרִים הֵם (*bitter were they*)—is very common in
nominal sentences (§ 13. 6) introduced by כִּי *that, for* : cf. Gen. 20⁷,
כִּי־נָבִיא הוּא *for he is a prophet*. See also the last sentence of this
Exercise.

³ The idea in עַל is that of "inclining or impending *over*" ; this
prep. is commonly used (as here) where persons or things are represented as beside water ; cf. 2 Kings 2⁷ עָמְדוּ עַל־הַיַּרְדֵּן *they stood by the
Jordan*.

⁴ יְאֹר is used almost exclusively of the Nile.

Note the absence of the daghesh forte from the י after the article,
§ 7. 5.

⁵ This, on the whole, is better than *had*. Cf. § 46. 1. 2 (2) and § 22. 6.
So Ps. 96¹⁰ יְהוָֹה מָלָךְ *Yahweh has entered on his sovereignty, and
reigns*.

⁶ Note that בְּהֵמָה is in the singular, and used collectively. The
plur. (בְּהֵמוֹת) is poetic and very rare. בְּהֵמָה is *beast* as distinguished

from man ; among beasts, it usually denotes *cattle* as distinguished from wild beasts : of the latter it is very seldom used.

Note that the prep. בְּ is repeated in the Hebrew with the next noun.

[7] Not always strictly "two," though always found in the dual except once (sing.).

[8] Rather than טוֹבוֹת : see § 4 (c).

[9] Note the force of זָכַר *remembers*, rather than *remembered*. See § 22. 6, and cf. Note 5 above.

זכר might also be pointed זְכֹר *remember, O Yahweh* (2nd sing. masc. imperative), as will be seen when we reach § 21, p. 76. Only the context could decide.

B.

1 זָכַרְתִּי אֶת־¹הַשָּׁרִים אֲשֶׁר שָׁמַעְתִּי בַּהֵיכָל : 2 מָרִים הַמַּיִם
הָאֵלֶּה : 3 הַשָּׁמַיִם הַהֵם רָמִים מְאֹד : 4 אֵלֶּה הַחֲמוֹרִים
אֲשֶׁר הֲרַגְנוּ : 5 מִי הַשָּׂרִים וְהַגִּבּוֹרִים הָאֵלֶּה : 6 שָׁמַעְתָּ
אֶת־הַפָּרוֹת : 7 זָכַר אֱלֹהִים אֶת־²הַצַּדִּיקִים : 8 יָשַׁבְנוּ
בֶּהָרִים יוֹמָיִם : 9 ³לֶחֶם אָכַל וּמַיִם שָׁתָה : 10 הַצַּדִּיקִים
כַּכּוֹכָבִים אֲשֶׁר ⁴בָּרָקִיעַ : 11 הַיַּרְכָתַיִם : 12 לָקַח ⁵פָּרִים
וּפָרוֹת וְסוּסִים וַחֲמוֹרִים : 13 שָׁמַעְנוּ אֶת־הַזְּאֵבִים ⁶בָּעֶרֶב :
14 סָפַרְתִּי אֶת־הַכּוֹכָבִים אֲשֶׁר נָתַן אֱלֹהִים בַּשָּׁמָיִם :
15 מַיִם ⁷מְהַבְּאֵרֹת : 16 ⁸נָתַן־לִי אֱלֹהִים שִׁיר חָדָשׁ :
17 שָׁפַכְתָּ דָּמִים :

[1] The masc. שִׁיר is much commoner than the fem. שִׁירָה.

Note the spelling שָׁרִים, § 4. c ; cf. Gen. 31²⁷. שִׁירִים, of course, would not be wrong ; cf. שִׁיר הַשִּׁירִים, the song of songs, *i.e.* the most excellent song (§ 47. 2 b), Song 1¹.

[2] Beginners commonly, but mistakenly, write צְדִיקִים. But this would only be possible if the sing. were צְדִיק. The word, however, is צַדִּיק (*çad-dîq*) ; and as the first syllable is closed, its vowel _ is unchangeable.

Note further that, in spite of § 4. c, the longer form of the plur. is much the most common, צַדִּיקִים, though both the other possible shorter forms are also found, צַדִּיקִם (Gen. 18²⁴) and צַדִּקִים (2 Kings 10⁹).

[3] The usual order of the verbal sentence is verb, subj., obj. (cf. § 13.

2

6) ; but the demands of emphasis may lead, as here in English, to a variation in this order. *E.g.* Deut. 5²¹ (E.V.²⁴) וְאֶת־קֹלוֹ שָׁמַעְנוּ *and his voice we heard*; 2 Kings 22⁸ סֵפֶר הַתּוֹרָה מָצָאתִי (cf. § 17) *the book of the law I have found*; Num. 11²¹ בָּשָׂר אֶתֵּן לָהֶם *flesh I will give them.* (For אֶתֵּן, cf. §§ 21, 33.)

⁴ The methegh is here, as usual, in the *second* syllable from the tone (*î*), as the *a* under ע, which is only furtive (§ 8. 1 a), does not count.

⁵ Not אֶת־פָּרִים, for את is used not with all, but only with *definite* accusatives, § 13. 7 a.

⁶ עֶרֶב pausal form of עֶרֶב, as אֶרֶץ is of אֶרֶץ, § 10. 4 a.

⁷ The methegh may appear on the third syllable (if open) from the tone, or even on the fourth, if the second syllable is shut.

⁸ Note the collocation of the two accented syllables (*thán-lí*) and the consequent retraction of the tone from *thán* to *nă*, § 10. 4 (c) iii. When the second word is a monosyllable, as here, it is frequently connected with the first by the maqqeph, § 10. 3, in which case the penult of the first word, which is now in the open syllable second from the tone, takes the methegh ; cf. 1 Kings 10¹³ נָתַן־לָהּ. Even when the maqqeph is not used, and the methegh would now be impossible within the first word, there is always some mark to indicate that the accent falls on the penult ; *e.g.* 2 Kings 22¹⁰ סֵפֶר נָתַן לִי חִלְקִיָּה *Hilqîyá* (Hilkiah) *has given me a book.*

§ 17.

A.

1. The people did not drink from the waters of the river. 2. David took Abigail to wife,¹ and she was a woman of good understanding.² 3. The poor of the people are righteous. 4. We have not kept the law of Yahweh, the God of Israel. 5. The prince did according to the king's commandment. 6. And in the law of Yahweh thou hast not walked. 7. These are the commandments of the God of all³ the earth which I have written this day.⁴ 8. The boy lay on the bed of the man of God. 9. There came a great army from the ends⁵ of the earth and from the four winds of heaven. 10. We ate of every tree of the garden. 11. Now⁶ the queen of the land was the daughter of a mighty man of valour. 12. There was a famine in the

land, and Abraham went down [7] into Egypt, for the famine was sore [8] in the land.

The law of Yahweh is good : תּוֹרַת יְהֹוָה טוֹבָה 13

בַּיּוֹם הַהוּא עָשָׂה יְהֹוָה יְשׁוּעָה [9] בְּיִשְׂרָאֵל: 14

On that day Yahweh wrought deliverance in Israel.

[1] For this phrase see Note 1 of Exercise 14 B.

[2] Lit. *good of* (or *in*) *understanding.*

[3] Notice that the possible daghesh is kept out of the כ in כְּל־, because of the very intimate connection of this word with the preceding אֱלֹהֵי, which ends in a vowel, § 7. 2 c. Cf. Jud. 10[6] אֱלֹהֵי בְנֵי־עַמּוֹן *the gods of the children of Ammon* (i.e. the Ammonites); אֱלֹהֵי פְלִשְׁתִּים *the gods of the Philistines*; Exod. 3[22] כְּלֵי־כֶסֶף *jewels of silver* (construct of כֵּלִים, plur. of כְּלִי, p. 153). Yet, though the connection of the construct with the absolute is obviously one of the most intimate possible, the omission of the daghesh is by no means universal. On the one hand we find דִּבְרֵי דָוִד *the words of David* (2 Sam. 23[1]), on the other דִּבְרֵי גַעַל *the words of Ga'al* (Jud. 9[30]). The difference depends on how the passage was meant to be read, and this again is indicated by the accents (*Grammar*, pp. 230 f.), with which (except *ṣillûq* and *athnāḥ*) the student need not trouble till he has fully mastered the Grammar. A good working rule will be to omit the daghesh in such cases, as this will accustom him to consider words not only by themselves but in their relation to one another, and to group together words which really go together.

[4] See, however, Note 3 of Exercise 13 B.

[5] יַרְכָתִים (dual) is used figuratively to express the idea of "recesses, remote parts."

[6] וְ is the general connecting particle, not necessarily always to be translated by *and*. It "is used very freely and widely in Heb., but also with much delicacy, to express relations and shades of meaning which Western languages would usually indicate by distinct particles," e.g. *now, then, but, or, notwithstanding, howbeit, so, thus, therefore* (*BDB*, p. 252).

[7] If Abraham's going down to Egypt was after the famine or in consequence of it, וְאַבְרָם יָרַד would not be the natural or normal way of expressing this, nor is it the mode of expression in Gen. 12[10], where we find וַיֵּרֶד אַבְרָם for reasons which will be clear when we come to § 23. 3 (4) and § 39. 2. 2 b. It would normally mean "but Abraham had gone down," or "*Abraham*"—i.e. he and not some one else—"went down" (see Note 2 of Exercise 15 A). But, important as this point is, it need not detain us now, and the above translation may be provisionally accepted.

The order in sentence 12 has simply been designed to avoid the normal, but as yet unfamiliar, construction.

[8] Note the Hebrew order—very frequent after כִּי. See Note 2 of Exercise 16 A.

[9] It is better to insert the daghesh here, for the connection of this word with the word before it is not close : there is a real, if slight, break. Cf. Isa. 59[17] וְכוֹבַע יְשׁוּעָה בְּרֹאשׁוֹ *and a helmet of salvation on his head.* The case is not really parallel to the אֱלֹהֵי כָל־ discussed in Note 3.

Note, on the other hand, the omission of daghesh in כָבֵד after כִּי in sentence 12 of this Exercise.

B.

1 יוֹם יְהוָה הַגָּדוֹל : 2 גָּדוֹל יוֹם יְהוָה : 3 מַלְכַּת הָאָרֶץ
[1]הַטּוֹבָה : 4 כָּל־עַם הָאָרֶץ : 5 כָּל־הָאֱמוֹרִי הַמֶּלֶךְ [2]הַטּוֹבִים :
6 פָּקַד [3]הַשַּׂר אֶת־כָּל־גִּבּוֹרֵי [4]הַחַיִל וְאֶת־כָּל־עַם הַמִּלְחָמָה :
7 בְּיַרְכְּתֵי הַהֵיכָל : 8 הָלַכְתִּי צָפוֹנָה : 9 יָרַדְנוּ [5]שְׁאוֹלָה :
10 הָלַךְ הָהָרָה : 11 הָרַגְנוּ אֶת־חֲמוֹר הָאִישׁ : 12 לֹא שָׁתָה
הָעָם מִמֵּי הַיְאֹר כִּי [6]דָם הֵם : 13 לֹא שְׁמַרְתֶּם אֶת־מִצְוֹת
אֱלֹהֵי [7]כָל־הָאָרֶץ : 14 רוּחַ אֱלֹהִים עַל־הַמָּיִם : 15 אֱלֹהֵי
[8]הָרוּחֹת לְכָל־בָּשָׂר : 16 נָתַצְתִּי אֶת־כָּל־[9]חוֹמֹת הָעִיר :
17 שָׁמַרְתָּ אֶת־אֶבְיוֹנֵי הָאָרֶץ מִכָּל־רָע : 18 אָכַלְתָּ מֵעֵץ
הַגָּן :

[1] This might equally well mean " the queen of the good land." But not even to prevent this ambiguity is it permissible to put הטובה after מלכת, as the construct must be *immediately* followed by the absolute with which it is connected in sense—" of the land " (הארץ) must immediately follow " queen " (מלכת).

[2] There is no such ambiguity here as in sentence 3, for הטובים can only refer back to the plur. חמורי. " The good king " would, of course, be הַמֶּלֶךְ הַטּוֹב.

[3] While פַּר *ox* is, with the article, always written הַפָּר, the word for *prince* שַׂר, takes, with the article, the form הַשַּׂר (and in pause, of course, הַשָּׂר).

[4] If, regarding this word as the middle of the verse, we add the *athnāḥ*, the pointing will then be הֶחָיִל : see *Grammar*, p. 43, footnote 3. Cf. Josh. 6[2].

⁵ This is the common form : cf. Num. 16³⁰ שְׁאֹלָה חַיִּים וַיֵּרְדוּ *and-they-shall-go-down* (§ 23. 3. 2) *alive to Sheol.* לִשְׁאוֹלָה is found only once—in Ps. 9¹⁸.

⁶ For absence of daghesh in ד see Note 3 of section A of this Exercise, and the last (Hebrew) clause in sentence 12 of same section.

⁷ For absence of daghesh in כ see references in preceding Note.

⁸ For spelling (so Num. 16²²) see § 4 c. On the same principle, רְחֹת is also found. But רוּחֹת is commoner than either.

⁹ See preceding note. The longer form חוֹמוֹת is also found (and even חֹמוֹת once). In the spelling of such words, usage is far from being uniform : *e.g.* we find קוֹלוֹת (*voices*), קֹלוֹת, and even קֹלֹת. In general it may be said that the shorter form, the *scriptio defectiva*, occurs in the earlier books of the Old Testament, and the longer form, the *scriptio plena*, in the later ; and there is a pronounced tendency to avoid the use of the same vocalic consonant in consecutive syllables. But the student need not trouble himself further with these forms, as the usage fluctuates so considerably.

§ 18.

A.

abs. sing.	cstr. sing.	abs. plur.	cstr. plur.
זָכָר	¹זְכַר	זְכָרִים	¹זִכְרֵי
דָּבָר	דְּבַר	דְּבָרִים	דִּבְרֵי
מָשָׁל	מְשַׁל	מְשָׁלִים	מִשְׁלֵי
כָּבֵד	כְּבַד and כֶּבֶד	כְּבֵדִים	כִּבְדֵי
נָמֵר	¹נְמַר	נְמֵרִים	¹נִמְרֵי
¹קָצֵר	קְצַר	¹קְצָרִים	קִצְרֵי
מָאוֹר	מְאוֹר	²מְאוֹרֹת	³מְאוֹרֵי
נָבִיא	¹נְבִיא	⁴נְבִיאִים	נְבִיאֵי
בָּרִיא	¹בְּרִיא	⁵בְּרִיאִים	בְּרִיאֵי
תָּמִים	תְּמִים	⁶תְּמִימִים	תְּמִימֵי
שָׂפָה	שְׂפַת	שְׂפָתַיִם (dual)	שִׂפְתֵי (dual)
בְּרָכָה	בִּרְכַּת	בְּרָכוֹת	בִּרְכוֹת
נְקָמָה	נִקְמַת	נְקָמוֹת	¹נִקְמוֹת
נְבֵלָה	נְבֵלַת	⁷נְבֵלוֹת	⁷נִבְלוֹת

¹ Not found.   ² So Gen. 1¹⁵ ; מְאֹרֹת in Gen. 1¹⁴·¹⁶.

³ This is the only form of the cstr. plur. which occurs (Ezek. 32⁸).

The masc. form of the absolute, מְאוֹרִים, which this presupposes, does not occur.

⁴ Much commoner than נְבָאִים.   ⁵ So 1 Kings 5³ (E.V. 4²³).

⁶ Also written תְּמִימִם.

⁷ Not found. The sing. can be used in a collective sense : *e.g.* Isa. 5²⁵ נִבְלָתָם *their dead bodies*; Jer. 7³³ נִבְלַת הָעָם הַזֶּה.

B.

בְּרִיאוֹת abs. *or* cstr. plur. fem. of בְּרִיא *fat.*

דְּגַת cstr. sing. of דָּגָה *fish* (almost always collective), fem. of דָּג.

נְבִיאֵי cstr. plur. of נָבִיא *prophet.*

יִשְׁרֵי cstr. plur. masc. of יָשָׁר *upright.*

רְקִיעַ cstr. sing. of רָקִיעַ *firmament.*

לְבָבוֹת abs. plu. of לֵבָב *heart.*

> Note that this plur. only occurs once—in 1 Chr. 28⁹ and is not to be imitated. The Hebrews practically always say " our, your, their *heart*" (in the sing.) not " hearts."

מְאוֹר cstr. sing. of מָאוֹר *luminary.*

מִשְׁלֵי cstr. plur. of מָשָׁל *proverb.*

כְּבַד cstr. sing. masc. of כָּבֵד *heavy.*

> This form occurs twice—in Exod. 4¹⁰, where Moses says כִּי כְבַד־פֶּה וּכְבַד לָשׁוֹן אָנֹכִי *for heavy of mouth and heavy of tongue* (*i.e.* an unready speaker) *am I.* The other form of the cstr. כֶּבֶד occurs once—in Isa. 1⁴ עַם כֶּבֶד עָוֹן *a people heavy* (*i.e.* laden) *with iniquity.*

פְּקִידֵי cstr. plu. of פָּקִיד *overseer.*

לְבַב cstr. sing. of לֵבָב *heart.*

שִׂפְתֵי cstr. dual of שָׂפָה *lip.*

נִקְמַת cstr. sing. of נְקָמָה *vengeance.*

בִּרְכוֹת cstr. plur. of בְּרָכָה *blessing.*

יָדַיִם abs. dual of יָד *hand.*

C.

1. And darkness was upon the face of the waters.
2. The prophet wrote all the words in a¹ book. 3. The

word[2] of Yahweh came to the prophets.   4. The law of
Yahweh is in the heart of the righteous.   5. I have written
for this people all the words of the law of Yahweh.
6. None[3] of the elders of Israel was there.   7. God set
the two[4] great luminaries in the firmament of heaven.
8. The prince gathered an army, great[5] as the stars of
heaven or[6] the sand on the seashore.   9. Isaac said, The
voice is the voice of Jacob, but[6] the hands are the hands of
Esau.   10. The aged prophet lifted the corpse of the man
of God[7] on to the ass.

I am heavy of tongue (*i.e.* slow of speech) כְּבַד לָשׁוֹן אָנֹכִי׃ 11

Ezra read in the book of ⎫ קָרָא עֶזְרָא [8] בְּסֵפֶר תּוֹרַת הָאֱלֹהִים׃ 12
the law of God   ⎭

---

[1] Or "the." See Note 8 of Exercise 14 A.

[2] Note the absence of the daghesh from ד, as the preceding word,
with which it is closely connected, ends practically in a *vowel* (*ā*). See
Note 3 of Exercise 17 A, and cf. Jer. 1[2].

[3] אִישׁ . . . לֹא *not a man*, the Hebrew concrete way of saying *no
one, none* ; § 13. 4. Note—"not a man *from*" ; see next Note.

[4] Note that, in spite of the construct, this does not mean "two of the
great luminaries." See § 48. 1 (2) a. שְׁנֵי הָאֲנָשִׁים means "the two men."
(For אֲנָשִׁים see *Grammar*, p. 153, אִישׁ.) It is important to notice this,
as failure to observe it may misrepresent a point in the narrative : *e.g.*
Gen. 22[3] שְׁנֵי נְעָרָיו strictly "his two servants," not "two of his servants" :
so Num. 22[22]. (This phrase, which in the Hebrew is identical in both
passages, is rendered differently in the English both in A.V. and R.V.)
Esth. 9[10] עֲשֶׂרֶת בְּנֵי הָמָן הָרְגוּ *the ten sons of Haman they slew* (not "ten
of the sons of Haman"). When Hebrew has to express the idea "two
of, five of," etc., it usually does so by a periphrasis with מִן. *E.g.*
Ruth 4[2] "he took *ten of the elders of the city*" עֲשָׂרָה אֲנָשִׁים מִזִּקְנֵי הָעִיר
(lit. "ten men from the elders of the city") ; Gen. 47[2] *he took five of
his brethren* מִקְצֵה אֶחָיו לָקַח חֲמִשָּׁה אֲנָשִׁים (lit. "from—מן—among his
brethren he took five men" : for omission of the daghesh in ק in מקצה
see § 7. 5, and for אֶחָיו see *Grammar*, p. 153, אָח and p. 43, footnote 3) ;
2 Kings 25[19] *five of those that look upon the king's face* חֲמִשָּׁה אֲנָשִׁים
מֵרֹאֵי פְנֵי־הַמֶּלֶךְ (lit. "five men from the beholders of the face of the
king"). In these three illustrations, notice, beside the מִן, the addition
of אֲנָשִׁים *men*.

⁵ כָּבֵד *heavy*, is sometimes used in the sense of *numerous* : cf. Exod. 12³⁸ מִקְנֶה כָּבֵד מְאֹד *very much cattle*.

⁶ For וְ in the sense of *or* or *but*, see Note 6 of Exercise § 17 A. Particles like אוֹ *or* and אוּלָם *but* (§ 49. 5) are reserved for cases in which special emphasis is required.

Note that the בְּ is repeated in Hebrew.

⁷ Note that only the *last* word has the article : *Grammar*, p. 61, footnote 1.

⁸ The בְּ has the daghesh (cf. Neh. 8¹⁸), because the preceding word, though ending in a vowel (*ā*), is not closely connected with it in sense : § 7. 2 c. Contrast Gen. 12¹⁸ פַּרְעֹה יִקְרָ֫א *and Pharaoh called* (so Exod. 10²⁴).

D.

1 תּוֹרַת יְהֹוָה ¹תְּמִימָה: 2 רָאָה הַמֶּ֫לֶךְ אֶת־הַפָּרוֹת הַבְּרִיאוֹת עַל־שְׂפַת הַיְאֹר: 3 אֲכַלְתֶּם בְּשַׂר פָּרִים ²בְּרִאִים: 4 יְשָׁרִים דִּבְרֵי שִׂפְתֵי יְהֹוָה: 5 לֹא אִישׁ דְּבָרִים ³אָנֹ֫כִי: 6 טוֹבִים דִּבְרֵי תוֹרַת יְהֹוָה: 7 הַמַּ֫יִם עַל־פְּנֵי הָאֲדָמָה: 8 שָׁמַ֫עְנוּ אֶת־דִּבְרֵי נְבִיאֵי אֱלֹהֵי כָל־הָאָ֫רֶץ: 9 שְׁמַרְתָּ אֶת־לֵבַב הָעָם הַזֶּה ⁴מֵרָע: 10 גְּדֹלוֹת מְאֹד צִדְקוֹת אֱלֹהִים: 11 בְּרוּכִים יִשְׁרֵי ⁵לֵב: 12 גְּדוֹלָה נִקְמַת הָעָם: 13 מִשְׁלֵי הַמֶּ֫לֶךְ הֶחָכָם תְּמִימִם⁶: 14 מָחָה אֶת־כָּל־⁷דְּגַת הַיְאֹר:

¹ תָּם should not be used at this stage, as this is not a First Declension word like דָּם, but belongs to the class discussed in § 43. As there are 2 *m*'s in the root (תמם), the second *m* must reappear (in the form of daghesh forte) when the word is enlarged by suffixes, as *fem.* תַּמָּה or *plur.* תַּמִּים ; and this has obviously the effect of reducing the long *ā* to the short *a* in the first syllable, which is now shut. The form here would be תַּמָּה : but in point of fact the fem. form is only found twice— in Song 5² 6⁹ תַּמָּתִי *my perfect one* (see § 19 for suffix).

² So spelt in 1 Kings 5³ (E.V. 4²³). The longer form בְּרִיאִים would, of course, not be wrong, though it does not happen to occur.

³ Notice the pausal form with the retraction of the accent, § 10. 4 b. In a non-pausal part of the verse, the first syllable has methegh, as the accent falls, in accordance with the rule, on the last syllable : thus אָֽנֹכִ֫י.

⁴ רַע masc.; cf. Am. 5¹⁵ שִׂנְאוּ־רָע וְאֶהֱבוּ־טוֹב *hate evil and love good.*
But the fem. (§ 16. 4. 7) would also be possible—מְרָעָה; cf. Jer. 7¹²
מִפְּנֵי רָעַת עַמִּי *by reason of the wickedness of my people.* (For רָעַת
with unchangeable *ā*, see § 43. 2).

⁵ The phrase יִשְׁרֵי לֵבָב is found only once (in 2 Chr. 29³⁴), and
that in prose. Elsewhere, in the Psalms, it always appears in the
shorter form יִשְׁרֵי־לֵב, cf. Ps. 32¹¹ 36¹¹. לֵב is a word of the type discussed in § 43 (see Note 1 of this Exercise). With the addition of a
suffix, the second ב of the root (obvious in לְבָב) is reinstated, and the
first vowel, being now in the shut syllable, is short; *my heart* is not
לְבִי but לִבִּי. (For pronominal suffix, see § 19.)

⁶ To this sentence הֵם might be added (*Grammar*, p. 46, lines 3–6),
but it is not necessary. (So sentence 1 might have ended with הִיא.)
Or תמימם might be put as the first word of the sentence.

⁷ So Gen. 1²⁶ (דְּגַת הַיָּם *the fish of the sea*), the fem. form דָּגָה being
collective. But דְּגֵי would be as good—cstr. pl. of דָּג (masc.); cf. Num.
11²² דְּגֵי הַיָּם.

§ 19.

A.

His law; his lips; thy (*m.*) blessing; thy (*m.*) sons;
your (*m.*) proverbs; her place; from my flesh;¹ your (*m.*)
flesh; before me; before thee (*f.*); thy (*m.*) lips; our sons;
our heart; their (*m.*) sons: my hands; his hand; their
law; their (*f.*) hands.

1. Lot went out to the men to² the doorway, and³ he
closed the door after him. 2. And Ehud blew a trumpet⁴
in the hill-country⁵ of Ephraim, and the Israelites⁶ went
down from the hill-country, with him at their head.⁷ 3.
He is Yahweh our God: in all the earth are his judgments.
4. He has remembered for ever his covenant, which he
made with⁸ Abraham. 5. The kindness of Yahweh is
from everlasting to everlasting upon them that fear him,⁹
and his righteousness unto children's children. 6. But as
for me,¹⁰ in thee have I trusted,¹¹ O Yahweh; I have said,
"Thou art my God." 7. How abundant is thy goodness,
which thou hast treasured up for them that fear thee,¹²

(which) thou hast wrought for them that trust in [13] thee, in the sight of the children of men. 8. How I have loved [11] thy law! all the day it is my meditation.

Yahweh our God has heard our prayer	9 שָׁמַע יְהוָֹה אֱלֹהֵינוּ אֶת־תְּפִלָּתֵנוּ: [14]
He went down to Sheol to his sons	10 יָרַד אֶל־בָּנָיו שְׁאוֹלָה:

[1] This is the famous phrase in Job 19²⁶, round which so much controversy has gathered. A.V. renders it "*in* my flesh," R.V. more literally "*from* my flesh," Amer. R.V. "*without* my flesh." It also occurs in Gen. 2²³.

[2] For the ה, at the end (the *He locale*) see *Grammar*, § 17. 3. Lit. "the-opening-wards," towards the opening or door-way.

[3] וְ *and* or occasionally *but*, as the context may demand. וְ has sometimes an adversative force; cf. § 49. 5 b. See Note 6 of Exercise 17 A and Note 6 of Exercise 18 C.

[4] Hebrew can say "he blew *a trumpet*" (direct acc.), but it says more frequently "he blew *on* (בְּ) a trumpet," as in this translated sentence from Jud. 3²⁷. As an illustration of the direct acc. cf. Jer. 6¹ תִּקְעוּ שׁוֹפָר בִּתְקוֹעַ *blow a trumpet in Tekoa'*, where note the word-play, which is an extremely common feature of Hebrew, even in elevated style.

[5] הַר may mean *hill-country, mountain range*, as well as *mountain*.

[6] It is better to render בני ישראל so, and not by "children of Israel," however familiar this phrase may be to our ears. It is like בְּנֵי אָדָם at the end of sentence 7 of this Exercise: "sons of man" is just the Hebrew way of saying "those who belong to the category of man," *i.e.* men. When Amos (7¹⁴) says לֹא בֶן־נָבִיא אָנֹכִי *no son of prophet am I*, he does not mean that his father was not a prophet, he means that he is not a member of any prophetic guild. The clause is practically equivalent to the preceding clause לֹא־נָבִיא אָנֹכִי *no prophet am I*, just as in Ps. 8⁵ בֶּן־אָדָם *son of man* is an exact parallel to אֱנוֹשׁ *man*. In the translation of poetry, of course, we may retain the phrase "*son of* man, *children of* men," but it tends to be misleading in prose: בְּנֵי־עַמּוֹן are *the Ammonites* rather than *the children of Ammon*.

The normal construction for *and . . . went down*, וַיֵּרְדוּ, is avoided for the reason explained in Note 7 of Exercise 17 A. All the remarks there made about the meaning of the order of the words in the text are applicable here.

[7] Lit. "and he before them." This is what is known as a circumstantial clause, the term used to describe a clause—usually introduced by וְ but frequently also without וְ—which expresses some circumstance

concerning the chief subject, or some concomitant of the main action (*Syntax*, § 137).

[8] אֵת is here the preposition *with*, not the sign of the accusative, though it has the same pointing (אֶת and אֶת־). For its suffixes, see *Grammar*, p. 142, footnote 1.

[9] Lit. "over his fearing ones" or fearers—plur. (יְרֵאִים) of יָרֵא *fearing* with 3rd sing. masc. suffix.

[10] When a pronoun is added (as אֲנִי here) which is not necessary to the sense, it usually implies emphasis, which must be brought out in translation—"but as for me."

[11] בָּטַחְתִּי "I have set my trust or reliance *upon*" (עַל).

As we shall learn in § 22. 6, these Hebrew perfects may equally well represent "I trust, I love."

[12] Lit. "for thy fearing ones"—plur. of יָרֵא, with 2nd sing. masc. suffix.

The first syllable of יְרֵאֶיךָ with לְ before it becomes first לִי by § 6. 2 (d) i, and then לְ by § 9. 1.

[13] This is the act. ptc. pl. from sing. בֹּטֵחַ or בֹּטֵחַ, § 21. 3 (§ 30. 1. 3). בטח may take after it בְּ (as here) or עַל (as in the preceding sentence) —trust *in* or *on*.

[14] This might also be imperative, שְׁמַע *hear our prayer*; § 21. 1, § 37. 1. 2 a.

B.

1 בִּרְכוֹתֵיכֶם : 2 נִבְלָתָהּ : 3 מִצְוֹתַי : 4 שְׂפָתֶיהָ : 5 (*m.*) דְּבָרֶיהָ :
(*f.*) דְּבָרֶיךָ : 6 פָּנָיו : פָּנֶיהָ : פָּנַי : 7 וְאֶת־דְּבָרָיו שָׁמַעְנוּ
מֵהָאֵשׁ : 8 תוֹרָתְךָ בִּלְבָבִי אֱלֹהָי : 9 פָּדָה אֱלֹהִים אֶת־
קְדוֹשָׁיו : 10 שָׁמַעְתָּ קוֹלִי מֵהֵיכָלֶךָ : 11 יָשַׁבְנוּ לְפָנֶיהָ :
12 דִּבְרֵי שְׂפָתֶיךָ כַּחוֹל אֲשֶׁר עַל־שְׂפַת הַיָּם : 13 בָּא
וּבְיָדוֹ חֶרֶב : 14 טוֹבִים מְאֹד מִשְׁלֵי שְׂפָתָיו : 15 מָכְרָנוּ
אֶת־חֲמוֹרֵינוּ : 16 אַתֶּם בָּנַי וּבְנוֹתַי אָמַר אֱלֹהֵיכֶם :
17 לְבָבִי בְתוֹרָתוֹ תָּמִיד : 18 שָׁמַרְתָּ אֶת־לְבָבֶם : 19 לֹא
שָׁמַרְנוּ אֶת־בְּרִית אֱלֹהֵינוּ בְּכָל־לְבָבֵנוּ : 20 יוֹם נְקָמָה
בְּלִבָּבוֹ : 21 שְׁמַרְתֶּם אֶת־תּוֹרָתִי וְאֶת־מִצְוֹתָי : 22 נָשָׂא
אֶת־נִבְלָתוֹ אֶל־הַחֲמוֹר : 23 בָּרִיא לְבָבָם : 24 תוֹרָתֶךָ

הַתְּמִימָה¹³ ‏: 25 ‏זֹאת בָּשָׂר מִבְּשָׂרִי ‏: 26 ‏בְּכָל־נְבִיאָיו
הַגְּדוֹלִים ‏:

¹ *Dual* (not plur.), in accordance with § 16. 5 a. See *Grammar*, p. 68, col. 4.

² אֶת־ may be used with the definite accus., even when the object precedes the vb.: cf. Gen. 3¹⁰ אֶת־קֹלְךָ שָׁמָעְתִּי *thy voice I heard*. It is rare in poetry (except in the later Psalms), and is not invariably found even in prose : cf. Dt 4³⁶ וּדְבָרָיו שָׁמַעְתָּ מִתּוֹךְ הָאֵשׁ *and his words thou didst hear out of the midst* (תּוֹךְ, cstr. of תָּוֶךְ, *Grammar*, p. 135, col. 3, מָוֶת) *of the fire.* מִתּוֹךְ הָאֵשׁ is the common phrase in such a connexion rather than מֵהָאֵשׁ.

³ So in Ezek. 15⁷. מִן־הָאֵשׁ would also be possible (§ 14. 2 c), and is found in Num. 18⁹ ; but the text there is doubtful, and not supported by the Septuagint. Generally speaking, however, in prose the fuller form is commoner. But for the more idiomatic turning of this particular phrase, see the preceding Note.

⁴ Without the אֶת־, if we regard the line as poetry. So Jonah 2³.

⁵ Not לְפָנֶיהָ, because יָהּ , having only one significant consonant, is a *light* suffix, § 19. 2, and the regular rules of vocalization (§ 6) apply.

⁶ A good illustration of the so-called circumstantial clause ; see Note 7 in section A of this Exercise. We should say idiomatically, " with a sword in his hand."

⁷ Pausal form of חֶרֶב, § 10. 4 a (also *Grammar*, p. 100, line 5).

⁸ The first ‍ is the *methegh* (two places from the tone), the second is the *silluq*, which marks the end of the verse.

⁹ Whether the ת will take the daghesh or not, will depend on whether we conceive a slight pause to intervene between this and the preceding word. Both forms could be theoretically justified. In Ps. 119¹⁰⁹ we find נַפְשִׁי בְכַפִּי תָמִיד *my soul is in my hand* (כַּף, § 43, col. 1) *continually*, *i.e.* my life is in continual jeopardy (note also the omission of the daghesh from ב : so in the translated sentence after לְבָבִי). On the other hand, cf. Exod. 25³⁰ לֶחֶם פָּנִים לְפָנַי תָּמִיד *shew-bread* (lit. bread of the presence) *before me continually.*

¹⁰ The article is never found with this phrase. It more commonly appears in the masc. form יוֹם נָקָם : cf. Isa. 34⁸ 61² 63⁴, Prov. 6³⁴. In Isa. 63⁴ the sentence (with "*my* heart") appears as יום נקם בלבי with the shorter form לֵב ; for the suffix, see *Grammar*, § 43, col. 3. So in the translated sentence we might write בְּלִבּוֹ.

¹¹ See sentence 10, in the Hebrew, of Exercise 18 C.

[12] Theoretically this might be בְּרָאִים לִבְבוֹתֵיהֶם, but לְבָבוֹת (pl. of לֵבָב)
is found only once: Hebrew prefers to say "their *heart*"—see Note on
לִבְבוֹת in Exercise § 18 B.   לִבּוֹת (pl. of לֵב) is found—always in poetry—
five times thus, and twice with the suffix ‍ָם ; לְבֹּתָם Isa. 44[18], לִבּוֹתָם
Ps. 125[4], in accordance with *Grammar*, p. 69, Note vi.

[13] For fem.—*this thing*—see § 16. 4. 7.

§ 20.

A.

1. Thou hast not kept my covenant.   2. They have
not kept thy law.   3. I have kept thy statutes with all my
heart.   4. She did not remember her latter end.   5. They
forgot their God.   6. Thy voice we heard out of the fire.
7. I am Joseph whom[1] ye sold into Egypt.[2]   8. Why is[3]
thy countenance fallen?   9. They shed blood[4] like[5] water.
10. Ye burned the city with[6] fire.   11. God saw all that
he had made, and, behold, it was very good.   12. Samuel
said to[7] the people, Whose ox[8] have I taken or whose ass
have I taken, or whom[9] have I oppressed, or from whose
hand have I taken a bribe?[10]   And all the people said,
Thou hast oppressed no one,[11] and thou hast not taken
anything from the hand of any one.   13. There flew to
me one of[12] the seraphs, with a glowing stone in his hand,[13]
which he had taken with the tongs[14] from off[15] the altar.
The woman stood before the king עָמְדָה הָאִשָּׁה לִפְנֵי הַמֶּלֶךְ: 14
15 שָׁבַת אֱלֹהִים בַּיּוֹם הַשְּׁבִיעִי מֵהַמְּלָאכָה אֲשֶׁר עָשָׂה:
God rested on the seventh day from the work which he
had[16] made.

---

[1] For this idiom read carefully § 13. 2.

[2] מִצְרַיְמָה pausal form of מִצְרַיִם, with *He locale*, § 17. 3.

[3] נפלו plur. in Hebrew, because פָּנִים is plur.   Note the absence of
the daghesh from פָּנֶיךָ because of the vowel at the end of the preceding
word; also its absence from ד in דָמִים of the next sentence, for the
same reason.

[4] דָּם is used in the singular "when the blood is regarded as an
organic unity," as, *e.g.*, "the blood of sacrifices (collected in the basin

and then sprinkled)." On the other hand דָּמִים (plur.) denotes *blood which is shed*. As this often suggests murder, דָּמִים "acquired the sense of *a bloody deed*, and especially of *blood-guiltiness*." See G.K. § 124 *n*.

[5] Note the use of the article in comparisons (see Note 2 of Exercise 14 B).

[6] Note the use of the article, as always, with this phrase—"burned in *the* fire," the fire which, as every one knows, burns. Cf. our "to fall into the water, into the fire." It is often used of familiar objects ; cf. Gen. 2[11] אֲשֶׁר־שָׁם הַזָּהָב *where there is gold*.

[7] After אָמַר, either אֶל־ or לְ may be used.

[8] Note this construction carefully. At first sight confusing, it is really quite normal—the ox (cstr.) of whom (abs.).

[9] For אֶת־מִי, see § 13. 7 c.

[10] Note the absence of the daghesh from כ after the vowel: see Note 9 of Exercise 19 B.

[11] "Not . . . a man, no one," § 13. 4. So with אִישׁ in next clause, "from the hand of a man," *i.e.* of any one.

[12] Note the מִן—one from, out of, the seraphs; for a discussion of the possible constructions after אַחד, see Note 20 of Exercise 46 B.

[13] Another good illustration of the circumstantial clause—"and in his hand a glowing stone." See Note 6 of Exercise 19 B.

[14] מֶלְקָחַיִם dual (from root לקח), "takers, catchers, tongs." The prefix מ sometimes denotes the *instrument*, § 30. 2 b.

[15] Hebrew says more accurately "from *on*," blending the prepositions מן and עַל. Cf. מִתַּחַת *from under*.

[16] As Hebrew has no plupf., the pf. in such connexions has to do duty for it, § 20. 9, § 46. I. 1 a (3).

B.

1 לֹא שְׁמַרְתֶּם אֶת־דְּבָרַי : 2 נָפְלָה אֵשׁ אֱלֹהִים מִן־הַשָּׁמַיִם :
3 נָתַן אֱלֹהִים [1]מְאוֹרֹת בִּרְקִיעַ הַשָּׁמָיִם : 4 נָפְלוּ כָל־הַגִּבֹּרִים
לִפְנֵי [2]הֶחָרֶב : 5 שְׁמֵי הַשָּׁמַיִם לֵאלֹהִים [3]וְהָאָרֶץ נָתַן לִבְנֵי
אָדָם : 6 נָפְלַת הָעִיר [4]בְּלֵבַב הַיָּם : 7 שָׁמַרְתִּי אֶת־לְשׁוֹנִי
מִדַּבֵּר רָעִים : 8 אֵלֶּה מִשְׁלֵי שְׁלֹמֹה מֶלֶךְ יִשְׂרָאֵל הֶחָכָם :
9 שָׁמַעְנוּ אֶת־קֹלוֹ מֵהֵיכָלוֹ : 10 נָפְלוּ פְנֵיהֶם : 11 סָמַכְנוּ
אֶת־יָדֵינוּ עַל־רֹאשָׁהּ : 12 [5]בִּרְכַּת יְהוָה עַל־בָּנֶיךָ : 13 יָשַׁבְנוּ

עַל־מֵי ⁶הַנְּהָרֹות הַגְּדֹולִים׃ 14 שְׂרַפְתֶּם אֶת־עִירָם בָּאֵשׁ׃
15 יָלְדָה לְאִישָׁה בֵּן לִזְקֻנָיו׃ 16 שָׁכְחוּ אֶת־דְּבָרַי וְאֶת־
מִשְׁלֵי שְׂפָתָי׃

¹ Without אֶת־ because indefinite, § 13. 7 a.

² Pausal form of הַחֶרֶב, § 10. 4 a and p. 43 (of *Grammar*), footnote 3.

³ Rather than וְאֶת־, in a poetic line like this.

⁴ The poetic form of this phrase is usually either בְּלֵב־יָם (for לֵב reduced to לֵב־, see § 10. 3 a: note also the omission of the article before יָם (or יָם)—בְּלֵב יַמִּים—§ 43, col. 1—being a plur. of majesty or amplification). In Jonah 2⁴ it appears as בִּלְבַב יַמִּים.

⁵ The cstr. sing. of בְּרָכָה always appears thus—with a daghesh in the ב (§ 18. 2); but with pronom. suffixes there is no daghesh, *e.g.* בִּרְכָתוֹ *his blessing*.

⁶ This plur. of נָהָר is commoner than נְהָרִים, but, as the word is masc. in the sing., the adjective which accompanies it would normally take the *masc.* plur. form : § 16. 4. 6

§ 21.

A.

(ﺍ) אֶשְׁמֹר 1 sing. impf. Qal of שָׁמַר.

(ﺏ) לִשְׁמֹר inf. cstr. Qal of שָׁמַר, with prepos. לְ prefixed.

(ﺕ) שִׁמְרוּ 2 plur. masc. imperat. Qal of שָׁמַר.

(ﺙ) שְׁמֹר 2 sing. masc. imperat. Qal of שָׁמַר.   Also inf. cstr.

(ﺝ) תִּשְׁמֹר 2 sing. masc. or 3 sing. fem. impf. Qal of שָׁמַר.

(ﺡ) יִשְׁמְרוּ 3 plur. masc. impf. Qal of שָׁמַר.

(ﺥ) נִשְׁמֹר 1 plur. impf. Qal of שָׁמַר.

(ﺩ) גְּנוּבִים plur. masc. abs. of passive ptc. Qal of גָּנַב.

(ﺫ) גָּנֹוב inf. abs. Qal of גָּנַב.

(ﺭ) תִּפְקְדוּ 2 plur. masc. impf. Qal of פָּקַד.

(ﺯ) תִּזְכְּרִי 2 sing. fem. impf. Qal of זָכַר.

(ﺱ) זְכֹר 2 sing. masc. imperat. Qal of זָכַר.   Also. inf. cstr.

(ﺵ) כֹּרְתִים plur. masc. abs. of active ptc. Qal of כָּרַת.

(ﺹ) דֹּרְשֵׁי plur. masc. cstr. of active ptc. Qal of דָּרַשׁ.

(ﺽ) רֹמֶשֶׂת sing. fem. abs. or cstr. of active ptc. Qal of רָמַשׂ.

(ﻁ) תִּשְׁמֹרְנָה 2 or 3 plur. fem. impf. Qal of שָׁמַר.

B.

1. Thou shalt not steal. 2. Ye shall not observe their judgments. 3. As for us,[1] we will cut down trees [2] from the mountain. 4. Pursue after him. 5. I have promised [3] to keep thy words. 6. The rulers [4] of this people. 7. Who shall dwell on the mount of Yahweh? One who walks perfectly,[5] and [6] works righteousness, and speaks truth in his heart. 8. Joseph came from the land of Egypt to bury [7] Jacob. 9. They buried the corpse of the aged prophet in the grave where [8] the man of God was buried.[9] 10. The sons of Jacob went down to Egypt to buy food. 11. And now gather to me all Israel to mount Carmel [10] and the prophets of the [11] Ba'al four hundred, that eat at [12] Jezebel's table. 12. Now Deborah, a prophetess,[13] was judging [14] Israel at that time, and she used to sit [15] under Deborah's palm in the hill-country [16] of Ephraim. 13. God said to Abimelech in a dream of the night, Behold, thou art a dead man because of the woman whom thou hast taken, for she is a married woman.[17]

Thine enemies will pursue after thee no more	14 אֹיְבֶיךָ לֹא [18]יִרְדְּפ עוֹד אַחֲרֶיךָ׃
On that day I will pour out my spirit upon all flesh	15 בַּיּוֹם הַהוּא [19]אֶשְׁפֹּךְ אֶת־רוּחִי עַל־כָּל־בָּשָׂר׃

[1] See Note 10 of Exercise 19 A.

[2] *i.e.* for wood : hence עֵצִים often=(pieces of wood, *i.e.*) *wood.*

[3] אמר is occasionally used in this sense, followed, as here, by לְ with the inf. cstr.

[4] Pl. cstr. of active ptc. of מָשַׁל, the ruling ones (of). This word (*môsh^elê*) could not be confused with מִשְׁלֵי *mish^elê* proverbs. The *ḥôlem* of the first word is absorbed in the point of the שׁ : § 3. 4 b.

[5] Or better, "in integrity." For Semitic feeling, תָּמִים is not a nominative ("he who walks as a perfect man"), but rather (as we may infer from Arabic, where the case-endings are easily recognized) an *accusative* (the case often used, in such connexions, to describe the *manner* in which an action takes place, and practically equivalent, as here, to an adverb). The passage Isa. 33[14f.], which very closely resembles Ps. 15[1f], has, as its corresponding phrase הֹלֵךְ צְדָקוֹת *he that walketh righteously* (lit. in righteousnesses), which proves conclusively

that תָּמִים here is not a nominative in apposition with the *he* implicit in הֹלֵךְ. For this adverbial accusative, see G.K. § 118 *n* (and for another possible explanation of these two passages, as a sort of cognate accusative—going *the way of* righteousness—see G.K. § 117 *r*, footnote 4).

⁶ וּ before the labial פ ; § 15. 1 c.

⁷ לְקְבֹּר first syllable closed, § 21. 2 (a) ii ; hence daghesh in ב.

⁸ שֵׁם . . . אֲשֶׁר : § 13. 2 a. בּוֹ (*in it*) . . . אֲשֶׁר־ would have been equally good.

⁹ The beginner is apt to suppose that a Hebrew sentence containing a ptc. must, like a Latin, Greek, or English sentence containing such a ptc. (sepultus, τεθαμμένος, ταφείς, having been buried), be completed by a finite verb. But while the Hebrew ptc. may be used like a real ptc. (*e.g.* Lev. 11²⁷ כֹּל הֹלֵךְ עַל־כַּפָּיו *every* [beast] *going on* [*i.e.* that goes on] *its paws*), and thus often partakes of the nature of a noun or an adjective (cf. Ps. 119¹⁵⁷ רַבִּים רֹדְפָי *many are those pursuing me, i.e.* my persecutors : and in sentence 11 of this Exercise אֹכְלֵי שֻׁלְחַן אִיזֶבֶל *those eating at, i.e.* who eat at, the table of Jezebel), it is also *very* frequently used *alone*, practically in the sense of a finite verb, just like a pf. or impf. (though, of course, with a different shade of meaning ; for which see § 46. IV. 2). So here the meaning is *not*, "the man of God, having been buried, was or did" something else, to be indicated by a finite verb. *The sentence is complete as it stands*, and קָבוּר alone means *was buried* (not with reference to the act of burial, which would rather be the *pf.* of a passive voice—*e.g.* Niph'al, § 25—but rather *lay* buried). This very frequent use applies to active and passive ptc. alike : see sentence 12 of this Exercise הִיא שֹׁפְטָה *she was judging*.

[handwritten margin note: Translation of the ptcp. as finite verb.]

¹⁰ Note that Carmel, as here, frequently has the article—a reminiscence doubtless of its ultimate meaning (*the* garden-land). So Jordan is *the* Jordan, הַיַּרְדֵּן *the* river that descends (from יָרַד), *the* rushing river.

¹¹ Note *the* Ba'al, not simply Ba'al. The Ba'al in question was the Ba'al of Tyre, Melkart. In the ancient Semitic world there were "gods many and lords many" (1 Cor. 8⁵).

¹² For ptc. see Note 9 above ; and note the construct which, like the English *of* which usually translates it (impossible here), covers a very wide range of relationships.

¹³ Lit. "a woman, a prophetess." Such pleonastic phrases are not uncommon ; cf. Jud. 6⁸ אִישׁ נָבִיא *a man, a prophet.* Cf. our "a widow woman."

¹⁴ For force of ptc. as practically equivalent to a finite vb., see Note 9 of this section.

¹⁵ Lit. "she was sitting" or "dwelling" : both meanings are possible in the context (Jud. 4⁵) : on the whole, "sitting" is better.

3

[16] See Note 5 of Exercise 19 A.

[17] Lit. "the owned of an owner, the ruled of a ruler," *i.e.* the wife of a husband. בְּעֻלַת is the cstr. sing. fem. pass. ptc. of בָּעַל : in the *scriptio plena* בְּעוּלַת, it would have been more readily recognizable. This is the word which has given rise to "Beulah land"; Isa. 62⁴ *thy* (f.) *land* אַרְצֵךְ shall be called בְּעוּלָה *Beʿûlâ, i.e.* married.

בַּעַל in the sentence before us is the pausal form of the *noun* בַּעַל (lord, husband). The accent shows that it could not be the verb, which takes the accent on the *last* syllable, and would be here, in pause, בָּעַל.

The last three words illustrate the circumstantial clause (see Note 7, Exercise 19 A).

[18] Note that as the first syllable of the impf. is closed, the ד at the beginning of the next syllable must take the daghesh.

[19] Daghesh in פ : see previous Note.

C.

1 אֶרְדֹּף אַחֲרֶיהָ: 2 אָמַרְתִּי לִרְדֹּף אַחֲרֵיהֶם: 3 רֹדֵף (*or* רֹדְפוּ) אַחֲרָיו: 4 נָתַן אֶת־הַכּוֹכָבִים בִּרְקִיעַ הַשָּׁמַיִם לִמְשֹׁל בַּלָּיְלָה: 5 יִשְׁפֹּט יְהוָה אֶת־הָעָם הַזֶּה: 6 עִיר שֹׁפֶכֶת דָּם כַּמַּיִם:[1] 7 שְׁמֹר לְשׁוֹנְךָ מֵרָע: 8 תִּשְׁמְרוּ אֶת־מִצְוֺת אֱלֹהֵיכֶם בְּכָל־לְבַבְכֶם:[2] 9 חָדְלוּ לִסְפֹּר אֶת־מִשְׁלֵי שְׂפָתָיו כִּי הֵם כַּחוֹל[3] אֲשֶׁר עַל שְׂפַת הַיָּם: 10 אֶת־מִצְוֺתָיו וְאֶת־דְּבָרָיו נָשָׁמֹר: 11 יִשְׁמְרוּ בָנָיו אֶת־בְּרִיתוֹ: 12 יָדַיִם שֹׁפְכוֹת[4] דָּם: 13 וַאֲנִי[5] אֶדְרֹשׁ אֶל־אֱלֹהִים:[6] 14 בָּא לִשְׁפֹּךְ דָּם: 15 נִשְׂרֹף[7] אֶת־עִירְכֶם בָּאֵשׁ: 16 קָבַר (*or* קָבְרוּ) אֶת־נִבְלָתִי[8] בַּקֶּבֶר אֲשֶׁר הַנְּבִיאִים[9] קְבוּרִים[10] שָׁם:

[1] For the article used in comparisons, see Note 2 of Exercise 14 B.
[2] Note 2nd pl. suffix *always* has the accent on the last syllable: here לְבַבְכֶם, so דְּבַרְכֶם, etc. Never, therefore, in pause, could this become דְּבַרְכֶם, לְבַבְכֶם. The sing., however, דְּבָרְךָ, לְבָבְךָ, etc. (where the , is the methegh, in the second place from the accented ךָ), takes in pause לְבָבֶךָ, דְּבָרֶךָ, etc., § 10. 4 (c) i, § 19. 2, Note 1 (p. 69 of *Grammar*).

[3] In dependent sentences, *e.g.* after כִּי, *for*, the predicate frequently stands first, especially if the subject be a pronoun ; cf. 1 Kings 18²⁷ קִרְאוּ בְקוֹל־גָּדוֹל כִּי־אֱלֹהִים הוּא *cry with a loud voice, for he is a god.* (See Note 2 of Exercise § 16 A.) In the translated sentence, however, הֵם is put first, to bring the antecedent immediately before the relative ; and, for the order, cf. Mal. 3² כִּי־הוּא כְּאֵשׁ מְצָרֵף *for he is like a refiner's fire* (מְצָרֵף, Pi'el ptc. of צרף, § 26. 4, § 36. 1 (3) *a*).

[4] *Plural*, for there is no dual of the ptc. ; see § 16. 5 b. The plur. of the ptc.—both masc. and fem.—will be better understood when we reach § 30.

[5] The *I* is here emphatic, hence it is expressed by the pronoun : Eliphaz is implicitly contrasting himself with Job (Job 5⁸).

[6] דָּרַשׁ is more usually construed with the simple accus.

[7] Or, as Hebrew seems usually to have turned such sentences so as to bring *burn* and *fire* together, we may render נִשְׂרֹף בָּאֵשׁ (אֶת־)עִירְכֶם.

[8] נָבַלְתִּי occurs once (Isa. 26¹⁹) ; cf. § 18. 2, small print. But the text is uncertain ; and, in view of the well-attested normal forms נָבַלְתּוֹ, נָבַלְתָּה, etc., there can be little doubt that we ought here to translate by נָבַלְתִּי.

[9] See Note 9 on section B of this Exercise.

[10] Or בּוֹ ; § 13. 2. Cf. Note on section B of this Exercise.

§ 22.

A.

תִּשְׁפַּלְנָה 2 or 3 plur. fem. impf. Qal of שָׁפֵל.

קָטֹנְתִּי 1 sing. pf. Qal of קָטֹן.

תִּקְפֹּן 2 sing. masc. or 3 sing. fem. impf. Qal of קָטֹן.

יָכְלָה 3 sing. fem. pf. Qal of יָכֹל.

יְכָלְתֶּם 2 plur. masc. pf. Qal of יָכֹל.   (See § 22. 1 b.)

אֶשְׁכַּל 1 sing. impf. Qal of שָׁכֵל.

לִבְשִׁי 2 sing. fem. imperat. Qal of לָבֵשׁ (לְבַשׁ is also found).

נִכְבַּד 1 plur. impf. Qal of כָּבֵד.

תִּכְבְּדִי 2 sing. fem. impf. Qal of כָּבֵד.

אֶגְדַּל 1 sing. impf. Qal of גָּדַל.

רָעֵבוּ 3 plur. pf. Qal of רָעֵב (pausal form of רָעֵבוּ, § 36. 1. (2), Ps. 34¹¹ ; § 10. 4 c).

B.

1. We shall not hear the sound of the trumpet, nor shall we be hungry for bread. 2. Thou art not able to count the stars. 3. The name of Yahweh will be great[1] for ever. 4. Draw near (*sing.*) and hearken to all the words which I am about to speak[2] unto thee. 5. Now I know that thou fearest God.[3] 6. O Yahweh, my God, thou art very great. 7. The memory of the righteous is blessed,[4] but the name of the wicked shall rot. 8. Nigh art thou, O Yahweh, and all thy commandments are truth, my ringing cry shall come near before thee. 9. In[5] the time of Solomon's old age his heart was not perfect with Yahweh his God, like the heart of David. 10. The king shall read in the book of the law all the days of his life, that he may learn to[6] fear[7] Yahweh his God. 11. No[8] flesh can be[9] righteous before thee.

12 קָדוֹשׁ אַתָּה יְהוָה מָלְאָה 10כָל־הָאָרֶץ כְּבוֹדֶךָ:

Holy art thou, O Yahweh, all the earth is full of thy glory.

13 שָׂבַעְתִּי 11עוֹלוֹת וְדַם פָּרִים לֹא חָפָצְתִּי:

I am sated with burnt-offerings, and in the blood of oxen I delight not.

---

[1] This may also mean "May (or) let the name of Y. be great (*i.e.* magnified)." Cf. Ps. 35²⁷ 40¹⁷ 70⁵ יִגְדַּל יְהוָה *Yahweh be magnified.* In that case יִגְדַּל would be jussive, rather than impf., though here, as usually, the forms would coincide. See § 23. I. 1.

[2] Note that the ptc. *by itself* means "*am* about to speak," and is practically equivalent to a finite vb. (See Note 9, Exercise 21 B.)

Note further this very common use of the ptc. to express the *imminent future, i.e.* to be *about to do* something : cf. § 46. IV. 1 (p. 159 of *Grammar*). This is a very common construction in Deuteronomy, specially in the frequently recurring phrase, "the land *which Yahweh thy God is about to give thee,*" אֲשֶׁר יְהוָה אֱלֹהֶיךָ נֹתֵן לָךְ, Deut. 4⁴⁰.

Note also the prep. אֶל־ after דָּבֵר.

The second imperative of the sentence might be more idiomatically rendered by *that thou mayest hearken.* The imperative sometimes has this force : *e.g.* Amos 5⁴ דִּרְשׁוּנִי וִחְיוּ *seek me and live,* i.e. *that ye may live* (see Driver, *Hebrew Tenses,* § 65).

3 Lit. "that a fearer of God art thou."

Note the order of the words after כִּי, and cf. 1 Kings 18²⁷ quoted in Note 3 of Exercise 21 C.

4 Lit. "is for a blessing"—a very frequent use of the prep. לְ to indicate "a transition into a new state or condition, or into a new character or office" (BDB, p. 512, col. 1). In this way הָיָה לְ = become in many different connexions, cf. Gen. 2⁷ וַיְהִי הָאָדָם לְנֶפֶשׁ חַיָּה "and the man became (for וַיְהִי see § 45. 2. 3) a living soul." לְ is thus often practically = so as to be or become : e.g. Exod. 21⁷ when a man sells his daughter לְאָמָה so that she passes into the state of a female slave, i.e. sells her for or as a slave ; Deut. 6⁸, thou shalt bind them (i.e. the words of the shᵉmaʿ) לְאוֹת for a sign.

Note the omission of the article before צַדִּיק and רְשָׁעִים. Poetry often omits the article where prose would insert it, e.g. Ps. 2² מַלְכֵי־אֶרֶץ the kings of the earth.

5 Or more correctly at. לְ expresses concurrence (at) rather than duration (in, בְּ). The meaning is, "when Solomon had grown old." לְ as an indication of time is much rarer than בְּ.

6 Notice the לְ which precedes the inf. after לָמַד, and so usually after vbs. signifying, "to begin, to cease, to desire, to be willing, to refuse, to be able," etc.

7 יִרְאָה is inf. cstr. of יָרֵא : § 22. 3.

יִרְאָה is also very frequently used as a noun (= fear), especially in such phrases as יְהֹוָה or יִרְאַת אֱלֹהִים the fear of God or Yahweh, the Hebrew phrase for "religion, reverence, piety."

8 כֹּל . . . לֹא, no : cf. § 13. 4.

9 This would illustrate the potential use of the impf. : cf. § 46. II. 4. It may, however, also simply mean "is righteous," as the impf. may be used to express a general truth : § 46. II. 5 c. Or, "in thy sight shall no flesh be justified."

10 For the omission of the daghesh from כ after â, cf. Isa. 34⁶ חֶרֶב לַיהֹוָה מָלְאָה דָם a sword has Yahweh (which) is filled with blood ; cf. Ps. 35²⁷ יֹאמְרוּ תָמִיד let them say continually.

11 In the original (Isa. 1¹¹) the waw is written only once עֹלֹת : cf. § 4. c. But as the absence of the first waw (representing ô) would make it difficult for the beginner to recognize the word in unpointed Hebrew, it has been added. Vocalic consonants are always welcome in unpointed texts : their absence aggravates the difficulty of pointing and interpretation.

C.

1 לֹא יָכֹלְתִּי ¹לְקָרֹב: 2 אֶגְדַּל: 3 (sing.) קְרַב or (plur.)
קְרֹבוּ: 4 אֶת־הָאֱלֹהִים אֲשֶׁר עָשָׂה אֶת־הַשָּׁמַיִם וְאֶת־הָאָרֶץ
אֲנִי יָרֵא: 5 לֹא יָכָלְתֶּם לִשְׁמֹר אֶת־פִּקּוּדֵי בְּכָל־לְבַבְכֶם:
6 (masc.) קְטֹנֶת or (fem.) קְטֹנֶת: 7 שְׁמַע לְמַעַן תִּלְמַד
לְיִרְאָה אֶת־יְהוָה אֱלֹהֶיךָ: 8 לֹא יָכְלוּ לִרְדֹּף אַחֲרָי:
9 ²שָׁכֹלְתִּי: 10 יָדַעְתִּי כִּי מָלוֹךְ ³תִּמְלֹךְ: 11 חָדְלוּ ⁴לְקָרֹב
לְפָנַי כִּי ⁵מָלְאוּ יְדֵיכֶם דָּמִים: 12 מַה־גָּדְלְתָּ אֱלֹהַי ⁶עָמְקוּ
מְאֹד מַחְשְׁבֹתֶיךָ:

¹ The inf. after יָכֹל is usually preceded by לְ. See Note 6 in section B of this Exercise.

² In וַאֲנִי כַּאֲשֶׁר שָׁכֹלְתִּי שָׁכָלְתִּי *and as for me, as I am bereaved, I am
bereaved* (Gen. 43¹⁴), the first שכלתי is the normal form and the second
the pausal. This illustrates the rare transition from *ŏ* or *ō* to *ā* in
pause: see G.K. § 29 *u*.

³ In the original the last two words appear as מָלֹךְ תִּמְלֹךְ (1 Sam.
24²¹). The inf. abs. may be written either as מָלוֹךְ or מָלֹךְ: the second
vowel (*ŏ*) is *unchangeably* long, whether it has consonantal representation (וֹ) or not. But the second vowel of the impf. Qal (and also, of
course, of the imperat. and—mark—the inf. *cstr.*) is only *tone*-long (*ŏ*):
how little it can hold its own, like an unchangeably long vowel, is clear
from the readiness with which it is depressed to shᵉwa—*e.g.* יִקְטֹל
yiqtŏl, יִקְטְלוּ yiqtᵉlû. Therefore it is, strictly speaking, incorrect to
represent this merely *tone*-long vowel by a consonant, as is done in
תִּמְלוֹךְ. The vocalic consonant is indeed occasionally found (cf. Ps. 1³
יִבּוֹל *shall wither*, from נָבֵל), but this ought not to be imitated. It is,
generally speaking, a sign of late date, when vocalic consonants tended
to multiply, and וֹ was used indiscriminately to represent either *ŏ* or *ō*.

⁴ For לְ before the inf. after חָדַל, see Note 6 in Section B of this
Exercise.

⁵ In Isa. 1¹⁵ the last three words appear in the following order:
מָלֵאוּ (pausal form) יְדֵיכֶם דָּמִים. "This collocation brings the subj. and
obj. into very close relation." *Syntax*, § 111. *c*.

⁶ The *vb.* עָמֵק is intended to be used here. If the *adj.* עָמֹק is used,
the proper form would be not עֲמֻקוֹת, as if it were a First Declension
word, but עֲמֻקּוֹת; see § 43. 4.

§ 23.

A.

1. I would keep thy law continually.   2. Let us make a covenant, I and thou, and it shall be for [1] a witness between me and thee.[2]   3. Abraham said to the Hittites,[3] Sell me a grave, that [4] I may bury my dead out of my sight.[5]   4. Be not very [6] angry, O Yahweh.   5. Draw not nigh hither, for the place whereon thou art standing [7] is holy ground.[8]   6. Jacob said to Esau, First sell me thy birthright; and he sold him his birthright. 7. Yahweh said, Behold,[9] the man is become as God, knowing [10] good and [11] evil; and now, lest [12] he put forth his hand and take [13] of the tree of life and eat and live for ever. 8. And the waters prevailed exceedingly [14] upon the earth, and all flesh expired that moved upon the earth, among birds and cattle, and all mankind.   9. And it shall be, like people, like priest,[15] and I will visit his deeds upon him;[16] and they shall eat, and not be satisfied,[17] for Yahweh they have forsaken.

10 נִקְרְבָה אֶל־יְהוָֹה וְיִשְׁפֹּט בֵּינִי וּבֵינֶךָ׃

Let us draw nigh to Yahweh, that he may judge between
    me and thee.

11 וַיִּשְׁכְּחוּ [18] בְנֵי־יִשְׂרָאֵל אֶת־יְהוָֹה אֱלֹהֵיהֶם וַיִּמְכֹּר אוֹתָם [19] בְּיַד מֶלֶךְ מוֹאָב׃

And the Israelites forgot Yahweh their God and he sold
    them into the hand of the king of Moab.

---

[1] For this very frequent use of לְ, see Note 4 of Exercise 22 B.

[2] Note that Hebrew repeats the preposition.   Cf. the repetition of בְּ towards the end of sentence 8 of this Exercise.

[3] So, rather than "the children of Ḥeth." See Note 6 of Exercise 19 A.

[4] This illustrates the *final* use of the *simple* waw with impf. (or rather cohortative); § 23. 3. 6.   The meaning is not "and I shall bury," which would normally be (after the imperat. as after an impf.; § 23. 3. 5 b) וְקָבַרְתִּי.

[5] Lit. "away from at my face."   Mark the blending of מִן and לְ, and see Note 15 of Exercise 20 A.

[6] מְאֹד though commonly used as an adverb = *very, exceedingly*, is

strictly and primarily a noun (=*abundance*); hence עַד־מְאֹד, lit. *unto abundance*, exceedingly.

⁷ For ptc. used like a finite vb., see Note 9 of Exercise 21 B.

⁸ Lit. "ground of holiness." קֹדֶשׁ is a *noun*, not to be confused with the adj. קָדוֹשׁ *holy*.

⁹ הֵן is not so common as הִנֵּה.

¹⁰ Note that יֹדֵעַ is sing., not plur. (יֹדְעִים). When אֱלֹהִים means *God*, it is nearly always construed with a sing.; when it means *gods*, it takes the plur.

Note also the use of the ptc. here, not as practically = a finite vb., but in simple apposition, like an adjective. See reference in Note 7. The original reads at this point לָדַעַת *in respect of* (לְ) *knowing* (cstr. inf. of יָדַע, § 39. 2. 2´ (*d*) i, ii). Gen. 3²².

¹¹ See § 15. 1 d.

¹² This might be explained as a pregnant use—"(I fear) lest," cf. Gen. 19¹⁹. But it is better to assume an *anacolouthon*—"lest he may eat (let us send him forth)." The latter clause is omitted, but it is implied in the next verse (Gen. 3²³), "so he sent him forth."

¹³ Note that after the first impf. (natural after פֶּן־) *all* the subsequent vbs. have the *pf.* with waw consec.

¹⁴ מְאֹד is occasionally duplicated for emphasis — "exceedingly, exceedingly."

¹⁵ *i.e.* the priest shall fare like the people. The *him* and the *his* of the next clause therefore probably refer to the priest. Grammatically, however, they could just as well refer to the people, as עַם is masc. sing.

Usually a phrase like this כעם ככהן would mean "the people shall fare as the priest (*Grammar*, p. 87, lines 2–6). But occasionally (as here, Hos. 4⁹, and in Isa. 24² where the same phrase occurs) the meaning is the reverse. So Isa. 24²—כַּעֶבֶד כַּאדֹנָיו—not "the servant shall fare as his master," but (as the servant, so his master) "the master shall fare as his servant." (Note in this last illustration the article with ַ instead of ָ before עבד—one of the very rare exceptions to the rule of § 11. b.)

¹⁶ This is a common Hebrew phrase for *punish*, פקד על to visit one's ways, deeds, etc. (accus.), upon one (עַל־); cf. Am. 3².

¹⁷ More idiomatically, "without being satisfied." Note for prose composition this way of rendering "without."

¹⁸ Notice the methegh in the open syllable, as the two words are linked by the maqqeph into a word-group, and practically constitute one word.

¹⁹ Hebrew says "into the *hand* of" rather than *hands*; cf. Jud. 2¹⁴ 3⁸ 4² 10⁷, and cf. Note 12 of Exercise § 19 B.

B.

1 לֹא תִשְׁכַּב בַּמָּקוֹם הַהוּא׃ 2 אֶשְׁכְּבָה׃ 3 אַל־תִּקְרְבוּ׃
4 יִשְׁפֹּט יְהוָה בֵּינִי וּבֵין הָעָם הַזֶּה׃ 5 [1]שְׁמַע [2]תְּפִלָּתִי
אֱלֹהֵינוּ׃ 6 [3]מִכְרוּ לִי אֶת־הַמְּעָרָה הַזֹּאת וְאֶקְבְּרָה [4]אֶת־
מֵתִי שָׁם׃ 7 אָכַל הָאִישׁ מִן־הָעֵץ אֲשֶׁר בַּגָּן וַיִּקְצֹף אֱלֹהִים
[5]מְאֹד׃ 8 וְאֶת־הָעֵגֶל לָקַחְתִּי וָאֶשְׂרֹף אֹתוֹ בָּאֵשׁ׃ 9 כֹּה
אָמַד יְהוָה [6]הִנֵּה אֲנִי [7]נֹתֵן אֶת־הָעִיר הַזֹּאת [8]בְּיַד [9]מֶלֶךְ
בָּבֶל וְשָׂרַף [10]אֹתָהּ בָּאֵשׁ׃ 10 יָלְדָה שָׂרָה לְאִישָׁהּ בֵּן וַיִּגְדַּל
הַיֶּלֶד׃ 11 וַיִּקְרָא אֱלֹהִים [11]לָאוֹר יוֹם וְלַחשֶׁךְ [12]קָרָא לָיְלָה׃
12 וְשָׁמַרְתָּ אֶת־תּוֹרָתוֹ [13]תָּמִיד׃ 13 וָאֶזְכֹּר אֶת־דְּבָרָיו׃
14 וְהָיָה הַנָּבִיא כַּכֹּהֵן׃

---

[1] Or שִׁמְעָה תְפִלָּתִי (emph. imperat., § 23. 2).

[2] אֶת־ omitted in poetry.

[3] *Plur.*: if *sing.* מְכֹר or even מִכְרָה (so Gen. 25[31], though we should
rather expect מָכְרָה, as the impf. is יִמְכֹּר. Conversely we find in Ps. 69[19]
קָרְבָה where we should expect קִרְבָה, as the impf. is יִקְרַב. See § 23. 2).

[4] In Gen. 23[4] אֶת־ is omitted before this word, in ver.[8] it is inserted,
which shows that usage was not uniform. אֶת־ is not indispensable
even in prose, though it is extremely common.

[5] This is the common form in prose; עַד־מְאֹד is found chiefly in
poetry.

[6] The pers. pronoun following הִנֵּה, instead of being written separately as here, very often appears in the form of a suffix. Here it would
be הִנְנִי. For the suffixes to הִנֵּה, see *Grammar*, p. 142, footnote 1.

[7] Am *about to give*: ptc. used of the imminent future. See Note 2
(2nd paragraph) of Exercise 22 B.

[8] Hebrew says, with נָתַן as with מָכַר (sell), "into the *hand* of"
rather than *hands*. See Note 19 in section A of this Exercise.

[9] In Jer. 34[2] מֶלֶךְ and בָּבֶל are joined by maqqeph; consequently
the first syllable of מלך has the methegh: מֶלֶךְ־בָּבֶל. See Note 18 in section A of this Exercise.

[10] Generally Hebrew appends the pronoun (unless it is emphatic) in
the form of a suffix to the vb. Here it would be וּשְׂרָפָהּ. A knowledge

of the pronominal suffixes, however, cannot be presupposed, as they are
not dealt with till § 31 ; hence the use of the separate accus. here
   [11] See Note 1 of Exercise 14 A.
   [12] The accent falls on the *first* syllable of this word ; see § 10. 4 (c) iii.
   [13] See Note 9 of Exercise 19 B.

§ 24.

Hardly any of the vbs. enumerated is found in all parts.
It will be sufficient, for purposes of illustration, to take two
—פקד, which is found in all parts, and קדשׁ in all but the
Hoph‘al.

The feature which beginners are apt to overlook, in
pointing, is that, as the first syllable of the pf. Niph‘al,
Hiph‘il and Hoph‘al is *closed* (like the first syllable of the
impf. Qal), the second letter of the root, starting as it does
a new syllable, will take a daghesh, if it be a *bᵉghadhkᵉphath*
letter.

Thus pf. Qal רָדַף, impf. Qal יִרְדֹּף, pf. Niph. נִרְדַּף.

Pf. Qal כָּבֵד, impf. Qal יִכְבַּד, pf. Niph. נִכְבַּד.

Pf. Qal גָּדַל, impf. Qal יִגְדַּל, pf. Hiph. הִגְדִּיל.

Pf. Qal סָתַר, pf. Niph. נִסְתַּר, pf. Hiph. הִסְתִּיר

Of פקד the parts are

Niph. נִפְקַד, Pi. פִּקַּד, Pu. פֻּקַּד, Hithpa. הִתְפַּקֵּד, Hiph. הִפְקִיד,
Hoph. הָפְקַד.

Of קדשׁ the parts are

Niph. נִקְדַּשׁ, Pi. קִדַּשׁ,[1] Pu. קֻדַּשׁ, Hithpa. הִתְקַדֵּשׁ, Hiph. הִקְדִּישׁ
(Hoph.[2] הָקְדַּשׁ).

   [1] In point of fact, however, the 3rd sing. masc. pf. Pi. of קדשׁ always
appears in the form קָדַשׁ : see § 26. 1 (a) i.
   [2] Not found.

§ 25.

A.

נִשְׁמָר sing. masc. ptc. Niph. of שׁמר.   It might also be
the *pausal* form (נִשְׁמָר) of 3 sing. masc. pf.
Niph. (נִשְׁמַר).

הִשָּׁפֵט 2 sing. masc. imperat. Niph. *or* cstr. inf. Niph. of שפט.

נִפְקַדְתֶּם 2 plur. masc. pf. Niph. of פקד.

אֶשָּׁבֵר 1 sing. impf. Niph. of שבר.

נִכְתְּבוּ 3 plur. pf. Niph. of כתב.

נִשָּׁפְטָה 1 plur. cohortative (§ 23. 1. 2) Niph. of שפט.

לְהִמָּלֵט cstr. inf. Niph. of מלט, with the prepos. לְ.

יִשָּׁקֵל 3 sing. masc. impf. Niph. of שקל.

תִּלָּחֵם 2 sing. masc. or 3 sing. fem. impf. Niph. of לחם.

נִלְחַמְתִּי 1 sing. pf. Niph. of לחם.

תִּזָּכַרְנָה 2 or 3 plur. fem. impf. Niph. of זכר.

As the imperfects are susceptible of so many interpretations, it is hardly worth while to translate the above words, in the absence of a context.

B.

1. The wicked shall not be written [1] in the book of the living.[2] 2. The snare is broken,[3] and, as for us, we [4] are escaped. 3. And the earth was corrupted before God, and the earth was filled with violence. 4. He that sheddeth man's blood, by man shall his blood be shed.[5] 5. And the child grew and was weaned. 6. I have been driven out this day from [6] the face of the ground, and from thy face shall I be hidden. 7. And Yahweh repented that he had made man on the earth. 8. Never again [7] shall all flesh be cut off by [8] the waters of the flood. 9. The enemy came to the city, but he was not able to fight against it.

10 And the city was burned with fire. וַתִּשָּׂרֵף הָעִיר בָּאֵשׁ: 9

11 הִשָּׁמֶר לְךָ פֶּן־תִּכְרֹת בְּרִית 11לְיוֹשֵׁב הָאָרֶץ 12וְלָקַחְתָּ מִבְּנוֹתָיו לְבָנֶיךָ:

Beware [13] lest thou make a covenant with the inhabitants of the land and take of [14] their [15] daughters for thy sons.

[1] Note the methegh, which shows that the *shᵉwa* is sounded (representing as it does the original ָ of the sing.), and also that the ָ is not *o* but *ā*. (Of course, if the *shᵉwa* were silent and the ָ consequently *o* this would have the further effect of putting a daghesh in the ב: thus בּ. But there is no such form.)

[2] So, rather than the "book of *life*." חַיִּים (*ḥay-yîm*) certainly is often

a noun, meaning *life* ; but it may also be the plur. of the adj. חַי *alive*, *living* (for duplication of י in pl. see *Grammar*, p. 140, § 43, col. 1) : and Ps. 69²⁹ where חַיִּים is paralleled with צַדִּיקִים *the righteous*, shows that חיים is to be taken in the sense of " the living." The book of the living is the book in which are written the names of those who are destined to life (*i.e.* who will not perish in the judgment) : cf. Ex. 32³².

Whether in the sense of *life* or *living*, we should normally, in prose, expect to find חיים accompanied by the article, in accordance with *Grammar*, p. 60, Rule 1. *b* (" *the* book of life " or " the living "), though the article is frequently omitted in poetry. In point of fact the word is found both with and without the article, but on the whole more frequently without it than with it. *The land of the living* appears, *e.g.*, as אֶרֶץ חַיִּים in Ps. 27¹³ 52⁷, Isa. 53⁸, Jer. 11¹⁹, Ezek. 26²⁰ 32²⁴· ²⁵· ²⁶· ²⁷· ³² ; but as אֶרֶץ הַחַיִּים in Job 28¹³, Ps. 142⁶, Isa. 38¹¹. So *the tree of life* appears in Gen. 2⁹ 3²²· ²⁴ (prose) as עֵץ החיים, but in Prov. 15⁴ (poetry) as עֵץ חיים.

³ By itself נִשְׁבָּר might be ptc., but the parallel נמלטנו, which can only be pf., makes it pretty certain that נִשְׁבָּר is also *pf.* (pausal form of נִשְׁבַּר).

⁴ אֲנַחְנוּ, which is unnecesary to the vb. in the 1st pers. plur., is emphatic—" *we* are escaped."

⁵ These six Hebrew words really constitute two lines of verse of three words each. Note the assonance—the play upon דָּם and אָדָם. Note further the use of the ptc. practically as a noun—" the one shedding, the shedder of." As a nominative it has strictly no grammatical construction in the sentence ; it hangs in the air, the vb. יִשָּׁפֵךְ having as its subj. דָּמוֹ ; but the meaning is quite clear.

⁶ Hebrew more pictorially, with the compound prepos. (מִן and עַל), "from *upon*" :—we might say "from *off*."

⁷ Lit. "not . . . any more " (עוֹד . . . לֹא).

⁸ מִן can describe not only the source or origin, but the *cause*, and so is often= "in consequence of, on account of, by reason of."

⁹ Not וַתִּשָּׂרֵף. The retraction of the accent (with the waw consec.) and the consequent shortening of the last syllable described in § 25. 2, takes place chiefly where the word following the vb. is a monosyllable (as in the last illustration in § 25. 5), or a word with the tone on the first syllable : see § 10. 4 (c) iii. There are certain forms, however, in which the retraction has become usual : *e.g.* וַיִּלָּחֶם *and he fought*, is always thus written, and וַיִּנָּחֶם often (always in the phrase וינחם יהוה *and Yahweh repented*).

¹⁰ The imper. Niph. of שמר is to be included among the words referred to in the last sentence of the preceding note : it is *always*

8. It was proving upon (the old man) the wall

9. Samuel promised on [?] the people an ox
whoever I took and an ass whoever I took
and whomever I oppressed and whomever's hand
whoever I took a bribe.

10. And all the people said: Thou didst not tell a
man and thou didst not take from the hand
of a man anything.

11. We present were pursuing
from the desert unto the mountain. and there we

אֲנַחְנוּ — wu

אֲנִי, אָנֹכִי — I, ni, ki   אַתֶּם / אַתֵּן — fem / ten

אֶתְכֶם   אַתֶּן / אֶתְכֶנָה — ten

אַתָּה / אַתְּ — ta / t   אֶתְכֶן / הֵנָּה — m

הוּא / הִיא — who   הֵם / הֵמָּה — m

הוּא / הִיא — y (ha)   הֵן / הֵנָּה — n

---

5. They were [running]...   He was

He people who were going down into death

He city and also they were spilling

blood like water.

2. All who write in the book we were watching

with all our heart.

S	3 m	קָטַל
	f	קָטְלָה
	2 m	קָטַלְתָּ
	f	קָטַלְתְּ
	1 c	קָטַלְתִּי
P	3 m	קָטְלוּ
	f	קָטְלוּ
	2 m	קְטַלְתֶּם
	f	קְטַלְתֶּן
	1	קָטַלְנוּ

5. And I unto thee ⟨that⟩ my trust in Yₒₕ...
the saying of his God thee.

3 m	קָטַל ✓	
3 f	קָטְלָה	
2 m	קָטַלְתָּ ✓	
2 f	קָטַלְתְּ	
1 c	קָטַלְתִּי ✓	
3 e	קָטְלוּ ✓	
2 m	קְטַלְתֶּם ✓	
2 f	קְטַלְתֶּן ✓	
1 e	קָטַלְנוּ ✓	

aṭärt	
aṭáli	
aṭaḷ	
aṭäḷ	
aṭáḷ	
aṭáṛ	

(except in Isa. 7⁴ הִשָּׁמֶר) written in the form הִשָּׁמֵר. When it stands before לְךָ as it nearly always does, it is a perfectly normal form, coming under the principle stated in § 10. 3 a that "the occurrence of two accented syllables in immediate succession is contrary to the rhythm":— normal, if we allow לְךָ to count as one syllable.

[11] יֹשֵׁב collective, as frequently, "inhabitants." Cf. Isa. 5³ יְרוּשָׁלֵַם וְאִישׁ יְהוּדָה "ye *inhabitants* of Jerusalem and ye *men* of Judah."

After כָּרַת בְּרִית "to make a covenant," *with*, which is here rendered by לְ, is also commonly rendered by אֶת־ (*i.e.* the prep.) or עִם (for both words see *Grammar*, p. 142, footnote 1). Cf. Gen. 15¹⁸ כָּרַת יְהוָה אֶת־ אַבְרָם בְּרִית Yahweh made a *covenant with Abraham* ; Gen. 26²⁸ נִכְרְתָה בְרִית עִמָּךְ (עִמָּךְ pausal form of עִמְּךָ) let us make (cohortative) a *covenant* (notice absence of daghesh from ב after vowel of preceding word with which it so closely goes in sense; see Note 10 of Exercise 22 B) *with thee.*

[12] Note: waw consec. with the *pf.* after the *impf.* which naturally follows פֶּן־. Note further, in this construction, that the accent is normally thrown forward from the penult to the *last* syllable (תָּ), and that consequently the vowel in the open syllable second from it (לְ) takes the methegh.

[13] Lit. "take heed to thyself."

[14] "From among": or it might be the partitive use of מִן "(some) from," "some of." מִן is occasionally used in this latter sense.

[15] Singular suffixes in Hebrew, because יֹשֵׁב is sing. For בֵּן and בַּת see *Grammar*, p. 153.

C.

1 קָרוֹב יְהוָה ¹לְנִשְׁבְּרֵי־לֵב : 2 נִסְתַּרְתִּי מִפְּנֵי אֱלֹהָי :
3 הִסָּתֵר מִפָּנָיו : 4 תִּסָּתְרוּ בַּיּוֹם הַהוּא : 5 וַתִּשָּׁחֵת הָאָרֶץ
וַיִּכָּרֵת כָּל־בָּשָׂר ²מִמֵּי הַמַּבּוּל : 6 ³זְרֹעוֹת ⁴הָרְשָׁעִים תִּשָּׁבַרְנָה :
7 אָמְלְטָה בְיוֹם הַלָּחֶם : 8 וַתִּמָּלֵא הָאָרֶץ ⁵דָּמִים : 9 נִקְבַּר
מֵתוּ מִלְּפָנָיו : 10 ⁶כֹּה אָמַר יְהוָה אֱלֹהֵי יִשְׂרָאֵל הִנְנִי נֹתֵן
אֶת־הָעִיר הַזֹּאת בְּיַד מֶלֶךְ־בָּבֶל וּשְׂרָפָהּ בָּאֵשׁ ⁷וְאַתָּה לֹא
תִמָּלֵט מִיָּדוֹ כִּי ⁸תִלָּכֵד ⁹וְנִתַּתָּ בְיָדוֹ : 11 בְּטַח ¹⁰בַּיהוָה
בְּכָל־¹¹לִבֶּךָ ¹²וְאַל־תִּשָּׁעֵן אֶל־בִּינָתֶךָ :

[1] In the only two places where this phrase occurs (both poetry), the shorter form לֵב appears (Ps. 34[19], Isa. 61[1] ; cf. Ps. 51[19] לֵב־נִשְׁבָּר *a broken heart*).

Note further that the words for *heart, soul, eyes*, etc., when preceded by an adjective, are usually without the article ; *e.g.* Ps. 7[11] יִשְׁרֵי־לֵב *the upright in heart* (*Syntax*, § 22, Rem. 3).

[2] For this use of מִן, see Note 8 of section B of this Exercise.

[3] Such is the order in Ps. 37[17]. In prose the vb. usually comes first, § 13. 6 ; but the order may be modified for a variety of reasons : see *Syntax*, §§ 110, 111.

[4] In the Psalm רְשָׁעִים is written without the article, as is also צַדִּיקִים (cf. *v.* 29). So in Ps. 1 these words are without the article (1[6]). They represent a party, and are almost equivalent to a proper name. See Note 4 (2nd paragraph) of Exercise 22 B.

[5] Naturally without אֶת, as it is indefinite : so Ezek. 9[9]. A similar phrase in 2 Kings 3[20] puts אֶת־ before the accusative וַתִּמָּלֵא הָאָרֶץ אֶת־הַמָּיִם *and the country was filled with the water*—which is permissible (though not obligatory), because the accus. is here *definite*, as the article and the preceding clause show (§ 13. 7 a).

For דָּמִים in the sense of *blood-shed*, see Note 4 of Exercise 20 A.

[6] For this sentence read carefully Notes 6–10 of Exercise 23 B.

[7] *Thou* is emphatic here in sense, if not in form, pointing as it does the contrast between the fate of the city and of the king (Zedekiah) :— *and as for thee*—hence the pronoun אַתָּה may be appropriately added, though it is not strictly necessary.

[8] Or תִּתָּפֵשׂ (as in Jer. 34[3], where notice the abs. inf. of the *Qal* תָּפֹשׂ before the *Niph.* תתפש). לכד, *to seize, capture*, is used chiefly of cities, sometimes of persons, תפש chiefly of persons, sometimes of cities.

[9] *Pf.* Niph. (with waw consec.) following the impf. In full it would be נִנְתַּנְתָּ, but the 2nd and the 3rd *n* are both assimilated to the following *t* : cf. § 33. 1a, 3a.

If the connexion between the *waw* and the vb. is broken, then the vb. takes the tense it would take if it were alone—here the impf. (thou shalt be given). This is how it appears in Jer. 34[3] וּבְיָדוֹ תִּנָּתֵן *and into his hand thou shalt be delivered*—here a rather more impressive order. See *Syntax*, § 111.

[10] בטח usually takes בְּ after it (to trust *in*), sometimes עַל־ (to trust or rely *on*), rarely אֶל־ (to trust *to*). In the original (Prov. 3[5]) אֶל־ is used here, perhaps the better to point the contrast with the next clause.

On the pointing בַּיהוָה (cf. § 10. 5 b), see G.K. § 102 *m*. "The divine name יְהוָה, which has not its original vowels (יַהְוֶה) but those of אֲדֹנָי, except that the ' has simple not compound *sheʷa*, takes the prefixes also, after the manner of אֲדֹנָי, thus מֵיהוָֹה, בִּיהוָֹה, לַיהוָֹה, וַיהוָֹה (since they are to be read מֵאֲדֹנָי, בַּאֲדֹנָי, לַאֲדֹנָי, וַאֲדֹנָי, for the א of אֲדֹנָי *quiesces* after the prefixes בְּ, כְּ, לְ, וְ but is *audible* after מְ (for מִן)."

¹¹ In Prov. 3⁵ לִבֶּךָ (pausal form of לִבְּךָ) from the shorter form לֵב —see Note 5 of Exercise 18 D.

¹² The order in the original is וְאֶל־בִּינָתְךָ אַל־תִּשָּׁעֵן, *and unto thine own understanding lean not*, in accordance with the principle that "it is a point of style, particularly in prophetic and poetic parallelism, to vary the order of words. So even in ordinary prose. Exod. 3⁷ רָאִיתִי אֶת־עֳנִי עַמִּי וְאֶת־צַעֲקָתָם שָׁמַעְתִּי 'I have seen the misery of my people, and their cry I have heard'" (Syntax, § 111, Rem. 3).

§ 26.

A.

1. Hear, O heavens, for it is Yahweh ¹ that has spoken: Sons have I brought up, but, as for them, they have rebelled against me. 2. Why then will ye harden ² your hearts, as the Egyptians ³ and Pharaoh hardened ⁴ their hearts? 3. The heavens are telling ⁵ the glory of God. 4. Remember the Sabbath day ⁶ to keep it holy. 5. Noah walked with ⁷ God. 6. And they heard the voice of Yahweh as he walked ⁸ in the garden in the cool ⁹ of the day, and the man and his wife hid themselves ¹⁰ from the presence of Yahweh. 7. And no expiation can ¹¹ be made for the land for the blood that has been shed ¹² in it, except by the blood of him that shed it.¹³ 8. What shall we speak, or how shall we justify ourselves? 9. The poor are seeking water, and there is none.

10   אֶת־פָּנֶיךָ יְהוָֹה אֲבַקֵּשׁ׃   Thy face, Yahweh, I will seek.

11   נִמְצְאוּ הָחֲמוֹרִים אֲשֶׁר הָלַכְתָּ לְבַקֵּשׁ׃

The asses are found which thou wentest to seek.

12   וַיִּקְרָא פַרְעֹה אֶת־כָּל־¹⁴חַכְמֵי מִצְרַיִם ¹⁵וַיְסַפֵּר לָהֶם אֶת־חֲלֹמוֹ׃

And Pharaoh called all the wise men of Egypt, and he related to them his dream.

¹ The order shows that יהוה is emphatic; no less an one than Yahweh is the speaker.

[2] Or "*do* ye harden"—expressing the action (which here is present, but may also be past) in a vivid and pictorial way ; see § 46. II. 1. 2.

[3] מצרים can mean the *people* (*Egyptians*) as well as the *land of Egypt*.

[4] The pf. is the natural tense here, as the action is a *fact* of the distant past (1 Sam. 6[6]).

[5] For this very common use of ptc., see Note 9 of Exercise 21 B.

The ptc. means "are telling *evermore*," as distinguished from the impf. which would mean "tell from time to time, from day to day" (§ 46. IV. 2), and the pf. which would mean, "told once for all."

[6] Lit. "the day of the Sabbath."

[7] אֶת־ is clearly here the prep. "with," not the sign of the accus.

[8] Lit. "walking"—Hithpa. ptc.

[9] Lit. "at the breeze of the day, *i.e.* towards evening, when in Eastern lands a refreshing wind springs up" (Skinner's *Genesis*).

For לְ = *at*, see Note 5 of Exercise 22 B.

[10] Notice the Hebrew *singular*. In the case of a compound subject, as here, "when the pred. is first, it perhaps oftenest agrees in gend. and numb. with the element of the subj. which is next it ; but it may be in plur. When the subj. has once been mentioned, the following vbs. are in the plur. ; cf. Gen. 31[14] וַתַּעַן רָחֵל וְלֵאָה וַתֹּאמַרְנָה *and Rachel and Leah answered and said* (תַעַן, 3 *sing.* fem. apocopated impf. Qal of עָנָה ; § 45. 1. (4) ; Num. 12[1] וַיִּדַבֵּר מִרְיָם וְאַהֲרֹן . . . וַיֹּאמְרוּ *and Miriam and Aaron spoke and said*" (*Syntax*, § 114. *b*). Note that the plur. vb. in the last illustration is *masc.*, while in the former (referring to two *women*) it is fem.

[11] Lit. "and for the land it (impersonal) cannot be atoned (or expiated) for the blood," etc. The general sense of the sentence shows that the potential meaning must be given to the impf. here. § 46. II. 4.

[12] The Niph. of שָׁפַךְ occurs 8 times. We met it in the impf. (יִשָּׁפֵךְ) in sentence 4 of the Hebrew into English of § 25. The Pu'al occurs 3 times, inclusive of this passage, which is from Num. 35[33]. The Pu'al is, generally speaking, the passive of the Pi'el, but the Pi'el of שָׁפַךְ does not occur in O.T.

[13] Lit. "the one shedding (ptc.) it" (*i.e.* the blood—masc. suffix agreeing with דָּם) or "its shedder." The formation of the suffixes (pronominal and plural) to words of the type of שֹׁפֵךְ is explained in § 30.

[14] For חַכְמֵי, see § 6. 2 (d) ii.

[15] Note that there is no daghesh forte in the י (§ 7. 5).

B.

1 אֵלֶּה הַדְּבָרִים אֲשֶׁר ¹דִּבַּרְתִּי׃ 2 אַל־תְּכַבְּדוּ אֶת־לְבַבְכֶם
פֶּן־יִקְצֹף יְהוָֹה אֱלֹהֵיכֶם׃ 3 ²בַּקְּשׁוּ אֶת־פָּנָיו׃ 4 הִתְהַלְּכוּ
לְפָנַי ³וְהִתְקַדִּשְׁתֶּם׃ 5 לֹא יָכֹלְתִּי לְדַבֵּר אֶל־הָעָם הַזֶּה כִּי
כִבְּדוּ אֶת־לְבָבָם׃ 6 שָׁמַעְנוּ אֶת־קוֹל יְהוָֹה מִתְהַלֵּךְ בַּגָּן
וַנִּתְחַבֵּא מִפָּנָיו׃ 7 אָמַר אֶל־הָאִשָּׁה ⁴דְּבָרִי וַתְּדַבֵּר הָאִשָּׁה׃
8 אֲכַבֵּד ⁵אֶת־מְכַבְּדָי׃ 9 וְעַתָּה הִנֵּה הַמֶּלֶךְ מִתְהַלֵּךְ לִפְנֵיכֶם
⁶וַאֲנִי זָקַנְתִּי ⁷וַאֲנִי הִתְהַלַּכְתִּי לִפְנֵיכֶם מִנְּעוּרַי עַד־הַיּוֹם
הַזֶּה׃

---

¹ Here, in pause, we should expect דִּבַּרְתִּי, and in other vbs. this is
the correct pausal form of this and similar parts, e.g. קְטַלְתִּי, קְטַלְתָּ, קְטַלְנוּ.
But with דבר and שבר the 1st pers. pf. Pi'el does not in pause raise the
_ to ָ ; the form is always דִּבַּרְתִּי and שִׁבַּרְתִּי (G.K. § 52 *l*).

² While the Pi. pl. *pf.*, *impf.*, and *ptc*. write the ק without the
daghesh forte, § 7. 5 (מְבַקְשִׁים, יְבַקְשׁוּ, בַּקְשׁוּ), the daghesh is always inserted (as above) in the *imperat*.

³ The *pf.* with waw consec. is the most common construction after
an imperat. (as after an impf.); § 23. 3. 5 b. But a succession of
imperatives is possible: cf. Gen. 17¹ הִתְהַלֵּךְ לְפָנַי וֶהְיֵה תָמִים *walk
thou before me and be thou* (imper. of הָיָה, § 45. 2. 3 *a*) *perfect*. So in
the translated sentence we might write וְהִתְקַדִּשׁוּ (pausal form of הִתְקַדְּשׁוּ;
§ 26. 3 *c*). Sometimes the perfect and imperative alternate; cf. Gen.
27⁴³ᶠ· וְקוּם בְּרַח . . . וְיָשַׁבְתָּ עִמּוֹ *and arise, flee, and dwell with him*;
עֲלוּ וַאֲמַרְתֶּם אֵלָיו *go up and say to him*. See Driver, *Hebrew Tenses*,
§ 112.

Note further הִתְקַדִּשְׁתֶּם instead of, as we should expect, הִתְקַדַּשְׁתֶּם,
by the attenuation of *a* to *i*; G.K. § 44 *d*. Cf. Lev. 11⁴⁴ 20⁷, Ezek. 38²³.

⁴ Pausal form of דְּבָרִי, § 10. 4 c.

⁵ Lit. "those honouring me"—ptc. with suffix, § 30. In poetry the
אֶת־ would be dispensed with (so 1 Sam. 2³⁰).

⁶ The אֲנִי brings out the contrast between the speaker and the king:
see Note 7 of Exercise 25 C. Then, after the intrusion of the אֲנִי, the
natural tense to express *I am old* is the pf., § 22. 6; and this again
would normally be continued by waw consec. with the impf., § 23. 3. 1 a

(but see next Note). In the original, however (1 Sam. 12²), אֲנִי is again repeated, and is, of course, followed by the natural tense to express " I have walked," viz. the pf. : וַאֲנִי הִתְהַלַּכְתִּי.

[7] In spite of the fact that the pf. is almost habitually followed by waw consec. with the impf., that construction (וָאֶתְהַלֵּךְ) would not be quite appropriate here ; for, strictly speaking, it implies a real *sequence*, whether chronological or logical : it represents "the *continuation* or *development* of the past which came before it" (Driver, *Hebrew Tenses*, § 67)—and that is not the case here The insertion of אֲנִי enables the pf. to stand in its full pf. force (I *have walked*) ; without it the meaning might be "and I *will walk*." In 1 Sam. 12² the אֲנִי has perhaps an additional justification in the contrast with the preceding בָּנַי (my sons).

§ 27.

A.

1. Thou[1] hast made me king instead of David my father. 2. Behold my face is against[2] this people and I will destroy them from off the face of the earth. 3. And God stationed the cherubim before the garden of Eden, to guard the way to the tree of life.[3] 4. God set luminaries in the firmament of heaven, to divide the day from the night.[4] 5. And I[5] will assuredly hide my face on that day. 6. Behold, his head will be thrown[6] to thee over the wall. 7. And they sent and called Jeroboam, and they made him king over Israel. 8. And the firmament permanently divided[7] the waters from[8] the waters.

9 אַל־[9]תַּסְתֵּר אֶת־פָּנֶיךָ מֵהָעָם הַזֶּה:

Hide not thy face from this people.

10 [10]וַיַּמְטֵר יְהֹוָה עַל־הָעִיר אֵשׁ מִן־הַשָּׁמַיִם [10]וַיַּשְׁמֵד אוֹתָהּ מֵעַל־פְּנֵי הָאֲדָמָה:

And Yahweh rained fire from heaven upon the city and destroyed it from off the face of the earth.

[1] The separate pronoun, usually emphatic, is not always so. Sometimes it "appears to be placed before the verb more on rhythmical grounds, *i.e.* in order to give the statement a fuller sound than that of the bare verbal form" (G.K. § 135 *a*). It is common, *e.g.*, in solemn promises ; cf. 1 Kings 2¹⁸, Bathsheba said טוֹב אָנֹכִי אֲדַבֵּר עָלֶיךָ אֶל־הַמֶּלֶךְ

Good : I will speak concerning thee to the king (notice עַל=*concerning*, common after vbs. of speaking and hearing). The addition of the pronoun is common "particularly in *responses* to preceding statements or requests, as Gen. 21²⁴ אָנֹכִי אִשָּׁבֵעַ *I will swear* (Niph. of שבע). And in prayers the *thou* is merely part of the solemnity of the sentiment, 1 Kings 3⁶" (*Syntax*, § 107, Rem. 1). The translated sentence (1 Kings 3⁷) is from a *prayer* of Solomon.

² A.V. and R.V. render "upon" (Am. 9⁸). But in this context "upon" has a definitely unfavourable, even hostile sense, and is practically = *against*. בְּ frequently means this : cf. Gen. 16¹² יָדוֹ בַכֹּל וְיַד כֹּל בּוֹ *his hand against all and the hand of all against him* ; 2 Sam. 20²¹ נָשָׂא יָדוֹ בַּמֶּלֶךְ *he has lifted up his hand against the king.* "*To fight against* an enemy" is usually נִלְחַם בְּ.

³ See *Grammar*, p. 61, line 5.

⁴ Lit. "to make a separation between the day and between the night." Note the repetition of בֵּין : this is normal.

⁵ The אנכי might be emphatic—"*as for me*, to whom they will certainly turn for help in their distress" (Deut. 31¹⁸) ; or it may simply be a mark of the solemn style referred to in Note 1.

⁶ Ptc. to indicate the (imminent) future—see Note 2 (2nd paragraph) of Exercise 22 B. The ptc. in this sense is frequently introduced, as here, by הִנֵּה (§ 46. IV. 1).

⁷ The ptc. by itself can express the idea of continuity or duration (§ 46. IV. 1 and 2 ; see Note 5 of Exercise 26 A). But in order to express the idea of duration more distinctly, the vb. הָיָה *to be*, is sometimes used with the ptc. ; cf. Gen. 37² יוֹסֵף הָיָה רֹעֶה *Joseph was shepherding*, and here in Gen. 1⁶ *was* (permanently) *dividing*. This usage is more common in the later style.

⁸ Besides בֵּין . . . בֵּין we may use לְ . . . בֵּין. Note the ָ in the pretone under the לְ ; § 14. 1 d.

⁹ Note the *jussive*—not the impf. (תַּסְתִּיר) ; while the *imperative* (הַסְתֵּר) after אַל־ would be impossible ; § 23. 1. 1. Note (i).

¹⁰ Note carefully the form taken by the Hiph. with waw consec. (וַיַּשְׁמֵד not וַיַּמְטִיר ; so וַיַּמְטֵר). In the Hiph. alone does the jussive differ from the impf. (§ 23. 1. 1), and it is the *jussive* form that is used in impf. Hiph. after waw consec., § 27. 1 (*a*) i.

B.

1 יֵשׁ־עֵת ¹לִשְׁמֹר וְעֵת לְהַשְׁלִיךְ : 2 אַל־תַּצְדֵּק אֶת־הָרְשָׁעִים :
3 אַסְתִּירָה ²פָּנַי מִן־הָעָם ³הָרַע הַזֶּה כִּי הִשְׁחִיתוּ לְפָנַי עַל־

הָאָֽרֶץ׃ 4 אָמַר הַמֶּלֶךְ הַשְׁלִיכוּ אֶת־רָאשׁוֹ אֵלֵינוּ בְּעַד
הַחוֹמָה וַיַּשְׁלִיכוּ אֶת־רֹאשׁוֹ אֲלֵיהֶם׃ 5 כִּי הַמָּטָר יַמְטִיר
עַל־הָעִיר הָרָעָה הַהִיא אֵשׁ מִן־הַשָּׁמַיִם וְהִשְׁמִיד אֹתָהּ וְלֹא
תִזָּכֵר עוֹד לְעוֹלָם׃ 6 מָצָא הַנָּבִיא אֶת־הַיֶּלֶד ⁴מִשְׁכָּב עַל־
מִטָּתוֹ׃ 7 יָרַדְנוּ אֶל־הָעִיר לְהִלָּחֶם ⁵עָלֶיהָ וְלֹא יָכֹלְנוּ
לְהַשְׁמִיד אֹתָהּ׃ 8 אָמַר רְאוּבֵן אַל־תִּשְׁפְּכוּ־דָם הַשְׁלִיכוּ
אֹתוֹ אֶל־הַבּוֹר הַזֶּה אֲשֶׁר בַּמִּדְבָּר וַיַּפְשִׁיטוּ אֶת־יוֹסֵף
וַיַּשְׁלִיכוּ אֹתוֹ ⁶הַבּוֹרָה וְהַבּוֹר רֵק׃

¹ The incorrect form שָׁמוֹר in Eccl. 3⁶ is a mark of the later style. It is incorrect, because the ō of the cstr. inf. is only a *tone*-long vowel and may pass into shᵉwa ; cf. § 31. 9, and Note 3 of Exercise 22 C.

² Daghesh omitted from פ after אסתירה : so Deut. 32²⁰. See Note 10 of Exercise 22 B.

³ In pause this always appears, of course, as הָרָע, but this form also appears in other places ; *e.g.* Exod. 33⁴ אֶת־הַדָּבָר הָרָע הַזֶּה, whereas this very same phrase appears in Deut. 17⁵ with הָרַע. The form depends upon the accent with which it is accompanied (*Grammar*, pp. 230 f.).

⁴ ֻ (*u*) is more general in the Hoph. *ptc.* than ָ (*o*), but in the other parts, while ָ predominates, usage occasionally varies even within the same vb. ; cf. Ezek. 32³² הֻשְׁכַּב (pf.) *was laid*, 32¹⁹ הָשְׁכְּבָה (emphatic imper. sing.) *be laid*.

⁵ "To fight *against* a city" is usually עַל. (See Note 2 of section A of this Exercise.) בָּהּ would therefore not have been so appropriate here ; but, had we used it, the previous word would then have become לְהִלָּחֶם (see Note 9 of Exercise 25 B) ; cf. Jud. 11²⁷·³² where this form is followed by בִּי and בָּם.

⁶ In Gen. 37²⁴ יַּשְׁלִכוּ and הַבֹּרָה are written in the *scriptio defectiva* (§ 4. d), and הַבֹּרָה is immediately followed by הַבּוֹר—which shows how fluctuating the usage was. So the sing. רֵק is usually written, as here, in the *scr. def.*, while the plur. usually appears in *scr. plena* רֵיקִים. But the student should not burden his memory with these details, as there is no solid principle behind the fluctuations. יַשְׁלִכוּ and יַשְׁלִיכוּ are written indifferently ; but the absence of the vocalic consonant makes the reading and accurate pointing of unpointed Hebrew more difficult. With the י a Hiph'il is immediately recognizable: without it, the

unpointed impf. Hiph. might equally well be impf. Qal, Niph., Pi., Pu., or Hoph.

§ 28.

כָּתַבְתִּי   1 sing. pf. Qal of כתב.

כֹּתְבִים   plur. masc. abs. act. ptc. Qal of כתב.

¹ כְּתוּבִים   plur. masc. abs. pass. ptc. Qal of כתב.

תִּכְתֹּב   2 sing. masc. *or* 3 sing. fem. impf. Qal of כתב.

יִכָּתֵב   3 sing. masc. impf. Niph. of כתב.

שְׁמֹר   inf. cstr. *or* 2 sing. masc. imperat. Qal of שמר.

נִשְׁמָר   sing. masc. abs. ptc. Niph.² of שמר.

נִשְׁמֹר   1 plur. impf. Qal of שמר.

³ הִשָּׁמֵר   2 sing. masc. imperat. (*or* inf. cstr.) Niph. of שמר.

מְשַׁמֵּר   sing. masc. abs. *or* cstr. ptc. Pi. of שמר.

יִרְדֹּף   3 sing. masc. impf. Pi. of רדף.

אֶשְׁבֹּר   1 sing. impf. Qal of שבר.

אֲשַׁבֵּר   1 sing. impf. Pi. of שבר.

מַזְכִּיר   sing. masc. abs. *or* cstr. ptc. Hiph. of זכר.

הַמְשֵׁל   inf. abs. *or* 2 sing. masc. imperat. Hiph. of משל.

רֻדַּף   3 sing. masc. pf. Pu. of רדף.

הָשְׁבַּר   3 sing. masc. pf. Hoph. of שבר.

זָכוֹר   inf. abs. Qal of זכר.

תַּמְשִׁילוּ   2 plur. masc. impf. Hiph. of משל.

תִּשְׁקְלִי   2 sing. fem. impf. Qal of שקל.

שְׁקֹל   inf. cstr. *or* 2 sing. masc. imperat. Qal of שקל.

⁴ שְׁכַב   2 sing. masc. imperat. Qal of שכב.

מֹלֶכֶת   sing. fem. abs. *or* cstr. act. ptc. Qal of מלך.

יַמְטִיר   3 sing. masc. impf. Hiph. of מטר.

⁵ יַפְקֵד   3 sing. masc. jussive Hiph. of פקד.

מִסְתַּתֵּר   sing. masc. abs. *or* cstr. ptc. Hithpa. of סתר.

יִקְדַּשׁ   3 sing. masc. impf. Qal of קדש.

תִּלְבַּשְׁנָה   2 or 3 plur. fem. impf. Qal of לבש.

תִּזְכֹּרְנָה   2 or 3 plur. fem. impf. Niph. of זכר.

---

¹ The name given to the third division of the Old Testament in Hebrew—"Law, Prophets, and *Writings*."

² Or pausal form of the 3 sing. masc. pf. Niph.

³ Always (except in Isa. 7⁴) appearing as הִשָּׁמֶר.

⁴ This form, as it happens, may also be the inf. cstr. Qal (cf.

2 Kings 14²² : with לְ, Gen. 34⁷). But such a form of inf. cstr. is very rare, natural as it might seem, in the case of stative vbs. ; the last vowel is usually *ō* not *a* : cf. 1 Sam. 12²³ חֲדֹל : § 22. 3.

⁵ This is the form used with a waw consec. after a pf., § 27. 1 (*a*) i.

§ 29.

A.

1. And God created man in his (own) ¹ image. 2. Your ways are not my ways.² 3. And now, ye inhabitants ³ of Jerusalem and ye men of Judah, judge, I pray you, between me and my vineyard. 4. And they hid the child and his nurse from the face of ⁴ the queen. 5. Thy word is a lamp to my foot ⁵ and a light to my path. 6. Make fat ⁶ the heart of this people and make heavy their ears.⁷ 7. And the broad open places of the city shall be filled ⁸ with boys and girls.⁹

8 ¹⁰ פְּנֵי יְהוָה בִּרְשָׁעִים לְהַכְרִית מֵהָאָרֶץ זִכְרָם׃

The face of Yahweh is against the wicked, to cut off the remembrance of them from the earth.

9 כַּסְפְּךָ וּזְהָבְךָ לֹא חָפַצְתִּי׃

Thy silver and gold¹¹ I do not delight in.

¹ If it be desired to emphasize the pronoun in the oblique case in Hebrew, this is done by adding the appropriate pronoun (necessarily in the nominative case, as there is no other, § 12), and the pronoun is then frequently preceded by גַּם, *also*, *even*. Here, *e.g.*, we might add גַּם־הוּא. Cf. 1 Kings 21¹⁹ דָּמְךָ גַּם־אַתָּה *thine own blood* (lit. *thy blood*, *even* [thou, of thee] *thine*) ; Gen. 27³⁴ בָּרֲכֵנִי גַם־אָנִי *bless* ME *also* (2 s. m. imperat. Pi. of ברך with 1 sing. suffix : *Grammar*, p. 211, last column). So after nouns : cf. Gen. 4²⁶ לְשֵׁת גַּם־הוּא *to Seth also.*

² For the order, see sentence 5, "a light to my foot is thy word."

³ See Note 11 (1st paragraph) of Exercise 25 B.

⁴ More idiomatically, the English Versions say simply *from*, omitting *the face of* (2 Kings 11²). Note this for prose composition. פָּנִים is very much commoner in Hebrew than *face* in English : cf. Jer. 42¹⁷ "none of them shall survive or escape מִפְּנֵי הָרָעָה *from the evil*" (*i.e.* calamity). (It is interesting to note that earlier in the sentence the same word has been used in its ordinary sense : "all the men that

שָׂמוּ אֶת־פְּנֵיהֶם לָבוֹא מִצְרַיִם have set *their faces* to go into Egypt.") So
Jer. 44²² מִפְּנֵי רֹעַ מַעַלְלֵיכֶם "*because of* the evil of your doings" (cf.
Deut. 28²⁰). Starting from this usage, it is even found, with אֲשֶׁר, in the
very next verse (and once again in Exod. 19¹⁸) as practically = a conjunction, מִפְּנֵי אֲשֶׁר קִטַּרְתֶּם "*because* ye have burned incense" (Jer. 44²³).

⁵ Another reading is רַגְלַי (dual) *feet*; so the Greek Version (τοῖς
ποσίν μου).

⁶ *i.e.* callous.

⁷ *i.e.* dull. Note the contrast in the order of these two clauses, and
see Note 12 of Exercise 25 C. Had the vb. in the second clause come
at the beginning, it might have been imperat. (co-ordinate with the first
imperat.) וְהִכָּבֵד, or, more usually, waw consec. with the *pf.*: וְהִכְבַּדְתָּ
(see Note 3 of Exercise 26 B). But the sentence as it stands gives a
better rhythmical balance.

⁸ This might seem to be a case of natural agreement—the masc.
plur. vb. agreeing with a masc. plur. noun (רְחֹבוֹת, despite its fem. plur.
ending, retaining the [presumably] masc. gender of the singular, in
accordance with § 16. 4. 6). But in point of fact רְחוֹב is *fem.*, so that
רחבות is *fem.* also. The masc. plur. of the vb. is in reality due to a
certain dislike of the 3rd plur. fem. impf.

⁹ For quiescent י in וִילָדוֹת see § 9. 1.
In the original (Zech. 8⁵) this word is followed by מְשַׂחֲקִים "boys
and girls *playing*" (Pi. ptc. of שָׂחַק, § 36. 1. 3 *a*). Note that the ptc. is
masc. in accordance with the rule that an adj. or ptc. accompanying two
or more nouns of different genders is put in the *masc.*: cf. Neh. 9¹³
חֻקִּים וּמִצְוֹת טוֹבִים *good statutes* (*Grammar*, p. 140, § 43, col. 4) *and
commandments.*

¹⁰ For בְּ, meaning *against*, see Note 2 of Exercise 27 A.

¹¹ After וֹ the construct of זָהָב is written in Gen. 2¹² (as occasionally
under other initial sibilants accompanied by shᵉwa) with the *composite*
shᵉwa, וּזֲהַב—"to emphasize the vocal character of the shᵉwa," G.K.
10 *g.* Cf. *Grammar*, p. 18, lines 5–8.

B.

1 מַלְכִּי: 2 מְלָכֵינוּ: 3 סְפָרָיו: 4 צְדָקָה: 5 ¹בְּרָכֵינוּ:
6 (*m.*) רַגְלַיִךְ or (*f.*) רַגְלָיִךְ: 7 קַרְנֵנוּ: 8 כַּסְפָּם: 9 נִסְתָּרָה
דַּרְכִּי מֵאֱלֹהָי: 10 כִּי הִשְׁחִית כָּל־בָּשָׂר אֶת־דַּרְכּוֹ עַל־הָאָרֶץ:

11 לֹא דָרְכִינוּ דַרְכֵיהֶם: 12 ²וַיִּכְרַע כָּל־הָעָם עַל־בִּרְכָּיו לִפְנֵי ³הַמֶּלֶךְ: 13 ⁴תְּדַבֶּר־נָא שִׁפְחָתְךָ בְּאָזְנֵי הַמֶּלֶךְ: 14 מָלַךְ אֱלֹהַי וּמַלְכִּי ⁵עַל־צִיּוֹן הַר קָדְשׁוֹ: 15 אַדַּרְתִּי: 16 גְּבִרְתָּהּ: 17 מַמְלַכְתּוֹ מַמְלֶכֶת ⁶עוֹלָם: 18 אַחֲרִית ⁷קַשְׁתָּם וְכָל־כְּלֵי מִלְחַמְתָּם:

¹ First syllable of dual closed, hence daghesh in כ (*Grammar*, p. 101, footnote 2).

² Or וַיִּכְרְעוּ and בִּרְכֵיהֶם. (Note that in Jud. 7⁶—the only place where this suffix occurs with בֶּרֶךְ—the first syllable is *not* closed, though it is closed, as we should expect, with the other suffixes, בִּרְכֵּי, בִּרְכָּיו, בִּרְכֶּיהָ. Conversely, in the *plur.* of such words—both with suffixes and in cstr.— the first syllable is sometimes, though very rarely, closed: *e.g.* Gen. 42²⁵· ³⁵ כַּסְפֵּיהֶם *their pieces of money*, Ezek. 17⁹ טַרְפֵּי from טֶרֶף *leaf*. But these irregularities are not to be imitated.)

A plur. vb. is frequent, and easy to understand, when the collective noun comes first; cf. 2 Sam. 15²³ כָּל־הָאָרֶץ בּוֹכִים *all the country was weeping*: but the vb. may be plur. even when it comes first; cf. Hos. 4⁶ נִדְמוּ עַמִּי *my people are destroyed* (Niph. of דָּמָה, § 44. 2), 2 Sam. 18⁷ וַיִּנָּגְפוּ עַם יִשְׂרָאֵל *and the people of Israel were smitten*. A collective noun may take the verb (and the subsequent suffixes alluding to it) either in the sing. or the plur. In sentence 6 of section A of this Exercise the suffix is sing.—"make heavy *its* ears." Singular may alternate with plur. even in consecutive verses: *e.g.* Jud. 9³⁶ people יוֹרֵד *are coming down*; 9³⁷ יוֹרְדִים (in both cases immediately preceded by עָם). Not infrequently the construction begins in the singular (especially when the predicate precedes), but is carried on, after the collective subject has been mentioned, in the plural: *e.g.* Exod. 1²⁰ וַיִּרֶב הָעָם וַיַּעַצְמוּ מְאֹד *and the people multiplied* (sing.) *and waxed very mighty* (plur.); G.K. § 145 *g*. (For ירב, apoc. impf. of רָבָה, see § 45. 1. 1 *d*.)

³ מֶלֶךְ is never written as מָלֶךְ in pause (*Grammar*, p. 100, line 7).

⁴ When the polite נָא is added to תְּדַבֵּר, the ֵ of the vb. naturally becomes ֶ (§ 10. 3 a).

⁵ בְּ is also used in connexion with הַר *mountain* (cf. Ps. 15¹).

⁶ *Everlasting*, before a noun, may be rendered thus: cf. Exod. 30²¹ חָק־עוֹלָם *an everlasting statute* (חֹק becomes חָק־ *hoq*, by § 10. 3 a). In Ps. 145¹³ the (chiefly late) word מַלְכוּת is used for *kingdom*, and the

sentence appears thus—מַלְכוּתְךָ מַלְכוּת כָּל־עֹלָמִים.   The plur. of עוֹלָם
is found only 10 times in the Old Testament.

[7] In the poetic style, אֵת־ is better omitted. See Mic. 5[9-12] where
וְהִכְרַתִּי and I will cut off (pf. Hiph. of כרת with waw consec.) occurs
four times over (and also with other cognate words) without אֶת־ before
the noun.

§ 30.

A.

It will be enough to say here that the words in the Vocabulary which
belong to the First Declension are עוֹלָם, מִשְׁפָּט, יָרֵחַ and חֻקָּה (fem.
form of חֹק: cf. Grammar, p. 140, § 43, col. 4); and to call attention
to points apt to be overlooked in some of the other words.

כֹּהֵן naturally takes with the ה a composite instead of a simple sh^ewa;
    hence plur. כֹּהֲנִים, with suffixes כֹּהֲנַי, כֹּהֲנֶיךָ, כֹּהֲנָיו, כֹּהֲנֶיהָ, etc.
    (see § 36. 2).

מִזְבֵּחַ cstr. sing. מִזְבַּח, with suffixes מִזְבְּחִי, מִזְבַּחֲךָ, מִזְבְּחוֹ, etc.; plur.
    מִזְבְּחוֹת (see § 37. 2).

מַקֵּל cstr. sing. both מַקֵּל and מַקַּל, with suffixes מַקְלִי (§ 7. 5), מַקְלוֹ,
    מַקֶּלְכֶם; pl. מַקְלוֹת.

אֹיֵב, with suffixes אֹיְבִי, אֹיִבְךָ (§ 30. I. 2 a), אֹיְבוֹ, etc.; pl. אֹיְבִים.

כִּסֵּא, with suffixes כִּסְאִי (§ 7. 5), כִּסְאֲךָ, כִּסְאוֹ, etc.; pl. כִּסְאוֹת (see
    § 38. 2).

The cstr. sing. of כֹּהֵן, אֹיֵב, and כִּסֵּא is the same as the absolute.

עוֹלֵל (as a First Declension word) takes plur. עוֹלְלִים.

עוֹלֵל (as a Third Declension word) takes plur. עוֹלָלִים.

B.

1. The Israelites ate the passover with their loins girt,[1]
their sandals on their feet, and their staff[2] in their hand.
2. Their king dealt kindly with our king, our[3] priests, and
our prophets.   3. I let mine enemy go[4] and he escaped.
4. Thine enemy is dead who sought[5] thy life.   5. And the
inhabitants of the land shall go (i.e. walk) like blind men,[6]
and their blood shall be poured[7] out like dust.

Thou art my son 6 בְּנִי ⁸אַתָּה:

Ye are my sons 7 אַתֶּם בָּנָי:

I will speak no more in his name 8 לֹא אֲדַבֵּר עוֹד בִּשְׁמוֹ:

9 וּלְקַחְתֶּם אֶת־מַקֶּלְכֶם בְּיֶדְכֶם:

And ye shall take your staff in your hand.

[1] This and the next two clauses are good illustrations of the circumstantial clause, which is very frequently introduced by waw, but is also quite frequently, as here, added without waw (see Note 6 of Exercise 19 B).

[2] Notice *staff* in the *sing.* with *hand* in the *sing.* (see Note on לבבות in Exercise 18 B).

[3] Note the repetition of the prep. with *each* of the nouns.

[4] Note שׁלח in the Qal, *to send*; in the Pi. *to send off, send away, dismiss*, and, as here, *to let go*, also *to let loose*.

[5] Note that the *daghesh forte* is not inserted in the מ of the Pi. ptc. after the article (§ 7. 5), but the vowel of the article is safeguarded by the methegh.

[6] Note that Hebrew commonly uses the def. article in comparisons, as we also may here ("like *the* blind," though later in the sentence, Hebrew says, as we do not, "like *the* dust"). See Note 2 of Exercise 14 B.

Note that the article before עורים is הַ, an exception to the rule in § 11 b. See Note 15 (2nd paragraph) of Exercise 23 A.

Note further the omission of the daghesh forte in the *waw*: § 7. 5.

[7] For Pu. of שׁפך see Note 12 of Exercise 26 A.

[8] Pausal form of אַתָּה; § 10. 4 b.

C.

1 זֶה בְּנִי וְאֵלֶּה ¹בָּנֵי בָנָי: 2 ²שִׁלַּח אֶת־³הַצְפַרְדְּעִים עַל־כָּל־הָאָרֶץ: 3 כָּל־נְבִיאָיו כְּלָבִים אִלְּמִים לֹא ⁴יֻכְלוּ לִנְבֹּחַ: 4 בִּירוּשָׁלֵם כִּסֵּא קָדְשִׁי: 5 לְקָחְנוּ אֶת־⁵מַקְלֵנוּ בְּיָדֵנוּ: 6 ⁶עָשׂוּ אֹיְבֵינוּ ⁷חֶסֶד עִם־בָּנֵינוּ: 7 אֵלֶּה הַחֻקּוֹת וְהַמִּשְׁפָּטִים אֲשֶׁר תִּשְׁמְרוּ בָאָרֶץ אֲשֶׁר אַתֶּם ⁸עֹבְרִים שָׁמָּה ⁹אַתָּה וּבִנְךָ וּבֶן־¹⁰בִּנְךָ: 8 ¹¹שָׁרְצָה אַרְצָם ¹²צְפַרְדְּעִים בְּחַדְרֵי מַלְכֵיהֶם:

[1] For the daghesh after אֵלֶּה, cf. Gen. 6⁹ אֵלֶּה תּוֹלְדֹת נֹחַ *these are the generations of Noah*.

[2] The Pi.—"let loose"—is better here than Qal; so Ps. 78⁴⁵, and cf. Note 4 of section B of this Exercise.

For the Pi. of שָׁלַח, see § 37. 1. 2 a.

³ The pathaḥ furtive with the ע of the singular does not really complicate matters. The plur. follows the exact analogy of קְטֵל, and the pathaḥ is simply ignored, as the guttural is now no longer final: § 8. 1 a. As the טֵל of קְטֵל gives טְלִים in the plur., so the דֵּעַ gives דֵּעִים.

⁴ In the original (Isa. 56¹⁰) the more vivid *impf.* is used—they are not at any time able to bark—יוּכְלוּ. For יָבֹל, see *Grammar*, p. 152. 2 (5).

⁵ The sing. is more in accordance with usage here than the plur. (see Exod. 12¹¹; also Note 2 in section B of this Exercise. The plur. of this word (מַקְלוֹת: cf. § 7. 5), which occurs occasionally (5 times in Gen. 30³⁷·⁴¹ and twice elsewhere), is not used in connexions like this. If used, the form would here be מַקְלוֹתֵינוּ. Note that *hand* is also in the sing.

⁶ For the manipulation of vbs. like עָשָׂה, see § 44. 2. 1.

⁷ Sometimes the חֶסֶד is put at the end of the phrase (*e.g.* "we will deal with thee *kindly*") esp. where the *with* is followed simply by a pronoun; cf. Jud. 1²⁴ וְעָשִׂינוּ עִמְּךָ חָסֶד *and we will deal with thee kindly* (note חסד in pause).

⁸ A good illustration of the use of the ptc. to indicate the (imminent) future—"ye (are) *about to cross*"—frequent in Deut. (see Note 2 of Exercise 22 B). In this construction the pronoun usually precedes the ptc. unless the ptc. be emphatic, or the clause begins, *e.g.*, with כִּי (see Note 2 of Exercise 16 A), *e.g.* Ps. 1⁶ כִּי־יוֹדֵעַ יְהוָה דֶּרֶךְ צַדִּיקִים *for Yahweh knows the way of the righteous.*

⁹ In Jud. 8²² this phrase appears as גַּם־אַתָּה גַּם־בִּנְךָ גַּם בֶּן־בְּנֶךָ, but in Deut. 6² with *waw* (וְ) as in the translation. The latter is much the commoner: cf. Gen. 6¹⁸.

¹⁰ For בֶּן, see p. 153. The pausal form of 2. s. m. suffix ךָ (effected by changing ָ to ֶ , cf. *Grammar*, p. 69, Note i.) is naturally treated as a *vocalic* suffix, and the rule of § 30. 1. 1 applies; *i.e.* the ֶ of בֶּן becomes ְ , just as it does in בְּנִי *my son.*

¹¹ "When the subj. precedes the pred. there is in general agreement in gend. and numb. whether the subj. be person or thing; cf. Gen 15¹² וְתַרְדֵּמָה נָפְלָה *and a deep sleep fell.* But when the pred. precedes"—as here in the sentence from Ps. 105³⁰—"while agreement in gend. and numb. is usual, esp. when the subj. is personal, the vb. is often in 3 *sing. masc.* even though the subj. be *plur.* or"—as here—"*fem.*; cf. Gen. 1¹⁴ יְהִי מְאֹרֹת *let there be* (masc. *sing.*) *lights* (masc. *plur.*); 2 Kings 3²⁶ חָזַק מִמֶּנּוּ הַמִּלְחָמָה *the battle* (*fem.* sing.) *was too strong* (*masc.* sing.) *for him* (lit. *stronger than he*: for comparative expressed

by מִן, see § 47. 1); 1 Kings 11³ וַיְהִי־לוֹ נָשִׁים שָׂרוֹת *and there were* (*masc.* sing.) *to him* (*i.e.* he had) *wives* (*fem.* plur.) *princesses* (*fem.* plur.).'' The *masc.* plur. is apt to be used for the *fem.* plur. in 3 pl. impf.; cf. 1 Kings 11³ וַיַּטּוּ נָשָׁיו אֶת־לְבּוֹ *and his wives perverted* (3 pl. *masc.* impf. Hiph. of נָטָה, §§ 33, 44) *his heart* (i.e. *his mind*). See *Syntax*, § 113. *a, b*.

¹² Not preceded by בְּ. Vbs. expressing the idea of *fulness* (as here) or *want*, are followed by the accusative ; § 38. 3 b.

§ 31.

A.

Thou (*m.*) hast kept me. I have kept thee (*m.*). And he will keep him. To keep thee.¹ And to keep her. Keep (thou) me. And he kept me. And it clothed itself in me.² Thou wilt keep them. ᴵ⁶(In order) that³ I may keep it (*or* her). He will keep him. She will keep thee.⁴ They judged me. ᴵ⁷They judged them.ᴵ⁸When thou judgest.⁵ Judge (*sing.*) me. Thou hast remembered them. I will remember her⁶ (*or* it, *fem.*).ᴵ⁹And he remembered her. ²⁰They will remember me. ²ᴵWhen he made mention of.⁷ ²²Put (*sing.*) me in remembrance. ²³She stole them.⁸ ²⁴They stole thee (*m.*). ²⁵And he will gather thee (*m.*). ²⁶He gathered them. ²⁷And I will gather them. ²⁸And those that gather it⁹ (*or* him). ²⁹When I gather. ³⁰I will gather thee (*f.*).¹⁰ ³ᴵ He will gather thee (*m.*).

¹ In spite of what is said in the last five lines of § 31. 3 (c), לִשְׁמָרְךָ (*lishmor^khâ*) is always written so, and never לְשָׁמְרְךָ (*l^shomr^khâ*).

² This does not mean "and he clothed me." לבשׁ in the Qal means *to put on* a garment, *be clothed with* (accus. of garment) : only the Hiph. could mean "he clothed me" (*me* accus., and *garment* accus. : § 38. 3 b) : cf. Gen. 41⁴² וַיַּלְבֵּשׁ אֹתוֹ בִּגְדֵי־שֵׁשׁ *and he clothed him in garments* (cstr. pl. of בֶּגֶד) *of fine linen*. The word in question is from Job 29¹⁴ צֶדֶק לָבַשְׁתִּי וַיִּלְבָּשֵׁנִי *I put on righteousness and it clothed itself in me*, it put me on, *i.e.* it became incarnate in me. Note that the word is not יַלְבִּשֵׁנִי : impfs. (and imperats.) in *a* (*e.g.* יִלְבַּשׁ) follow the analogy of the *First* Declension (cf. דְּבָרֵנוּ) not of the Third : § 31. 3 (a) i.

³ Cf §23. 3. (6). The termination is 3rd sing. fem. suffix with *nûn energicum* ; § 31. 7.

⁴ Said of חָכְמָה *wisdom*, in Prov. 4⁶. The suffix is 2nd sing. masc. with *nûn energicum*. Notice the dagh. forte in the ך by way of compensation for the lost *nûn*. (In Jer. 22²⁴ the *nûn* is retained, אֶתְּקֶנְךָ *I will tear thee off*—1 s. impf. Qal. of נתק, § 33. 1, in pause ; cf. Ps. 72¹⁵ יְבָרֲכֶנְהוּ *he will bless him*. But this is very unusual.)

⁵ Pausal form (§ 19, p. 69, Note i.) of cstr. inf. Qal.

⁶ 3 s. f. suffix with *nûn energicum*). The next word is the ordinary form of same suffix.

⁷ זָכַר Qal, *to remember* ; Hiph. to cause to remember, therefore *to remind* (as in the next word הַזְכִּירֵנִי), *to keep in remembrance*, and *to mention* (as here, כְּהַזְכִּירוֹ אֶת־אֲרוֹן הָאֱלֹהִים *when he made mention of the ark of God*, 1 Sam. 4¹⁸). כְּ is often used (as בְּ more frequently) with the cstr. inf. : cf. Gen. 27³⁴ כִּשְׁמֹעַ עֵשָׂו אֶת־דִּבְרֵי אָבִיו *when Esau heard the words of his father*.

⁸ The accent falls on the penult בָ (note carefully in the Paradigms, *Grammar*, p. 210, where the accent falls), therefore the last syllable is unaccented, and the normal ם (*ām*) becomes ם (*am*). From Gen. 31³².

⁹ Cf. Isa. 62⁹ where the masc. suffix refers to תִּירוֹשׁ *new wine*.

¹⁰ The fem. suff. in Isa. 54⁷ refers to Zion, regarded as a woman.

B.

1. *Thou*¹ hast requited me good,² whereas *I* have requited thee evil.² 2. They honoured³ me with their lips. 3. Keep thou the words of Yahweh, write them on the tablet of thy heart. 4. Seek peace and pursue it. 5. Make me to tread in the path of thy commandments, for in it do I delight. 6. Seek ye Yahweh, while he letteth himself be found.⁴

7 הָרַג מֹשֶׁה אֶת־הַמִּצְרִי וַיִּטְמְנֵהוּ בַּחוֹל:

Moses slew the Egyptian and hid him in the sand.

8 יְהוָֹה יִשְׁמָרְךָ מִכָּל־רָע יִשְׁמֹר אֶת־נַפְשֶׁךָ:

Yahweh will keep thee from all evil, he will keep thy soul.⁵

¹ The pronouns help to point the contrast between David and Saul (1 Sam. 24¹⁸).

² Note the fem. (§ 16. 4. 7).

³ *Honour me* (imper.) would be כַּבְּדוּנִי.

[4] Niph. inf. cstr. (הִפָּצֵא) with the 3rd sing. masc. suffix. Such infinitives, though they look like First Declension words of the type of קֵן, add their suffixes in accordance with the principles of the *Third Declension* (§ 30). This use of the Niph'al is known as the *Niph. tolerativum* : cf. Isa. 65[1] נִדְרַשְׁתִּי *I let myself be inquired of.*

(The Niph. ptc. plur. of vbs. ending in א springs a similar surprise. נִמְצָא (*m. sing.*), נִמְצָאָה (*f. sing.*) and נִמְצָאוֹת (*f. plur.*) follow the principles of the First Declension ; sometimes also the *m. pl.*, *e.g.* נִקְרָאִים. But sometimes the *m. pl.* follows the Third Declension : *e.g.* נִמְצָאִים always, except once וּמְצָאִים—in pause, Ezra 8[25].)

[5] נפשך means little more than *thee.* נֶפֶשׁ is hardly *soul* in our sense of the word : it is often practically=*person*, expressing the idea of *self* : cf. Am. 6[8] נִשְׁבַּע יְהֹוָה בְּנַפְשׁוֹ *Yahweh has sworn by himself.*

C.

[1] קִבַּצְתִּיהָ or קִבַּצְתִּיךְ : 2 אֲקַבְּצֶה מִיַּרְכְּתֵי הָאָרֶץ : 3 וּשְׁמַרְתַּנִי בַדֶּרֶךְ : 4 שְׁמָרֵהוּ : 5 לִפְנֵי שָׁמְרֹה אֶת־הָאִישׁ : 6 בְּיוֹם פָּקְדִי אֶת־יִשְׂרָאֵל [2] וְהִשְׁמַדְתִּי אֶת־מִזְבְּחוֹת [3] בֵּיתְאֵל : 7 שָׁפְטֵנִי כְצִדְקִי : 8 אַל[4]־נָא תִקְבְּרֵנִי [5] בְּמִצְרָיִם וְשָׁכַבְתִּי עִם[6]־אֲבוֹתַי וּקְבַרְתַּנִי בִּקְבֻרָתָם : 9 מֶה[7]־אָדָם כִּי [8]תִזְכְּרֶנּוּ וּבֶן־אָדָם כִּי [8]תִפְקְדֶנּוּ : 10 צָרוּפָה אִמְרָתֶךָ וְעַבְדְּךָ אֲהֵבָהּ : 11 לִפְנֵי כָרְתוֹ [9]כָל־בָּשָׂר [10]מִמֵּי הַמַּבּוּל : 12 אָמַר לְהַזְכִּירוּ לִפְנֵי לְהַנֵי הַהֵיכָל :

[1] Masc. and fem. suffixes respectively.
[2] A little more idiomatic than אַשְׁמִיד. Waw consec. with pf. may be used to form the apodosis (=then ye will or shall . . .) to temporal sentences *or their equivalents*, as, *e.g.*, a temporal phrase ; *e.g.* Gen. 3[5] בְּיוֹם אֲכָלְכֶם וְנִפְקְחוּ עֵינֵיכֶם *on the day of your eating* (=when ye eat) *then your eyes shall be opened* (just as the last two Hebrew words would naturally follow תֹּאכְלוּ [§ 35]—*ye shall eat*, and your eyes shall be opened). 1 Kings 13[31] בְּמוֹתִי וּקְבַרְתֶּם אֹתִי *when I die, ye shall bury me.* So Exod. 16[6] עֶרֶב וִידַעְתֶּם *at evening, then ye shall know* (practically=the simple תֵּדְעוּ, § 39. 2. 2 *b*, ye shall know). For the cognate use of waw consec. with *impf.* after a temporal *phrase*, see § 23. 3. 5 a.

³ Always written with *methegh*. In some editions it appears as בֵּית־אֵל, where the methegh is intelligible on the principle that it is used "to emphasize a long vowel in a closed syllable immediately before *maqqēph*; *e.g.* Deut. 17⁸ בֵּין־דָּם, Gen. 4²⁵ שָׁת־לִי (*shāth* not *shoth*)," G.K. § 16*f.*

⁴ The polite נָא־ of entreaty. After *â* the daghesh is naturally omitted from the following ת. Cf. Note 10 of Exercise 22 B.

⁵ This is the middle of the sentence, in respect of the sense : hence the *athnāḥ*.

⁶ For plur. of אָב, see *Grammar*, p. 153.

⁷ Not אִישׁ : the general term for *humanity* is אָדָם. But the original (Ps. 8⁵) has appropriately the poetic אֱנוֹשׁ (usually=mankind, *humanity*). Note that מָה is mostly written without maqqeph (and מַה with maqqeph).

⁸ The *nûn energicum* occurs principally in *pausal* forms of the impf.

⁹ For the omission of the daghesh after the inf. cstr. with vocalic suffix, cf. Amos 3¹⁴ בְּיוֹם פָּקְדִי פִשְׁעֵי־יִשְׂרָאֵל *in the day when I visit the transgressions of Israel* ; and even when the connexion is less intimate, cf. Amos 1¹¹ עַל־רָדְפוֹ בַחֶרֶב אָחִיו *because he pursued* (lit. on account of his pursuing) *his brother with the sword.*

¹⁰ For מָן in this sense, see sentence 8 of Exercise 25 B, with Note 8.

§ 32.

קרא 'Ayin guttural,¹ and lamedh aleph. אכל Pe aleph.² שלח Lamedh guttural. שחט 'Ayin guttural. שאף 'Ayin guttural. בין 'Ayin yodh. ילד Pe waw.³ ישע Pe waw³ and lamedh guttural. בקש Strong⁴ vb. רום 'Ayin waw. ברך 'Ayin guttural.¹ עבר Pe guttural. שקל Strong⁴ vb. נחה 'Ayin guttural and lamedh he.⁵ נחם Pe nun⁶ and 'ayin guttural. נגף Pe nun. רעע Double 'ayin. קלל Double 'ayin. בוא 'Ayin waw.⁷ סבב Double 'ayin. קרע 'Ayin guttural¹ and lamedh guttural. רדף Pe guttural. ירא Pe waw,³ 'ayin guttural, and lamedh aleph. ירה Pe waw,³ 'ayin guttural, and lamedh he.⁸

¹ For the purposes of these vbs. a medial ר usually counts as a guttural : cf. § 36. 1. 3 *a.*

² Cf. § 35. 1 a : not *Pe gutturaι* (§ 34). But the student need not trouble himself with this distinction till he reaches the relevant paragraphs.

[3] The student cannot understand why this is a *Pe waw* rather than a *Pe yodh* vb. till he reaches § 39. 2.

[4] A strong vb. is one whose stem contains no weak letter. The weak letters are enumerated in § 32. 2.

[5] נחה is not, in the strictest sense, to be regarded as a Pe nun vb., as the *n* is not assimilated ; see § 33. 1 d.

[6] See § 33. 1 d (last sentence).

[7] This would hardly be described as a Lamedh aleph vb., as this term is usually reserved for dissyllabic vbs. like מָצָא (rather than monosyllabic vbs. like בּוֹא).

[8] This vb., however, does not occur in any part which illustrates the peculiarities of the ʿAyin guttural group.

As the nomenclature is not in itself of first-rate importance, and certain ambiguities incidental to it, such as the distinction between *Pe yodh* and *Pe waw* vbs., cannot be resolved till later sections are reached, the student may be content meantime with a general appreciation of it.

§ 33.

A.

Give (*sing. masc.*). Take (*pl. m.*). Fall (*sing. m.*).[1] Be thou (*m.*) smitten (*Niph.*).[2] I will cause to fall (*Hiph.* of נפל). Thou (*m.*) hast delivered (*Hiph.* of נצל). Delivering (*Hiph. ptc.*). And they were delivered (*Niph.*). Give (2 *m. s. emphatic imper.*, § 23. 2). Thou (*m.*) wilt deliver them, *or* she will deliver them. Ye shall touch (*impf. Qal* of נגע). Smitten (*Niph. ptc.* of נגף). It was told *or* announced (*Hoph.* of נגד). Tell *or* declare ye (*Hiph.*). Look (2 *s. m. jussive Hiph.*[3] of נבט ; § 27. 1 (a) i). To fall. To approach.

[1] Besides being 2 s. m. imper. Qal it might be inf. cstr., as in the last word but one of this group.

[2] Or Niph. inf. cstr.

[3] Or 3 s. f. jussive Hiph.—"let her look."

B.

1. Deliver me from blood-guiltiness,[1] O God of my salvation, and my tongue shall declare[2] thy righteousness.

2. When thou vowest [3] a vow to Yahweh, do not forget to pay it.[4] 3. His enemies were afraid [5] to approach him. 4. Look now [6] toward heaven,[7] and count the stars. 5. And Yahweh caused a deep sleep to fall [8] upon the man, and he took one [9] of his ribs; and the rib which he had taken he built into [10] a woman. 6. The man said, The woman whom thou gavest (to be) with me, she [11] gave me of the tree. 7. Yahweh said to Abram, Walk [12] through the land in [13] the length of it and the breadth [14] of it, for to thee [15] will I give it; [16] and Abram fell upon his face. 8. Jacob dreamed, and, behold,[17] a ladder set up [18] on the earth,[19] and the top of it reached [20] to heaven. 9. We have been delivered [21] into the hands [22] of the kings of the lands.

10 [23]שַׁל [24]נְעָלֶיךָ מֵעַל רַגְלֶיךָ כִּי הַמָּקוֹם אֲשֶׁר [25]אַתָּה עוֹמֵד עָלָיו אַדְמַת [26]קֹדֶשׁ [27]הוּא :

Put off thy sandals from off thy feet, for the place whereon thou art standing is holy ground.

11 וַיֹּאמֶר לוֹ הַמֶּלֶךְ [28]תְּנָה־לִּי בְכֶסֶף וַיֹּאמֶר לֹא־אֶתֵּן לְךָ אֶת־כַּרְמִי :

And the king said to him, Give me thy vineyard for money; and he said, I will not give thee my vineyard.

---

[1] See Note 4 of Exercise 20 A.

[2] תַּגִּיד fem. (3 sing. Hiph. of נגד) because לְשׁוֹן is here, as usually, fem.

[3] The *scriptio plena* is incorrect (see Note 3 of Exercise 22 C). In Deut. 23[22] and Eccl. 5[3] it is written correctly as תִּדֹּר. This is a good illustration of the force of the impf. to indicate repetition (§ 46. II. 2). The meaning is not so much " when *once* in the *future* thou shalt vow " (though, of course, it could quite well mean this, § 46. II. 3), but rather " when *at any time* thou vowest, *every time* thou vowest."

[4] שַׁלְּמוֹ is the Pi. inf. cstr. (שַׁלֵּם), with the 3rd sing. masc. suffix— the whole treated like a word of the Third Declension, § 30. Cf. § 31. 3 b. What is true of the Pi. *impf.* is, of course, equally true of the imper. and inf. cstr., § 21. I (c) and 2 (a) i ; see *Grammar*, p. 211, last column.

[5] After יָרֵא, לְ or מִן may be used with the following inf.: cf. Gen. 26[7] יָרֵא לֵאמֹר אִשְׁתִּי " he was *afraid to* say, My wife " (*Grammar*, p. 153, אִשָּׁה), Ex. 3[6] יָרֵא מֵהַבִּיט אֶל־הָאֱלֹהִים " he was *afraid of* looking on God."

[6] The נָא־ softens the imperative. For the change of the ״ in הַבֶּט to ״, see § 10. 3 a.

⁷ *He locale*, § 17. 3.

⁸ Note וַיַּפֵּל (always so with waw consec. and impf. Hiph.) not וַיַּפִּיל, § 27. 1 (*a*) i.

⁹ For אַחַת, see *Grammar*, p. 164. For מִן after אַחַת (or אֶחָד, *m.*), see Note 12 of Exercise 20 A.

¹⁰ A very common use of לְ ; almost = "so as to produce or result in"; cf. Gen. 12² אֶעֶשְׂךָ לְגוֹי גָּדוֹל "I will make thee (§ 44. 2. 1) *into* a great nation." So "to make *into* a desolation" לְשַׁמָּה ; and so very frequently with the vb. הָיָה *to be* : see Note 4 of Exercise 22 B.

¹¹ The subj. is sometimes resumed by the corresponding personal pronoun, especially where it "is encumbered with complementary elements (as here), so that it needs to be disentangled and re-stated" (*Syntax*, § 106).

¹² For הִתְהַלֵּךְ, see § 26. 3 (*b*) iv.

¹³ More strictly "*according to* (*i.e.* to the full extent of) its length and breadth." לְ is used of "reference to a norm or standard, *according to, after, by*" (*BDB*, p. 516): cf. Gen. 1¹¹ לְמִינוֹ *according to* its kind; Gen. 10⁵ אִישׁ לִלְשֹׁנוֹ "each (§ 13. 4) *according to* his tongue" (*i.e.* language); Num. 1² לְבֵית אֲבֹתָם "*by* their fathers' houses" (*Grammar*, p. 153, אָב and בֵּית).

¹⁴ אֶרֶךְ is a normal word of Second Decl., here with 3 s. f. suffix (*Grammar*, p. 101, col. 3), and רֹחַב (though under the influence of the guttural the ֶ becomes ַ) is also normal (cf. § 36. 2, column 5).

¹⁵ Note the order—for emphasis.

¹⁶ 3 s. f. with *nûn energ.*, which occurs chiefly, as here, in pause (see sentence 9 of Exercise 31 C).

¹⁷ הִנֵּה with the ptc. does not *necessarily* refer to the future (§ 46. IV. 1. iii), though it is frequently added to the ptc. when used in this sense. Here, however, it is merely vivid.

¹⁸ Hoph. ptc. of נצב. For the ָ in the Hoph. ptc., see Note 4 of Exercise 27 B.

¹⁹ *He locale*, § 17. 3. So הַשָּׁמַיְמָה at the end of the sentence.

²⁰ Hiph. ptc. of נגע.

²¹ 1 pl. pf. Niph. of נתן : in full it would be נִנְתַּנְנוּ (never written): see *Grammar*, p. 213. See Note 9 (1st paragraph) of Exercise 25 C.

²² Hebrew says *hand* : see sentence 1 of section B of Exercise 30, and references in Note 19 of Exercise 23 A.

²³ 2 s. m. imper. of נשל.

²⁴ We should rather have expected the *dual* (§ 16. 5 a) נַעֲלֶיךָ. But the dual only occurs twice (Am. 2⁶ 8⁶), and never with the suffix. This

passage occurs in Exod. 3⁵ and Josh. 5¹⁵ (in the latter passage in the sing. נַעְלֶךָ, § 36. 2. 2, though some MSS. read plur.).

²⁵ As a rule the subj., as here, *precedes* the ptc.

²⁶ See Note 8 of Exercise 23 A.

²⁷ The unemphatic resumption of the subject (§ 12, p. 46).

²⁸ Emphatic imper. (§ 23. 2)—תֵּן being treated like a Third Declension word.

Note carefully the *daghesh forte conjunctivum* in לְ after a word ending in הַ . This is one of the cases referred to in § 7. 6 : a word ending in הַ accented, *which is immediately preceded by a vocal sh^ewa* (as here), is joined by maqqeph to the next word, which then takes the daghesh forte, *e.g.* Num. 22⁶ לְכָה-נָּא *come* (imp. לֵךְ from הלך, § 39. 2. (2) (*d*) i) *I pray thee* ; נָתְנָה-לִּי in sentence 6 of this Exercise. The dagh. forte is written chiefly when the word is a monosyllable as in the above cases, or a word accented on the first syllable ; and in such cases it is written also when the preceding word ends in an unaccented ָ ; cf. Gen. 15⁶ וַיַּחְשְׁבֶהָ לּוֹ *and he reckoned it to him.* The dagh. is also written with ה ָ ; cf. Gen. 33⁵ אֵלֶּה לָּךְ *these are thine* ; Gen. 11⁴ נִבְנֶה-לָּנוּ *let us build for ourselves.*

C.

1 תְּנוּ : 2 לֹא אֶתֵּן אֶת-כַּסְפִּי וְאֶת-זְהָבִי : 3 אַל-תַּגִּידוּ ¹בְנַת : 4 אַל-²תַּבִּיטִי אַחֲרַיִךְ פֶּן-³יִגַּף אֱלֹהִים : 5 הַצִּילֵנִי כִּי יְשׁוּעָתִי אָתָּה : 6 יִתְּנוּ לַיהוָה כָּבוֹד ⁴עַל-חַסְדּוֹ : 7 בִּתִּי אֶת-הָאִשָּׁה לָאִישׁ לְאִשָּׁה : 8 אַצִּילֵךְ ⁵וּלְשׁוֹנֵךְ תַּגִּיד צִדְקָתִי : 9 הַשִּׁיאָה הַנָּחָשׁ וַתִּקַּח מִן-הָעֵץ וַתִּתֵּן לְאִישָׁהּ : 10 יְרָאוּ ⁶מִגֶּשֶׁר פֶּן-יִנָּגְפוּ לִפְנֵי אֹיְבֵיהֶם : 11 הִפַּלְתָּ עָלַי תַּרְדֵּמָה : 12 וַיִּגַּשׁ אֶת-הָאִישׁ ⁷וַיְחַבְּקוּ-לוֹ וַיְנַשְּׁקוּ-לוֹ :

¹ "Sometimes the ָ (*a*) is intentionally retained in pause, especially if the following consonant is strengthened (doubled), *e.g.* יֻכַּתּוּ Job 4²⁰ (Hoph. impf. of כתת) *they are crushed,* or if it ought to be strengthened : *e.g.* בְּנַת " ; G.K. § 29 *l*. The derivative גִּתִּי Gittite (with *two t's*) points to a lost *t* (or more strictly *n* : the root is יגן, hence ideally גִּנְתִּי). That is why we do not write בְּנַת.

² Though the 2 sing. masc. jussive Hiph. has ֵ (תַּבֵּט), the 2 s. *fem.*

and *plur.* naturally revert, in the open syllable, to י (תַּבִּיטִי, תַּבִּיטוּ, just like the imperative הַקְטֵל, הַקְטִילִי, הַקְטִילוּ).

[3] An interesting form יִגְּפֶנּוּ (*yiggᵉphénnû*) occurs in 1 Sam. 26[10] (as if in our sentence we might have written יִגְּפֶךָ) *he will smite him* (*nûn energ.*), though 2 Chr. 13[20] has the more normal form יִגְּפֵהוּ. The ֶ (very seldom written with other consonants than gutturals, § 3. 3 b) is due to an attempt to preserve, so far as possible, the original *ō* sound (יִגֹּף yiggᵒph). Such forms are rare : see G.K., § 10 *h*.

[4] עַל־ *on the ground of*; cf. Ps. 138[2] אוֹדֶה אֶת־שִׁמְךָ עַל־חַסְדֶּךָ "I will give thanks (Hiph. of יָדָה, §§ 39, 44) unto thy name *because of* thy kindness."

[5] See Ps. 51[17]. The normal prose construction would be וְהִגִּידָה (waw consec. with pf.) The English sentence should end, "*my* righteousness."

[6] Or לָגֶשֶׁת, § 33. 3 d. See Note 5 of section B of this Exercise.

[7] So Gen. 29[13]. The phrase "to take in the arms" (which would here be וַיִּקָּחֵהוּ בִּזְרוֹעֹתָיו) does not seem to be used in the O.T.: the nearest approach to it, if the text is sound, is Hos. 11[3], but the idea there is different—taking a child *on* (עַל) the arms. חבק *to embrace*, should be used (in the Pi'el): it is usually followed by לְ (though also by the accus., cf. Gen. 33[4] וַיְחַבְּקֵהוּ *and he embraced him*).

נשק *to kiss*, chiefly in the Qal, though also (as in Gen. 29[13]) in the Pi'el. It is usually followed by לְ, but sometimes by the accus. (cf. Gen. 33[4] וַיִּשָּׁקֵהוּ *and he kissed him*). *And he kissed him* is several times rendered וַיִּשַּׁק־לוֹ. The juxtaposition of the two accented syllables in this last sentence (as also in the sentence translated above) explains the maqqeph, § 10. 3, and the methegh is put with the vowel on what is now the secondary tone, though this is in a *shut* syllable : cf. the frequent וַיִּתֶּן־לוֹ *and he gave to him*, Gen. 24[35f.] 30[6], Jud. 1[13].

§ 34.

A.

1. And he left all that he had in Joseph's hand.
2. Behold, the two kings[1] did not stand before him, and how shall *we*[2] stand? 3. And God remembered Noah, and he caused a great wind to pass over the earth. 4. And he and I dreamed a dream in one night.[3] 5. Be strong and of a good courage,[4] for thou[5] shalt cause this

people to inherit the land [6] which I swore [7] to their fathers [8] to give them.[9] 6. And Abraham trusted [10] in Yahweh, and he counted it [11] to him as righteousness. 7. Give us [12] this land and do not send us over [13] the river. 8. Yahweh sent me to bind up the broken-hearted.[14] 9. If thine enemy [15] be hungry, give him bread to eat.[16] 10. Touch [17] the mountains, that [18] they may smoke.

אַל־תַּעֲזֹב חָכְמָה אֱהָבֶהָ [19] וְתִשְׁמְרֶךָּ: 11

Forsake not Wisdom : love her, that she may keep thee.[20]

וְאַתֶּם אַל־[22]תַּעֲמֹדוּ רִדְפוּ אַחֲרֵי אֹיְבֵיכֶם כִּי נְתָנָם יְהוָה אֱלֹהֵיכֶם[21] 12
בְּיֶדְכֶם:[23]

Do not *ye* stand : pursue after your enemies, for Yahweh your God has delivered them into your hand.

[1] Not "two of the kings." See Note 4 of Exercise 18 C.

[2] Pronoun added for emphasis.

[3] Literally, "and we dreamed a dream . . . I and he." Note for prose composition. Idiomatically, "one night he and I dreamed," etc.

For the וְ in וְהוּא, see § 15. 1 d.

[4] Note the initial vowels in חֲזַק and אֱמַץ, and see § 8. 2 b.

[5] Note the emphatic אַתָּה. Moses is dead (Josh. 1²) ; but it will be *thy* (*i.e.* Joshua's) task to cause the people to inherit the land.

[6] Note the two accusatives, each with את, after the Hiph., § 27, 1 *d*.

[7] Note that שבע *to swear* takes the *Niph.* : it is also used in *Hiph.*, with the meaning *to cause to take an oath.*

[8] For אבותם, see *Grammar*, p. 153, אָב.

[9] Note that we write לָתֶת־לָנוּ (Ezra 9⁸ᶠ·) to avoid the juxtaposition of the two accented syllables תֶת and לְ (§ 10. 3 a—note further the methegh with the vowel now second from the tone) : so לָתֶת־לְךָ *to give thee*, לְךָ being treated as a monosyllable. But we do not write לָתֶת־לָהֶם, because the accented syllables are no longer juxtaposed, the accent on להם being on the *second* syllable ; we therefore write instead לָתֵת לָהֶם.

[10] The tense (pf.) would suggest the single act of trust illustrated by the story (Gen. 15), and the more normal construction would have been וַיַּאֲמֵן. This is actually read, as Kittel notes, by one MS. and by the Samaritan Pentateuch. But the original (Gen. 15⁶) reads וְהֶאֱמִן, which, if the text be correct, would have the force of an impf. (יַאֲמִין)—no doubt (in this context) in the frequentative sense (cf. § 46. III.)—*he repeatedly trusted*, or, with reference to the single incident in question, *he maintained his trust.*

[11] *It, i.e.,* his trust in Yahweh—*fem.,* § 16. 4. 7. Notice the second obj. צְדָקָה (in apposition) in the accus. But the construction with לְ is also possible ; cf. Ps 106[31] וַתֵּחָשֶׁב לוֹ לִצְדָקָה " and it was reckoned unto him *for* righteousness."

[12] For the לְ, see Note 28 (2nd paragraph) of Exercise 33 B.

[13] Lit. " do not cause us to come over." It is usually worth while to find some single English word to represent the Hiph. rather than resort to the cumbrous periphrasis "to *cause* some one *to do* something " : *e.g.* עָלָה *to go up*, הֶעֱלָה (§ 34. 2) *to bring up* ; יָצָא *to go out,* הוֹצִיא (§ 39. 2. 1 a) *to bring out.*

תַּעֲבִרֵנוּ 2 sing. m. jussive Hiph. : *scriptio def.* (§ 4. d) for תַּעֲבִירֵנוּ. Note Hiph. with two accusatives : cf. Note 6 of this section.

[14] For this phrase, see Note 1 of Exercise 25 C.

[15] One who hates thee (ptc. שֹׂנֵא). Sometimes the .. is retained with this suffix : cf. שֹׁלְחֶךָ *one who sends thee* : sometimes it is modified to _ as here (cf. Isa. 43[1] בֹּרַאֲךָ *thy creator*).

[16] Lit. " cause him to eat bread."

[17] Imper. of נגע, which usually takes בְּ.

[18] § 23. 3. 6.

[19] 3rd sing. fem. impf. of שׁמר with 2 s. m. suffix, with *nûn energ.,* § 31. 7. Note daghesh forte in ךָ. Were this not in pause, it would be pointed וְתִשְׁמְרֶךָ.

[20] Cf. sentence 10. But "and she will keep thee " may be justified, if we regard the *waw* as a simple copulative *waw* : in that case the impf. would be independent and would have its ordinary force. To convey such a meaning, however, the usual construction is waw consec. with pf. (For this construction after the imperative, see Note 3 of Exercise 26 B.)

[21] אַתֶּם perhaps in contrast to the sentinels in the preceding verse (Josh. 10[18]). Cf. sentence 2 of this Exercise.

[22] The pause in the sense is here so strong as to demand the pausal pointing (rather than simply תַּעֲמֹדוּ), even though, as in Josh. 10[19], it is not accompanied by one of the two great pausal accents, but by *zāqēph qāṭôn* (*Grammar,* p. 230, 2 d).

[23] Not בְּיֶדְכֶם : see *Grammar,* p. 106, footnote 2. Note that Hebrew says your *hand* (not *hands* : see Note 8 of Exercise 23 B. So *heart,* not *hearts*).

B.

1 רָאָה אַבְרָהָם אַיִל נֶאֱחַז [1]בְּקַרְנָיו: 2 אַל־תַּעַבְרוּ אֶת־
הַנָּהָר פֶּן־תִּנָּגְפוּ לִפְנֵי אֹיְבֵיכֶם: 3 לֹא תַעֲבֹד אַרְצֵנוּ כִּי

יַעַמְדוּ אֹיְבֵינוּ בְּקִרְבָּה׃ 4 ²אֶעְבְּרָה־נָּא אֶת־הַנָּהָר ³וְאַנְחִילָה
אֶת־הָעָם הַזֶּה אֶת־הָאָרֶץ אֲשֶׁר נִשְׁבַּע יְהוָה ⁴לַאֲבֹתָם לָתֶת
לָהֶם׃ 5 אֲהַב חָכְמָה אַל־תַּעַזְבֶנָּה⁵׃ 6 אָמְרוּ ⁶לוּ לְאֶסְרָךְ
יְרַדְנוּ ⁷לְתִתְּךָ בְּיַד אֹיְבֶיךָ׃ 7 ⁸וַיַּעַבְדוּ הָעָם אֶת־אֱלֹהֵיהֶם
⁸כָּל־יְמֵי יְהוֹשֻׁעַ ⁹וְכֹל־יְמֵי הַזְּקֵנִים אֲשֶׁר הֶאֱרִיכוּ יָמִים אַחֲרֵי
יְהוֹשֻׁעַ׃ 8 וַיַּעֲבֵר אֶת־¹⁰בָּנָיו בָּאֵשׁ׃

¹ Dual (קַרְנַיִם) not plur. (קְרָנוֹת, which would here give קַרְנוֹתָיו). In the (late) Book of Daniel, the dual appears in a longer form as קְרָנַיִם (8³·⁶·²⁰), and with the suffix consequently as קַרְנָיו (8⁷).

Between the dual and the plural "a difference of meaning appears in several names of members of the body, the dual denoting the living members themselves, while the plur. in וֹת expresses something like them, but without life : e.g. יָדַיִם hands. יָדוֹת artificial hands, also, e.g., the arms of a throne ; כַּפַּיִם hands, כַּפּוֹת handles ; קַרְנַיִם horns, קְרָנוֹת horns (of the altar)." G.K. § 87 o.

² The cohortative of אֶעְבֹר, which we should expect to be אֶעְבְּרָה, always appears in this form, with the first syllable closed (but in pause אֶעְבֵּרָה). So also the cohortative pl. of נַעְבֹר always appears as נַעְבְּרָה, cf. Num. 20¹⁷, Jud. 11¹⁹ (but in pause נַעֲבֵרָה). Note the daghesh in the following נ, and see Note 28 (2nd paragraph) of Exercise 33 B.

³ § 23. 3. 6. Note the double accus. after the Hiph. (§ 27. 1 d).

⁴ Rather than אֲבוֹתֵיהֶם ; see Grammar, p. 153.

⁵ With nûn energ. in the pausal form (from תַּעֲזֹב). In Prov. 4⁶ the form is not in pause, and therefore תַּעַזְבֶהָ.

⁶ Or אֵלָיו.

⁷ Not לְתִתְּךָ (though we say לָתֶת, § 33. 3 d), because the ל is not now pre-tonic.

⁸ For the plur. vb. with the sing. collective noun, see Note 2 (2nd paragraph) of Exercise 29 B.

⁹ In Jud. 2⁷ (=Josh. 24³¹) the more emphatic כֹּל and וְכֹל (i.e. without the maqqeph) are used.

¹⁰ Or יְלָדָיו.

§ 35.

A.

1. And Yahweh said to the man, Of every tree of the garden thou mayest freely eat.[1]   2. If ye be willing and hearken,[2] ye shall eat[3] the good of the land.   3. And I will cause them to eat the flesh of their sons and the flesh[4] of their daughters.   4. Take unto thee of every kind[5] of food that is eaten,[6] and it shall be for food for thee and for them.   5. O Yahweh, do not, we entreat thee, let us perish for[7] this man's life, and lay not upon us innocent blood.   6. And the king said to the woman, What aileth thee?[8] and she said, This woman[9] said to me, Give thy son that we may eat him[10] to-day, and my son[11] we will eat to-morrow.   So we boiled my son and ate him; and I said to her the next day,[12] Give thy son that we may eat him, but she hid[13] her son.

7 וַתִּקַּח הָאִשָּׁה מִפְּרִי הָעֵץ וַתֹּאכַל וַתִּתֵּן גַּם־לְאִישָׁהּ[14] וַיֹּאכַל׃

And the woman took of the fruit of the tree and ate, and she gave also to her husband, and he ate.

8 הֶאֱכַלְתֶּם לֶחֶם בַּמִּדְבָּר׃

Thou gavest them bread to eat[15] in the wilderness.

[1] A good illustration of the potential use of the impf. (§ 46. II. 4), and of the abs. inf. (§ 21. 2 b).

[2] Note the (thoroughly normal) sequence of tenses—waw consec. with impf. (natural after אִם) followed by the *pf.* (§ 23. 3. 2 a).

שְׁמַע *to hearken* (to the voice of Yahweh), is often practically=*to be obedient* (as here).

[3] The apodosis—"then ye shall eat"—might equally well have been introduced by waw consec. with the *pf.* (וַאֲכַלְתֶּם) instead of the simple impf. תֹּאכְלוּ (pausal form of תֹּאכֵלוּ, § 10. 4 c). Cf. Gen. 44[9] אֲשֶׁר יִמָּצֵא אִתּוֹ וָמֵת *with whomsoever it be found, he shall die.* This form of apodosis (waw cons. with pf.) is very common after a protasis introduced by כִּי or אִם; *e.g.* Deut. 22[2] אִם־לֹא קָרוֹב אָחִיךָ אֵלֶיךָ וַאֲסַפְתּוֹ "if thy brother be not near thee, *then thou shalt bring it . . .,*" where תֶּאֶסְפֵהוּ (from תֶּאֱסוֹף; cf. § 34. 3 b) would have been possible. (The *then* of the English apodosis in such sentences should be translated by וְ (with pf.); it is hardly ever represented by אָז, and then only where

special emphasis is desired : Driver, *Hebrew Tenses*, § 136, 1*a. Obs.* 2.)
An excellent illustration of the practical equivalence of these constructions occurs in 2 Kings 7⁴ אִם־יְחַיֻּ֫נוּ נִחְיֶה וְאִם־יְמִיתֻ֫נוּ וָמָ֑תְנוּ *if they spare
us, we shall live, and if they kill us, we shall (but) die.* (יְחַיֻּנוּ, Pi. impf.
of חיה with suffix, § 26. 1 (*b*) ii ; יְמִיתֻנוּ, Hiph. impf. of מות with suffix,
§ 40. 3 *a*.)

⁴ Note the repetition of בְּשַׂר. "There is nothing unusual in several
genitives after *one* construct : *e.g.* Deut. 8⁸ אֶ֫רֶץ חִטָּה וּשְׂעֹרָה *a land of
wheat and barley.*" But "in the broader or emphatic style, the construct is *repeated* before each genitive" as here : cf. Gen. 24³ אֱלֹהֵי
הַשָּׁמַ֫יִם וֵאלֹהֵי הָאָ֫רֶץ *the God of heaven and the God of earth (Syntax,*
§ 28, Rem. 4). English idiom : "the flesh of their sons *and daughters.*"

⁵ Generally speaking, כֹּל (lit. *entirety*) before a determinate noun
means *all* : cf. כָּל־הָאָ֫רֶץ *all the earth* ; but before an indeterminate noun,
it means *of all kinds, every kind of.* The second part of this rule,
however, is not strictly observed : *e.g.* כָּל־בָּשָׂר *all flesh* ; כָּל־עֵץ may
mean not only *every kind of tree,* but *all trees.*

⁶ A good illustration of the frequentative impf.—"that is *regularly*
or *customarily* eaten" (§ 46. II. 2. 1).

⁷ בְּ *on account of* : *e.g.* Deut. 24¹⁶ they shall be put to death
אִישׁ בְּחֶטְאוֹ, "each *on account of* his own sin"; Gen. 18²⁸ הֲתַשְׁחִית
בַּחֲמִשָּׁה אֶת־כָּל־הָעִיר "wilt thou (הֲ, § 49. 2. 2 a) destroy the whole city
on account of five" (§ 48)? This is possibly an extension of what is
known as the בְּ *pretii*, which indicates price, risk, etc.

⁸ "What hast thou?" like "*qu'as tu ?*" "*was hast Du ?*"="what is
the matter, what aileth thee ?"

⁹ The הַזֹּאת must go with the הָאִשָּׁה : for if we attempt to separate
the two, and to translate, "and the woman (הָאִשָּׁה) said, This (one) said
to me," we should have the impossible הַזֹּאת instead of the simple זֹאת
(§ 13. 1) as subject to אָמְרָה.

¹⁰ Note the suffix with *nûn energ.* here in a non-pausal place, and in
the next sentence the ordinary form הוּ in a pausal place. *Nûn energ.*
is specially frequent in pause.
Note, twice, the simple waw with impf. in final sense : § 23. 3. 6.

¹¹ Note the order, for emphasis. The unemphatic form would have
been וְאָכַ֫לְנוּ אֶת־בְּנִי (not וַאֲכַלְנֻהוּ : see § 23. 3. 4).

¹² Note the בְּ : so usually, though הַיּוֹם by itself can mean *this day,
to-day* : cf. Gen. 40⁷ מַדּוּעַ פְּנֵיכֶם רָעִים הַיּוֹם "why are your faces sad
to-day ? "

¹³ We should rather have expected וַתֵּחָבֵא (§ 38, p. 221, col. 4). But

in the jussive, impf. consec., and imper. Hiph. of Lamedh aleph vbs. "a number of cases occur (of which this is one) with *i* in the final syllable. If the tradition be correct, the retention of the *i* is to be attributed to the open syllable" (G.K. § 74 *l*). The א being quiescent (§ 9. 1), the syllable is virtually open.

[14] Note that in the ordinary non-pausal form of this word the accent is retracted, as always (with waw consec. impf.) when the first syllable is open (§ 23. 3. 4), as it is virtually here : therefore וַיֹּאכַל. In pause, the accent is naturally restored to the last syllable, but (though the pausal form of impf. of אכל is, *by itself*, יֹאכֵל) the pausal of impf. *consec.* is not וַיֹּאכֵל but וַיֹּאכַל (so *fem.* in the previous clause וַתֹּאכַל): see Gen. 3⁶.

[15] Lit. "thou didst cause them to eat."

B.

וַ אֶלְ־נָא נֹאבְדָה בְּנַפְשׁוֹ׃ 2 תֹּאכְלוּ מִפְּרִי דַרְכֵיכֶם׃ 1
וַיֹּאמְרוּ בְנֵי יִשְׂרָאֵל 4 [2]וַיֹּאכֵלוּ [1]לֶאֱכֹל 3 וַיִּקְרָא אֶת־הָעָם
לַגֵּר תִּתְּנֶנָּה [3]לֹא תֹאכְלוּ כָל־נְבֵלָה 5 מִי יַאֲכִלֵנוּ בָּשָׂר׃
[5]וְאָכֵל׃ [4]הַנָּחָשׁ הִשִּׁיאַנִי 6 וַתֹּאמֶר הָאִשָּׁה וַאֲכָלָה׃
8 לֹא יֵאָכֵל בָּאֵשׁ יִשָּׂרֵף׃ [8]וַאֲכָלָה׃ [6]תְּנָה־לִּי בָשָׂר 7
וַיִּשְׁכֵּם הָאִישׁ 10 וַיֹּאכְלוּ הַכְּלָבִים אֶת־בְּשַׂר עֶגְלִי׃ 9
בְּאָזְנֵי עֲבָדָיו׃ [10]אֶת־כָּל־הַדְּבָרִים הָאֵלֶּה [9]וַיַּגֵּד בַּבֹּקֶר
[13]וַיַּאַסְרֻהוּ [12]וַיֹּאחֲזוּ אֶת־שִׁמְשׁוֹן [11]פְּלִשְׁתִּים נֶאֱסְפוּ 11
[14]בַּנְחֻשְׁתָּיִם׃

---

[1] Not לְאָכֹל : cf. § 35. 3 b, also § 14. 1 c.

[2] The pausal form of the *plural* : for the *sing.*, see Note 14 of section A of this Exercise.

[3] Not necessarily אַל, though it is a virtual prohibition : cf. § 23. 1. 1. ii.

[4] This deviation from the customary order (vb., subj.) gives special prominence to the subject : "it was not on my own initiative, *it was the serpent that deceived me.*"

[5] So always the pausal form of the *first* pers. sing. (Non-pausal, אֹכַל.) See Note 2 for *third* pers.

[6] Or, less emphatically, תֶּן־לִי ; § 10. 3.

[7] For the *daghesh*, see Note 28 (2nd paragraph) of Exercise 33 B.

[8] Cf. § 23. 3. 6.

⁹ Not וַיִּגַּד : the accent cannot here be retracted from the last syllable to the penult, because the penult is not open, § 23. 3. 4 ; therefore וַיַּגֵּד. But וַיַּגֶּד־לָהּ *and he told her* (Jud. 14¹⁷ 16¹⁷), is quite correct and normal ; § 10. 3.

¹⁰ אָזְנֵי *dual* cstr. of אָזְנַיִם—first syllable closed.

¹¹ פְלִשְׁתִּים is usually written without the article.

¹² אָחַז may take the accus. as here, but it is also very frequently followed by בְּ ; *e.g.* Gen. 25²⁶ יָדוֹ אֹחֶזֶת בַּעֲקֵב עֵשָׂו *his hand was seizing* (*i.e.* had hold on : ptc.) *Esau's heel.*

¹³ When the tone is moved one place towards the end, ֳ ָ becomes ֳ ֳ ; thus יַאְסֹר (or יֶאְסֹר) becomes וַיַּאַסְרֵהוּ : cf. § 34. 3 b.

¹⁴ Note the article—*the* fetters which are used to bind men (see Note 8 of Exercise 14 A).

This phrase is so spelt five times, and once (Jer. 39⁷) בַּנְּחֻשְׁתַּיִם. For the omission of *daghesh* from the נ, see § 7. 5 ; and note the compensation in the *methegh.* See Note 5 of Exercise 30 B.

§ 36.

A.

Cleanse thou me (*Pi. imperat. with* 1 *s. suffix : pf.* טִהַר, *impf.* יְטַהֵר). Taste ye (*Qal*). Bless ye (*Pi.*). He will serve (*Pi.*). Cry thou (*f. Qal*). And they fought (*Niph.*). He will cleanse (*Pi.*). I will wash (*Qal*). Thou (*f.*) hast been washed (*Pu.*). I will wash (*Qal*) thee (*f.:* see § 31. 3 (a) i). Let us choose (1 *pl. cohortat. Qal*). Crying aloud (*Pi. ptc. m.*). My lord (בַּעַל *with* 1 *s. suffix.*[1] *So far as the form goes, it might also be* 2 *s. f. imper. Qal of* בָּעַל). Thy (*f.*) gates.

[1] Curiously enough, with the 3 s. f. suffix, the first syllable of this word is closed, בַּעְלָהּ *her husband*, 2 Sam. 11²⁶, Prov. 31¹¹ ; also with 3 pl. f. suff., בַּעְלֵיהֶן *their husbands*, Esth 1¹⁷· ²⁰. So זַעַם *indignation*, takes with suffixes זַעְמִי and זַעְמוֹ.

B.

1. Let there now[1] be fetched a little[2] water, and wash your feet, and rest[3] yourselves under the tree, and let me fetch[4] a morsel of bread, and sustain ye your hearts : after-

wards ye shall pass on.[5] 2. And Yahweh drove out[6] the man and sent him forth[7] from the garden of Eden to till the ground whence he had been taken. 3. The meal-offering[8] and the drink-offering are[9] cut off; the priests, the ministers[10] of Yahweh, mourn. 4. And the priests blessed the Israelites, saying, Yahweh bless thee and keep thee,[11] Yahweh lift up his face towards thee. 5. And the Israelites cried to Yahweh, saying, We have forsaken our God and served the Baals. 6. And I will bless thee[12] and make thy name great, and I will bless[13] those that bless thee,[14] and by thee shall all the families of the earth bless themselves.[15]

7 [16]בָּרְכִי נַפְשִׁי אֶת־יְהוָה וְאַל־[16]תִּשְׁכְּחִי [17]כָּל־חֲסָדָיו׃

Bless Yahweh, O my soul, and forget not any of his kindnesses.

8 בַּיּוֹם הַהוּא תֹּאמְרִי לִי אִישִׁי וְלֹא תִקְרְאִי־[18]לִי עוֹד בַּעְלִי׃

In that day thou shalt say to me, My husband, and thou shalt no more call me, My lord.[19]

[1] נָא polite—"I pray you."

[2] Construct—"a little of water." The form of the absolute is the same : in pause מְעַט (Isa. 10[7]). The plur. מְעַטִּים *few*, occurs twice (Ps. 109[8], Eccl. 5[1]).

[3] Lit. "lean"—*Niph.* שָׁעַן is the vb. from which מִשְׁעֶנֶת comes in Ps. 23[4] מִשְׁעַנְתֶּךָ *thy staff*, that on which one *leans* : § 29. 3).

[4] A more emotional form (§ 23. I. 2) than וְלָקַחְתִּי (*and I will fetch*, § 23. 3. 5 b) would have been.

[5] Pausal form of תַּעֲבֹרוּ, § 10. 4 c.

[6] יְגָרֵשׁ becomes, with waw consec., וַיְגָרֶשׁ : the tone can be, and is, retracted, because the penult is open : § 23. 3. 4. So וַיִּלָּחֶם *and he fought* (Niph.) ; cf. Note 9 of Exercise 25 B.

[7] שִׁלַּח in *Pi.*, not Qal. See Note 4 of Exercise 30 B.

[8] Primarily מִנְחָה is simply *offering* ; then it came to be *grain-offering*. R.V.'s *meal-offering* is preferable to A.V.'s *meat-offering*, which is now entirely misleading.

[9] Note the Hebrew *singular*. For the use of a *sing.* vb. (coming first) with a compound subject, see Note 10 of Exercise 26 A. As a rule the vb. agrees in gend. and numb. with the first subj. as being nearest to it. Here, however, the subj. מִנְחָה is *fem.*, while the vb. is *masc.* The pred., however, may appear in the masc. sing.— "before collectives fem. and masc."—in this order : cf. 2 Sam. 12[2]

לְעָשִׁיר הָיָה צֹאן וּבָקָר a rich man haa (הָיָה m. s.) sheep (f.) and oxen (G.K. § 146 f). So here.

[10] Cstr. Pi. ptc. of שרת.

[11] Note the co-ordination of the two impfs. by the simple waw; § 23. 3. 7. The illustrations of co-ordination there given happen to be with perfects; but the construction, though rare, is equally possible with imperfects, whether in a future or (as here) in a jussive sense (Driver, *Hebrew Tenses*, § 134). *E.g.* Exod. 24[7] "all that Yahweh has spoken נַעֲשֶׂה וְנִשְׁמָע *we will do and be obedient*"; Josh. 7[3] יַעֲלוּ וְיַכּוּ *let them go up and smite* (Hiph. of נכה, § 44. 2. 1).

[12] The more normal (prose) construction would have been waw consec. with pf.—וּבֵרַכְתִּיךָ (not וּב; cf. § 8. 4 b), followed by וְנִדְלְתִי and וּבֵרַכְתִּי; exactly like וְנִבְרְכוּ later in the sentence. But the impf. with simple copulative *waw* "gives the various actions more independence and force than if the ordinary secution with *waw consec. pf.* had been adopted" (*Syntax*, § 59).

In the context, however, this sentence (Gen. 12[2]) is preceded by an imperative (12[1]) לֶךְ־לְךָ מֵאַרְצֶךָ *get thee* (לֶךְ, imper. Qal of הָלַךְ, § 39. 2. 2 (d) i) *out of thy country*, so that the clause may well be final (§ 23. 3. 6), *that I may bless thee*. It may equally well, however, be a simple future, as the following clause, *and I will bless those that bless thee*, is much more naturally interpreted as future—a promise—than as final.

[13] Notice the emotional force of the cohortative אֲבָרְכָה, § 23. 1. 2.

[14] Pi. ptc. pl. with suffix, "thy blessers."

[15] The use of the Hithpaʻel (which can only be reflexive) in the very similar sentences, Gen. 22[18] 26[4] וְהִתְבָּרְכוּ, strongly suggests that the Niph. here (Gen. 12[3]), which might theoretically have a passive meaning —"in thee *shall* all the families of the earth *be blessed*"—should rather be taken reflexively (§ 25. 3. i); and the meaning really is that other nations in invoking blessings on themselves will use such words as "God make thee like Abram" (see Skinner's *Genesis*, p. 244; T. H. Robinson (*Genesis in Colloquial English*, p. 17), well brings out the meaning by "all the nations of the world shall regard you as a type of the prosperous man."

[16] The vbs. are *fem.*, ageeing with נֶפֶשׁ.

[17] Not "forget not *all*," but "forget not *any*," "forget *none*" (§ 13. 4).

[18] For קרא with לְ in the sense of "to name," see Note 1 of Exercise 14 A.

[19] "My Baʻal." Yahweh was the Baʻal, the lord, of Israel; but so perilous were the associations of the Baʻal worship that the name of Baal, in any application to Yahweh, is to disappear (Hos. 2[18f. (A.V. 16f.)]).

C.

1 בְּעֵבֶר נַהֲרֵי כוּשׁ׃ 2 תַּעֲמֹדְנָה רַגְלֵינוּ בִּשְׁעָרַיִךְ יְרוּשָׁלִָם׃
3 תְאֵהַב אֶת יְהֹוָה אֱלֹהֶיךָ וְאֹתוֹ תַעֲבֹד׃ 4 וַיִּזְעֲקוּ
אֵלַי אֲבֹתֵיכֶם וַיֹּאמְרוּ נֹאבַד מֵחֲמַס אֹיְבֵינוּ׃ 5 וַתֹּאמֶר
לָאִשָּׁה גָּרֵשׁ אֶת הַשִּׁפְחָה הַזֹּאת וְאֶת בְּנָהּ׃ 6 וַיִּשְׁכְּחוּ
אֶת יְהֹוָה וַיִּמְכְּרֵם בְּיַד אֹיְבֵיהֶם וַיִּלָּחֲמוּ בָּם׃ 7 וַיִּקְחוּ
לָהֶם נָשִׁים מִכֹּל אֲשֶׁר בָּחָרוּ׃

[1] Cf. Deut. 1[1] בְּעֵבֶר הַיַּרְדֵּן. Or more idiomatically—as in Isa. 18[1] and Zeph. 3[10]—מֵעֵבֶר לְנַהֲרֵי כוּשׁ: cf. Num. 22[1] מֵעֵבֶר לְיַרְדֵּן *beyond the Jordan*; Deut. 30[13] מֵעֵבֶר לַיָּם *beyond the sea*. Locality is often thus indicated—with מִן before the first word followed by לְ before the second: cf. Gen. 3[24] מִקֶּדֶם לְגַן־עֵדֶן *on the east of the garden of Eden* (lit. *off* the east *with reference to*); Josh. 8[13] מִצְּפוֹן לָעִיר *on the north of the city*; Exod. 26[33] מִבֵּית לַפָּרֹכֶת *within the veil*; Gen. 19[16] מִחוּץ לָעִיר *outside the city* (for מִחוּץ, see § 14. 2 b). Note that in this phrase the noun following מִן is in the *construct*.

[2] יַעֲמְדוּ would be possible, on the principle of dislike for the 3 pl. fem. impf. when the vb. precedes (see Note 8 of Exercise 29 A), and even sometimes when the vb. follows; cf. Prov. 1[16] רַגְלֵיהֶם לָרַע יָרֻצוּ *their feet run* (impf. of רוּץ, § 40. 2 a) *to evil*. In Ps. 122[2], the Hebrew rendered in A.V. by "our feet shall stand," is עֹמְדוֹת הָיוּ רַגְלֵינוּ, and should be rendered "our feet *were standing*" (ptc.)—it is really a retrospect. Note that הָיָה is sometimes (but not necessarily) added, as here, to give express emphasis to an idea continuing in the past (see Note 7 of Exercise 27 A). Ptc. fem. agr. with noun.

[3] Curiously enough, "thou shalt love" (without *and*) only seems to occur twice—both times as תְאֵהַב (so יֶאֱהַב twice—in pause); but as יֶאֱהַב also occurs without waw and many times with waw (consec.), we may fairly enough write as above. The commoner phrase is "*and* thou shalt love" וְאָהַבְתָּ (so Lev. 19[18. 34], Deut. 6[5] 11[1]). אהב usually takes the accus., but in two or three late passages (*e.g.* Lev. 19[18. 34]) it is followed by לְ.

[4] So (not אֶת־) in Deut. 6[5] 11[1] where a similar phrase occurs. The slower pace enhances the solemnity of the injunction.

[5] In sentences like this, where the vb. is accompanied by a preposi-

tional phrase, a good working rule, which, however, is by no means invariable, is to put that phrase immediately after the vb., if the preposition has a pronominal suffix, but to put the subject immediately after the vb., if the preposition is followed by a noun. *E.g.* Gen. 24[6] וַיֹּאמֶר אֵלָיו אַבְרָהָם (cf. 16[9. 10. 11] : וַיֹּאמֶר לָהּ מַלְאַךְ יְהוָֹה : also cf. 24[5]) but 24[2] וַיֹּאמֶר אַבְרָהָם אֶל־עַבְדּוֹ. Cf. Note 7 of Exercise 30 C and Note 10 of Exercise 39 B.

[6] שִׁפְחָה is used for *handmaid* in the J source, and אָמָה in the E.

[7] I Sam. 12[9] has the daghesh here, with this same phrase.

[8] Daghesh omitted from ק : § 7. 5.

[9] לָהֶם is idiomatically added—"they took *to themselves*."

[10] Plur. of אִשָּׁה : *Grammar*, p. 153.

§ 37.

A.

I will hear.   Let me hear *or* I would (fain) hear (*cf.* Ps. 85[9]).   When it was heard (*cstr. inf. Niph.*).   Cause to hear (*not " thou shalt cause to hear," which would be* תַּשְׁמִיעַ. *The form is* jussive Hiph.—*proper after* אַל: cf. Jud. 18[25] אַל־תַּשְׁמַע קוֹלְךָ, literally, *do not cause to hear thy voice,* i.e., *let not thy voice be heard*).   He (*or* one) who sends thee (*ptc. Qal*).   To send (*inf. cstr.*).   Send thou (*imper. masc.*).   He sent thee (*m.*) away (*Pi.: not* simply *" he sent thee," which would be Qal* שְׁלָחֲךָ).   I will send thee (*m.*).   He will forget him.   Thou (*f.*) hast forgotten.   Thou (*f.*) that hast been forgotten.[1]

[1] This is a difficult form.   It looks like the fem. ptc. Niph. ; but in the context (Isa. 23[15]) it is very doubtful if it can be that.   In the following verse [16] the ptc. appears in the form נִשְׁכָּחָה.   The context is וְהָיָה בַּיּוֹם הַהוּא וְנִשְׁכַּחַת צֹר *and it will come to pass on that day that Tyre will be forgotten.*   The normal construction would be waw consec. with *pf.* (וְנִשְׁכְּחָה, exactly like וְהָיָה) ; besides, if this were a ptc., the noun (Tyre) should precede it.   If the text be retained, it may be regarded as an Aramaizing form of the 3 s. f. pf.   It could not, of course, be 2 s. f. of the Hebr. pf. which would end in תְּ, not ת.

B.

1. Behold, I am sending[1] an angel before thee to keep thee in the way: take thou heed[2] before him and hearken unto his voice.   2. The poor of Zion I will satisfy with bread, and her priests I will clothe with salvation.   3. And Yahweh planted a garden in Eden, and he made to grow out of the ground every kind of tree,[3] desirable[4] in[5] appearance and good for food.   4. And Jacob took his wives and his children and crossed the ford of the Jabboḳ; and he took them and sent them across[6] the stream, and he sent across what he had.   And there wrestled a man with Jacob; and the man said, Let me go, for the dawn has risen.   And he said, I will not let thee go, unless thou bless[7] me.   And the angel said to him, Thy name shall no more be called Jacob, but Israel; and he blessed him there.   And the sun rose upon him as he passed over Penu'el, and he was limping upon his thigh.

5 וַיַּשְׁבִּיעֵנִי לֵאמֹר לֹא־תִקַּח אִשָּׁה לִבְנִי מִבְּנוֹת [8]הַכְּנַעֲנִי אֲשֶׁר אָנֹכִי יֹשֵׁב בְּאַרְצוֹ:

And he made me swear, saying, Thou shalt not take a wife
     for my son from the daughters of the Canaanites, in
     whose land I am dwelling.

6 הַשְׁמִיעֵנִי [9]בַבֹּקֶר חַסְדֶּךָ כִּי־[9]בְךָ [9]בָטָחְתִּי:

Make me to hear thy kindness in the morning, for in thee
     do I trust.

---

[1] *i.e.* am about to send—ptc. of imminent future (§ 46. IV. 1).

[2] הִשָּׁמֶר see Note 10 of Exercise 25 B.

[3] For כָּל־עֵץ see Note 5 of Exercise 35 A.

[4] For this meaning of Niph. ptc., see § 25. 4.   The Niph. ptc. may have the sense of the Latin gerundive or an adjective in—*bilis*; *e.g.* נוֹרָא (from יָרֵא, § 39. 2. 1 *a*) *to be feared*, terrible, נִכְבָּד *honourable*, נִתְעָב *detestable*.   So also sometimes the Puʿal, *e.g.* מְהֻלָּל (Ps. 48[2]) *worthy to be praised*.   But the passive ptc. of the *Qal* always corresponds to a Latin or Greek pf. ptc. passive.   See *Syntax*, § 97, Rem. 1 (2nd paragraph); G.K. § 116 *e*.

[5] לְ, *as regards, in respect of, in point of.*

[6] Hiph. without the י.

⁷ Pf. Pi. with the force of a fut. pf., *shalt* first *have blessed me.*
§ 46. I. 1 (a) 4. Note בַּ, not בְּ ; § 8. 4 b.

⁸ Gentilic names, with the article, are frequently used as collectives
in the *singular*, like *the Turk* ; cf. Gen. 15¹⁹⁻²¹, Exod. 4¹⁷. The plur. of
כנעני occurs only twice.

⁹ Dagh. omitted in all three cases in Ps. 143⁸.

C.

1 לֹא תִשָּׁכַח הַשִּׁירָה הַזֹּאת ¹לְעוֹלָם: 2 בְּיוֹם הִמָּשַׁח
²אֹתוֹ: 3 וְעַתָּה פֶּן־יִשְׁלַח ³אֶת־יָדוֹ וְלָקַח מֵעֵץ הַחַיִּים וְאָכַל
וָחַי לְעוֹלָם: 4 יִתֵּן יְהוָה לָכֶם בָּעֶרֶב בָּשָׂר לֶאֱכֹל וְלֶחֶם
בַּבֹּקֶר לִשְׂבֹּעַ: 5 הִשְׁמִיעַךָ אֶת־דְּבָרָיו ⁴מִתּוֹךְ הָאֵשׁ: 6 יֹאמְרוּ
אֹהֲבֵי יְשׁוּעָתֶךָ יִגְדַּל אֱלֹהִים: 7 שָׁמוֹעַ תִּשְׁמְעוּ בְּקוֹל מַלְאָכַי
⁵בְּשָׁלְחִי אֹתוֹ אֲלֵיכֶם: 8 וַיֹּאמֶר שְׁמוּאֵל דַּבֵּר יְהוָה ⁶כִּי
שֹׁמֵעַ עַבְדֶּךָ: 9 וַיִּלָּחֶם ⁷עַל־הָעִיר כָּל־הַיּוֹם הַהוּא ⁸וַיִּלְכֹּד
אֶת־הָעִיר וְאֶת־הָעָם אֲשֶׁר בָּהּ הָרָג וַיִּתֹּץ אֶת־הָעִיר וַיִּזְרָעֶהָ
⁹מֶלַח:

¹ *Never* may be rendered by לֹא . . . לְעוֹלָם ; cf. Jud. 2¹.
בְּרִיתִי אִתְּכֶם לְעוֹלָם *I will never break* (1 s. impf. Hiph. of פרר, § 42. 2 (b) i ;
Grammar, p. 227, col. 2) *my covenant with you* (אִתְּכֶם, *Grammar,*
p. 142, footnote 1) ; Joel 2²⁶ᶠ· לֹא־יֵבֹשׁוּ עַמִּי לְעוֹלָם *my people shall never
be ashamed* (impf.—note the *plur.*—of בּוֹשׁ, § 40. 2 a). עַד־עוֹלָם is found
in 2 Sam. 12¹⁰ לֹא־תָסוּר חֶרֶב מִבֵּיתְךָ עַד־עוֹלָם *the sword shall never depart*
(impf. Qal of סור, § 40. 2 a) *from thy house.*

² Every time the phrase *his being anointed* occurs, it always appears
in the above form (3 times after בְּיוֹם, Lev. 6¹³, Num. 7¹⁰· ⁸⁴, and once
after אַחֲרֵי, Num. 7⁸⁸). This—to us—curious construction is explained
thus. The passive (*i.e.* Niph. Pu. Hoph.) may be used impersonally
(3 s. m.) and governs in the same way as the active : cf. Gen. 27⁴²
וַיֻּגַּד לְרִבְקָה אֶת־דִּבְרֵי עֵשָׂו *and there were told* (*i.e.* one told) *to Rebekah
the words of Esau* ; Exod. 21²⁸ לֹא יֵאָכֵל אֶת־בְּשָׂרוֹ *its flesh shall not be
eaten* ; 1 Kings 2²¹ יֻתַּן אֶת־אֲבִישַׁג *let Abishag be given* (יתן, § 33. 3 c).
Naturally this construction can also be used (as in the sentence translated above) in the inf. cstr. ; cf. Gen. 21⁸ בְּיוֹם הִגָּמֵל אֶת־יִצְחָק *on the day
when Isaac was weaned* (lit. of Isaac's weaning). Of course the simpler

6

הַפִּשְׂחוֹ would also have been possible; cf. Isa. 55⁶ דִּרְשׁוּ יְהֹוָה בְּהִמָּצְאוֹ *seek ye Yahweh while he may be found* (or rather *letteth himself be found*—Niph. tolerativum: see Note 4 of Exercise 31 B.

³ In Gen. 3²² the אֵת is omitted.

⁴ Rather than simply מִן. See Note 2 of Exercise 19 B.

⁵ For a sentence of the same type, cf. Exod. 3¹² בְּהוֹצִיאֲךָ אֶת־הָעָם מִמִּצְרַיִם תַּעַבְדוּן אֶת־הָאֱלֹהִים עַל־הָהָר הַזֶּה *when thou bringest forth* (*i.e.* shalt have brought forth: Hiph. inf. cstr. of יצא, § 39. 2. 1 a) *the people from Egypt, ye shall serve God upon this mountain.*

⁶ The subj., as a rule, precedes the ptc., but after כִּי the pred. generally precedes the subj. whether the former is adj. or ptc.: cf. Gen. 12¹⁰ כִּי־כָבֵד הָרָעָב *for the famine was sore*; Gen. 3⁵ כִּי יֹדֵעַ אֱלֹהִים *for God knows.*

⁷ After *to fight* (לחם, Niph.) *against* is usually rendered by בְּ of the enemy, and by עַל־ of a city (see sentence 9 of Hebrew into English of Exercise 25). בְּ, however, *may* be used of the city: in the above sentence Jud. 9⁴⁵ uses בָּעִיר. It also reads כָּל הַיּוֹם.

⁸ Not וַיִּקַּח. לקח is *to take* in the more general sense, but to capture is לכד.

⁹ This double accus. may be brought under the general rule affecting vbs. of clothing (cf. § 38. 3, § 27. 1 d). So with vbs. of *planting* and *anointing*: cf. Isa. 5² וַיִּטָּעֵהוּ שֹׂרֵק *and he planted it* (*with*) *the choicest vines* (note the *sing.*—collective); Ps. 45⁸ מְשָׁחֲךָ זָ֗וְךָ שֶׁמֶן שָׂשׂוֹן *he hath anointed thee* (*with*) *the oil of gladness.*

§ 38.

A.

We will create (1 *pl. impf. Qal*); *or* he was created (3 *s. m. pf. Niph.*); *or* (the) one (*or* thing) that has been created (*ptc. Niph.*). Thou wilt cause to sin (*Hiph.*). And ye will sin (*pf. Qal*). Ye will sin (*impf. Qal*). I have filled (*Pi.*) thee (*m.*). Call ye (2 *plur. fem. imper. with loss of the* ה—*for* קְרֶאנָה: Ruth 1²⁰; cf. Exod. 1¹⁷ וַתִּירֶאןָ *and they* (f.) *were afraid*—impf. of ירא, § 39. 2. 2 a). And they found him. He will cause him¹ to find (*Hiph. with nûn energ.*, Job 34¹¹). We fear (§ 22. 6, cf. Hos. 10³) *or* we feared (1 *pl. pf. Qal*). I will *or* would (*or* let me) be filled (*cohortative Niph.*, § 23. 1. 2).   He will lift me up (*or* take me away; cf. Job 32²²: impf. Qal of נשׂא; see § 31. 3 (a) i).

¹ Not *us*. The *nûn energicum* is not found with the 1st plur. suffix (נו).

B.

1. And Jacob said to his sons, Gather yourselves together,¹ that I may tell² you what shall befall³ you in the days to come.⁴ 2. And the king of Israel said, I hate him, for he never prophesies⁵ good concerning⁶ me, but⁷ evil. 3. And he said to them, Take me up and cast me⁸ into the sea, that the sea may grow calm (and cease) from (raging) against you.⁹ 4. And the Israelites swarmed and grew strong, and the land was filled with¹⁰ them. 5. Thus saith Yahweh, I¹¹ am about to shake all the nations, and I will fill¹² this house with glory. 6. I have let myself be found¹³ by¹⁴ those who did not seek¹⁵ me; I have said, Here am I,¹⁶ here am I, to a nation that was not called¹⁷ by my name.

7 אָמַר הַכֹּהֵן הַגָּדוֹל סֵפֶר הַתּוֹרָה מָצָאתִי וַיִּתֵּן אֶת־הַסֵּפֶר ¹⁸אֶל־הַסֹּפֵר
¹⁹וַיִּקְרָאֵהוּ׃

The high priest said, I have found the book of the law, and he gave the book to the secretary, and he read it.

8 ²⁰וַיִּמְצָאֵהוּ אִישׁ ²⁰וַיִּשְׁאָלֵהוּ לֵאמֹר מַה־²¹תְּבַקֵּשׁ׃

And a man found him and asked him, saying, What seekest thou?

¹ Niph. imper. of אסף.

² Final use of simple waw with impf. (or rather cohortative : Hiph. נגד). See § 23. 3. 6.

³ Not "call." קָרָא and קָרָה (which would here give יִקְרֶה, § 44. 1 b) having the same sound are readily confused : § 38. 1. 5. Note that the person after קרה *to befall* (or *meet*) is usually put in the *accus.*, and not preceded by ל (as if the meaning were "to happen *to*").

⁴ Literally, "in the end of the days"—a fairly common phrase in the prophetical books (the "latter" or "last days" of A.V.).

⁵ The frequentative impf.—he does not *at any time*—i.e. *never* (§ 46. II. 2).

⁶ . . . עַל *concerning*, after vbs. of speaking, hearing, commanding, prophesying, etc.

⁷ כִּי אִם after a negative=*but, except, unless*. See two occurrences of this phrase in sentence 4 of the Hebrew into English of § 37 ; and cf. Ps. 1² "he takes not his seat in an assembly of scoffers, *but in the law of Yahweh is his delight* כִּי אִם בְּתוֹרַת יְהוָה חֶפְצוֹ.

⁸ Notice the two co-ordinate imperatives connected by simple waw : § 23. 3. 7. The second vb. might have been rendered by waw consec. with pf. (Note 3 of Exercise 26 B) וְהִשְׁלַכְתּוּנִי ; but suffixes to the 2 pl. pf. are extremely rare (§ 31. 5 c).

⁹ מֵעֲלֵיכֶם is a very pregnant and pictorial phrase, which shows how much Hebrew can pack into a compound preposition.

¹⁰ Not בְּ, but the accus., which is the usual construction after *to be full* or *filled*—מָלֵא in Qal or Niph. See, for illustration, sentence 8 of Exercise 30 C.

¹¹ אֲנִי is not here emphatic : it is necessary with the ptc., which gives no indication of its subject. Had הִנְנִי been written (*behold, I* . . .; *Grammar*, p. 142, footnote 1) the אֲנִי would, of course, not have been necessary.

¹² Waw consec. with *pf.*—quite normal after a ptc. equivalent to an impf. (§ 23. 3. 5 b).

¹³ Niph. tolerativum (see Note 4 of Exercise 31 B).

¹⁴ For לְ of the agent after passive, see § 25. 5.

¹⁵ Pi'el. For omission of daghesh from ק, see § 7. 5.

¹⁶ Or "behold me." הִנֵּנִי, pausal form of הִנְנִי (*Grammar*, p. 142, footnote 1).

¹⁷ Pf. Pu'al. There is no Pi'el of קרא, and the Pu'al is very rare. Hence some propose to read this simply as a Qal, קָרָא "which *has not* called upon my name."

¹⁸ This is not quite the same as לְסַפֵּר ; it is more pictorial. אֶל implies motion to, or *direction towards*, and so, of course, can be used with any verb expressing motion, even with נתן *to give* ; *e.g.* Gen. 21¹⁴ וַיִּתֵּן אֶל־הָגָר *and he gave* (them, *i.e.*, bread and water) *to Hagar* ; Deut. 13² וְנָתַן אֵלֶיךָ אוֹת *and he shall give thee a sign*. But this construction is not to be imitated.

¹⁹ 2 Kings 22⁸. It is worth noting that the Chronicler, for whom the discovered book was not simply Deuteronomy (in whole or in part) but the whole Pentateuch, which was obviously much too long to have been read through on the occasion described, alters the text to וַיִּקְרָא־בוֹ "and he read *in* it" (2 Chr. 34¹⁸).

²⁰ The suffixes to these impf. in *a* are added on the analogy of the

First Declension, § 31. 3 (a) i—hence not יִמְצָאֵהוּ nor יִשְׁאָלֵהוּ, but צָ
and אָ.

²¹ For the impf. to describe the present pictorially, see § 46. II. 1 (2).

C.

1 יִשְׁמַע יְהֹוָה בְּקָרְאֲךָ אֵלָיו: 2 מָלֵאתִי ¹רוּחַ מִשְׁפָּט
וּגְבוּרָה לְהַגִּיד לְיַעֲקֹב פִּשְׁעוֹ וּלְיִשְׂרָאֵל ²חַטָּאתוֹ: 3 וַתִּמָּלֵא
הָאָרֶץ חָמָס: 4 ³הַמְצָאתַנִי אֹיְבִי וַיֹּאמֶר ⁴מְצָאתִיךָ:
5 מִלֵּאתָ אֶת־הַבַּיִת הַזֶּה ⁵אֶת־כְּבוֹדֶךָ: 6 שָׂנֵאתָ כָּל־פֹּעֲלֵי
אָוֶן: 7 ⁶וַתִּשָּׂאֵהוּ רוּחַ יְהֹוָה וַתַּשְׁלִכֵהוּ ⁷אַרְצָה: 8 ⁸תֶּאֱהַב
⁹אֶת־¹⁰אֹיִבְךָ לֹא תִשְׂנָאֵהוּ בִּלְבָבֶךָ: 9 לוּלֵא חֲרַשְׁתֶּם
בְּעֶגְלָתִי לֹא מְצָאתֶם ¹¹חִידָתִי:

¹ A prophetic utterance of this kind in poetic style would dispense with את before the accus. True, it does occur in this passage (Mic. 3⁸) before one accus.—*not* the first—in a way which shows the phrase to which it is attached (רוּחַ יְהֹוָה) to be an almost certain intrusion. This conclusion, based upon grammar, is supported both by the sense and the metre.

² Or חֲטָאוֹ (from חָטָא).

³ For the pointing of the interrogative, see § 49. 2. 2 b.

⁴ The original (1 Kings 21²⁰), more idiomatically, has simply מָצָאתִי =our "Yes, I have."

⁵ As it happens, the second accus. after the Pi. of מלא in O.T. seems always to be indefinite—to fill with *water, grain, oil,* etc.—and consequently does not take את (§ 13. 7 a). Cf. sentence 5 in section B of this Exercise (from Hag. 2⁷)—"I will fill this house (definite, therefore את) with glory" (no את). But here the pronom. suffix makes the word definite (*thy* glory), § 13. 7 a, and justifies the את. For the double את, cf. Gen. 37²³ וַיַּפְשִׁיטוּ אֶת־יוֹסֵף אֶת־כֻּתָּנְתּוֹ *and they stripped Joseph of his coat* (*kuttontô* from כֻּתֹּנֶת or כְּתֹנֶת; Josh. 7⁷ לָמָה הַעֲבַרְתָּ אֶת־הָעָם הַזֶּה אֶת־הַיַּרְדֵּן *why hast thou brought this people over the Jordan?* (הַעֲבַרְתָּ) for the more usual הֶעֱבַרְתָּ, "evidently with the intention of strengthening the countertone-syllable," G.K. § 63 *p*: note, further, that לָמָה—not לָמָּה—is used before the gutturals א, ה, and ע); Josh. 1⁶ תַּנְחִיל אֶת־הָעָם הַזֶּה אֶת־הָאָרֶץ *thou wilt cause this people to inherit the land.*

⁶ רוּחַ is more often fem. than masc. If masc., then וַיִּשָּׂאֵהוּ and וַיִּשְׁלְכֵהוּ.

⁷ Pausal form of אַרְצָה. The *he locale* does not take the accent; § 17. 3.

⁸ See Note 3 of Exercise 36 C.

⁹ אָהֵב takes the accus. In a very few late passages it is followed by לְ; cf. Lev. 19¹⁸ וְאָהַבְתָּ לְרֵעֲךָ כָּמוֹךָ *and thou shalt love thy neighbour* (רֵעַ) *as thyself* (for כָּמוֹךָ, see *Grammar*, p. 87, footnote 1).

¹⁰ Pausal form of אֹיִבְךָ : § 30. 1. 2 *a*.

¹¹ Without אֵת in poetry. This is a rhymed couplet—a rare phenomenon—with three accents in each line.

§ 39.

A.

רְדָה 2 sing. masc. emph. imper. (from רֵד) Qal of ירד. *Come down.*

לָרֶדֶת inf. cstr. Qal of ירד; with לְ. *To go down.*

דַּע 2 sing. masc. imper. Qal of ידע. *Know (thou).*

דַּעַת inf. cstr. Qal of ידע. Frequently used as a noun = *knowledge.*

נֵלְכָה 1 plur. cohortative Qal (from נֵלֵךְ) of הלך. *Let us go.*

אִינַק 1 sing. impf. Qal of ינק. *I will suck.*

תִּירָא 2 sing. masc. or 3 sing. fem. impf. Qal of ירא. *Thou wilt (or she will) fear.*

הַנּוֹרָא masc. sing. ptc. Niph. of ירא, with article. *The one who is feared,* or *to be feared* (see Note 4 of Exercise 37 B), *the terrible*—used of God, the wilderness, the day of Yahweh, etc.

אִוָּרֵשׁ 1 sing. impf. Niph. of ירשׁ. *I shall be (dispossessed =) impoverished, come to poverty* (opposed in Prov. 30⁹ to אֶשְׂבַּע).

וַיּוֹרֶשׁ 3 sing. masc. impf. Hiph. of ירשׁ, with waw consec. *And he dispossessed, i.e.* drove out (*e.g.* the Amorites, Num. 21³²). The Hiph. of ירשׁ (הוֹרִישׁ) means either *to cause to possess,* or

to cause (others) to possess; i.e. *to dispossess.*
Even in the Qal יָרֵשׁ to *possess, take posses-*
sion of (a land), easily passes into the meaning
of *dispossessing* (a people).

וָאִישָׁנָה 1 sing. cohortative Qal of יָשֵׁן. *And I slept*; the
ה, here (Ps. 3⁶) possibly with a certain
emphasis, but sometimes with little or none
(see *Grammar*, p. 117, footnote 1). In Ps. 4⁹
the simple וָאִישָׁן even after the cohortative
אֶשְׁכְּבָה, *I will lie down*, with which it is co-
ordinated. (C. A. Briggs, *Psalms*, vol. i.
p. 37, thinks, however, that in view of the
co-ordination, the form here should be אִישָׁנָה,
as in Ps. 3⁶).

תּוּקַד 3 sing. fem. (or 2 sing. masc.) impf. Hoph. of יקד.
It shall be kindled, burn, *kept burning*—of the
altar-fire (Lev. 6². ⁵f. Heb. (9. 12f. E.V.)).

בְּהוֹרִידִי inf. cstr. Hiph. of ירד with בְּ and 1 sing. suffix (Ezek
31¹⁶). *When I brought down.*

תֵּרַדְנָה 2 or 3 plur. fem. impf. Qal of ירד. *Ye* or *they*
will come down.

וַיּוֹרִדֻהוּ 3 plur. masc. impf. Hiph. with waw consec. and
3 sing. masc. suffix—*scriptio defectiva* for
וַיּוֹרִידוּהוּ. *And they brought him down* (1 Kings
1⁵³).

הֻצַּע 3 sing. masc. pf. Hoph. of יצע, § 39. 3 (for ֻ, see
§ 7. 7). *It was spread.* (Of יצע only impf.
Hiph.—3 s. יַצִּיעַ, 1 s. אַצִּיעָה—and impf. Hoph.
יֻצַּע are found.)

מַצִּיג masc. sing. ptc. Hiph. of יצג (Jud. 6³⁷). *One who*
sets or *places* (יצג is found only in Hiph. and
once, if the text be correct, in Hoph., יֻצַּג
Exod. 10²⁴).

וַנֵּדָעֵם 1 plur. impf. Qal (נֵדַע) of ידע with waw consec.
and 3 plur. masc. suffix (Ps. 78³). *And we*
knew them.

יִירָשׁוּם 3 plur. masc. impf. Qal of ירשׁ, with 3 plur. masc.
suffix. *They will possess them.* In Deut. 2¹²,

where this phrase occurs, the reference is to
the *past*, and the meaning of the impf. will
strictly be, "and they (the descendants of
Esau) *proceeded to possess* (or dispossess)
them," *i.e.* the Ḥorites. Cf. § 46. II. 1. 1.

B.

1. And Abram went down into Egypt, and he said to
his wife, Say,[1] I pray thee, thou art my sister, in order that
it may be well with[2] me for thy sake. And the king took
her, and with Abram[3] he dealt well for her sake. But
Yahweh plagued him with great plagues, and he learned[4]
that she was his wife. 2. Yahweh said to Abram, I am
Yahweh who brought thee out of Ur of the Chaldees to
give thee[5] this land to possess it.[6] And he said,[7] O Lord
Yahweh,[8] whereby shall I know that I shall possess it?[9]
3. And the sons of Jacob said to him,[10] The man *asked*[11]
about[12] us and about our kindred,[13] saying, Is your father
still[14] alive? have you[15] a brother? and we told him[16]
according to the tenor[17] of these words. Could[18] we possibly
know[19] that he would say, Bring your brother down?[20]
4. And he forsook the counsel which the old men had given
him,[21] and he took counsel[22] with[23] the young men.
5. Those that trust in Yahweh shall walk and not be weary.[24]

6 וְזָכַרְתָּ אֶת־כָּל־הַדֶּרֶךְ אֲשֶׁר [25] הוֹלִיכְךָ יְהוָה אֱלֹהֶיךָ [26] זֶה [27] אַרְבָּעִים שָׁנָה
בַּמִּדְבָּר לְמַעַן דַּעַת אֶת־אֲשֶׁר בִּלְבָבְךָ [28] הֲתִשְׁמֹר מִצְוֹתָיו אִם־לֹא:

And thou shalt remember all the way which Yahweh thy
God hath led thee now for forty years in the wilderness, to know what was in thy heart, whether thou
wouldst keep his commandments or no.

[1] אִמְרִי, *fem.* imperat.

[2] Lit. *for*—dat. of advantage.

[3] The obj. is sometimes put first for emphasis: cf. 1 Sam. 2[19]
וּמְעִיל קָטֹן תַּעֲשֶׂה־לּוֹ אִמּוֹ *and a little robe his mother* (אֵם, *Grammar,* p.
140, col. 3) *used to make for him* (frequentative impf., § 46. II. 2. 2). Note
the dagh. in לֹ, and see Note 28 of Exercise 33 B. The more normal
order would have been וַיֵּיטֶב לְאַבְרָם (*Grammar,* p. 152. 2 (2)). Penult
open, therefore accent retracted, and טֹב reduced to טֹב (§ 23. 3. 4).

⁴ Not so much *knew* as *gained knowledge, got to know.* יָדַע often bears this meaning—*very* frequently in Ezekiel; cf. 6⁷ וִידַעְתֶּם כִּי־אֲנִי יְהוָֹה "*then ye shall know* (*i.e.* learn) that I am Yahweh."

⁵ For לָתֶת לְךָ, see Note 9 of Exercise 34 A.

⁶ לְרִשְׁתָּה, inf. cstr. Qal (רֶשֶׁת) of יָרַשׁ, with 3 sing. fem. suffix, and לְ.

⁷ Note וַיֹּאמֶר (not וַיֹּאמַר) in *pause.* The athnaḥ comes very early, but this is the middle of the verse, according to the sense.

⁸ In the original (Gen. 15⁸) יהוה is pointed, as always when it is accompanied by אֲדֹנָי, with the vowels of אֱלֹהִים (thus יֶהְוִֹה) to avoid, in public reading, the repetition of אֲדֹנָי (see *Grammar*, § 10. 5 b).

⁹ אִירָשֶׁנָּה, I sing. impf. Qal with 3 s. f. suff. and *nûn energ.* (§ 31. 7).

¹⁰ In the previous clause the customary order would be that אֵלָיו should immediately follow the vb.; cf. 2 Kings 23¹⁷ וַיֹּאמְרוּ אֵלָיו אַנְשֵׁי הָעִיר *and the men of the city said to him.* With the much less common order of the translated sentence, cf. Exod. 10⁷ וַיֹּאמְרוּ עַבְדֵי פַרְעֹה אֵלָיו *and Pharaoh's servants said to him.* In general, for the order with prepositional phrases, see Note 5 of Exercise 36 C.

¹¹ The inf. abs. does not here mean, though, of course, it could mean, "asked *straitly*" (so A.V.). It means that they did not volunteer the information—the man *asked* them (Gen. 43⁷).

¹² "Asked *in regard to* (לְ) us," not "asked us": the person asked is usually put in the accus., *e.g.* Gen. 44¹⁹ אֲדֹנִי שָׁאַל אֶת־עֲבָדָיו *my lord asked his servants.*

¹³ מוֹלֶדֶת with suffixes (here I pl.) exactly like קְטָלֶת, *Grammar*, p. 102, col. 2.

¹⁴ הַעוֹד. For הַ interrogative, see § 49. 2. 2 c.

¹⁵ Note יֶשׁ לָכֶם; but יֶשׁ־לָנוּ, יֶשׁ־לִי, יֶשׁ־בִּי (Gen. 44²⁰), by § 10. 3 a; to avoid the juxtaposing of two accented syllables.

¹⁶ וַנַּגֶּד־לוֹ (I pl. impf. Hiph. of נגד with waw consec.); but וַיַּגֵּד לָכֶם (Deut. 4¹³); see previous Note.

¹⁷ עַל־פִּי *according to the mouth of*, sometimes means *according to the commandment of* (*e.g.* Pharaoh, Gen. 45²¹; Yahweh, Exod. 17¹). But פֶּה is used sometimes in the secondary sense of *portion* (*e.g.* Deut. 21¹⁷ פִּי שְׁנַיִם *a portion for two, a double portion*), and quite frequently in the sense of *proportion, measure, e.g.* Exod. 16²¹ אִישׁ כְּפִי אָכְלוֹ (in 12⁴ לְפִי) *each in proportion to his eating;* even כְּפִי שָׁנָיו, Lev. 25⁵² *according to* the number of *his years*; and in a conjunctional phrase, with אֲשֶׁר, *e.g.* Mal. 2⁹ כְּפִי אֲשֶׁר אֵינְכֶם שֹׁמְרִים אֶת־דְּרָכַי *according as ye do not keep my ways* (for אַיִן with ptc. see Note 3 (2nd paragraph) of Exercise 41 B).

It is in this sense that עַל־פִּי is used in the translated sentence—*according to the measure of, in accordance with* (these words).

[18] נֵדַע : 1 plur. impf. Qal of ידע ; a good illustration of the potential use of the impf., as the following יֹאמַר (not, of course, יֹאמֶר, as it is not preceded by waw consec.) illustrates its conditional use (§ 46. II. 4).

[19] Abs. inf.: cf. Note 11. We might say idiomatically, "How could we know?"

[20] 2 plur. imper. Hiph. of ירד.

[21] Lit. "the counsel of the old men which they had counselled him"—cognate accus. (cf. sentence 1 of this Exercise—"plagued him (with) plagues." יְעָצֻהוּ is 3 pl. pf. Qal (יָעֲצוּ) of יעץ with 3 sing. masc. suffix.

[22] וַיִּוָּעֵץ is 3 sing. masc. Niph. of יעץ (with waw cons.) *he exchanged counsel*—the reciprocal use of the Niph. (§ 25. 3. ii). This part of the Niph. occurs eleven times, and always with _ (not .. or ָ) in the last syllable.

[23] אֵת. Not, of course, the sign of the accus., but the prepos.

[24] Or *faint*, Isa. 40[31]. יִיעָפוּ is the pausal form of יִיעֲפוּ which occurs in the previous verse (*scr. defectiva*, יָעֵפוּ)—3 pl. impf. Qal of יָעֵף.

[25] 3 sing. pf. Hiph. of הלך with 2 sing. masc. suffix, "he caused thee to go."

[26] This does not and could not mean "*these* forty years." זֶה is often used with a sort of enclitic force, *e.g.* מִי־זֶה *who then?* לָמָּה־זֶּה *wherefore now?* Besides being used to emphasize interrogatives, it is also frequently prefixed (as here) to expressions denoting a period of time: *e.g.* Gen. 27[36] וַיַּעְקְבֵנִי זֶה פַעֲמַיִם "and he has supplanted me *now* (not *these*) two times" (dual of פַּעַם). In this latter case, however, it is better —as J. A. Montgomery suggests in the *Journal of Biblical Literature*, 1924, vol. xliii., p. 227—to regard זה, not as an enclitic (which it clearly is not), but rather as what Nöldeke calls a "demonstrative relative pronoun," the exact equivalent of the ancient Arabic *ḏū*. The strict meaning would then be "a matter of forty years."

[27] *Grammar*, p. 165.

[28] For the interrog. particles אִם · · · הֲ, see § 49. 5 (c) i.

C.

1 וַתֵּלֶךְ הַתֵּבָה עַל־פְּנֵי הַמָּיִם : 2 הוֹדִיעֵנִי נָא [1]אֶת־דְּרָכֶיךָ :
3 וַיֹּאמְרוּ אֵלֶיהָ הֲתֵלְכִי עִם־הָאִישׁ הַזֶּה וַתֹּאמֶר [2]אֵלֵךְ :
4 וַיֹּאמֶר הוֹצִיאוּ כָל־אִישׁ מִן־הַבַּיִת וְלֹא־עָמַד אִישׁ [3]אִתּוֹ
[4]בְּהִתְוַדַּע [5]אֶל־אֶחָיו : 5 וַיִּפְתַּח הָאִישׁ אֶת־[6]דַּלְתוֹת הַבָּיִת

וַיֵּצֵא לָלֶכֶת לְדַרְכּוֹ : 6 וַתֹּאמֶר־לָהּ בַּת־פַּרְעֹה קְחִי אֶת־הַיֶּלֶד
הַזֶּה ⁷וְהֵינִקִהוּ לִי וַתִּקַּח אֶת־הַיֶּלֶד ⁸וַתְּנִיקֵהוּ : 7 הִנֵּה
שָׁמַעְתִּי כִּי ⁹יֶשׁ־שֶׁבֶר בְּמִצְרָיִם וְרִדוּ־שָׁמָּה ¹⁰וְשִׁבְרוּ־לָנוּ מֵעַט־
אֹכֶל : 8 וַיֹּאמֶר אֵלָיו יְהוָה אַל־תֵּרַד מִצְרָיְמָה ¹¹שֵׁב בָּאָרֶץ
אֲשֶׁר אֹמַר אֵלֶיךָ : 9 וַיִּירָא וַיֹּאמַר מַה־נּוֹרָא הַמָּקוֹם הַזֶּה :
10 וַיֹּאמֶר לֹא־אֵרֵד בְּנִי כִּי־¹²אָחִיו מֵת וְהוּא לְבַדּוֹ נִשְׁאָר
¹³וּקְרָאָהוּ אָסוֹן בַּדֶּרֶךְ אֲשֶׁר תֵּלְכוּ־בָהּ וְהוֹרַדְתֶּם אֶת־שֵׂיבָתִי
בְּיָגוֹן שְׁאוֹלָה :

¹ So Exod. 33¹³ (prose). In the similar sentence in Ps. 143⁸, the אֵת
is omitted—also the נָא.

² The vb. is repeated alone, without עִמּוֹ (for suffix, see *Grammar*,
p. 142, footnote 1), exactly as in sentence 4 of English into Hebrew of
§ 38—"I have found" (without *thee*). Our idiom would be simply
"Yes."

³ Or עִמּוֹ. For the suffixes to both words, see *Grammar*, p. 142,
footnote 1.

⁴ Cstr. inf. Hithpa. (הִתְוַדַּע, *Grammar*, p. 219, col. 2) with 3 s. m.
suffix.

⁵ The only other time the Hithpa. of יָדַע occurs, it takes, as here
(Gen. 45¹), אֶל after it—Num. 12⁶ בַּמַּרְאָה אֵלָיו אֶתְוַדָּע *I will make myself
known unto him in a vision* (מַרְאָה, *f.* very rare, for the familiar מַרְאֶה *m.*).

⁶ דַּלְתֵי dual cstr., would also have been possible ; but the *plur.*
(דְּלָתוֹת) and esp. the plur. *cstr.* דַּלְתוֹת, are considerably more frequent
than the dual (דְּלָתַיִם and דַּלְתֵי). Cf. Note 24 of Exercise 33 B.

⁷ For *scriptio plena* הֵינִיקִהוּ, 2 s. *f.* imperat. Hiph. of ינק. Waw
consec. with pf. would also have been possible after the imper. (see
Note 2 of Exercise 26 B) וְהֵינַקְתִּיהוּ or וְהֵינַקְתִּי (*Grammar*, p. 210, last
col.).

⁸ In Exod. 2⁹ this appears as וַתְּנִיקֵהוּ ; but this is almost certainly an
error, as the first syllable (*yê*) of the impf. Hiph. יֵינִיק is obviously firm
—as firm as the *yaq* in יַקְטִיל. The alternative would be to suppose
that there was a form נוק (which nowhere else occurs) alongside of ינק
(cf. טוב and יטב, *Grammar*, p. 152) ; this would give the Hiph. pf. הֵנִיק,
with impf. יָנִיק (§ 40. 3 a, *Grammar*, p. 225, col. 2) whose first vowel
would be changeable, and which would consequently yield the form in
the printed text. Conceivably also this form may be an "irregular

shortening of the first syllable, caused by the forward movement of the tone " due to the suffix (G.K. § 70 e). But it is more probably an error.

⁹ Not יֵשׁ—to avoid the collocation of two accented syllables יֵשׁ and שֵׁבֶר. See Note 15 of section B of this Exercise.

¹⁰ Or וּשְׁבַרְתֶּם.

¹¹ Or, as in Gen. 26² שְׁכֹן. שָׁבָה would also have been possible (§ 23. 2), שֵׁב is rather more frequently used. In the same phrase in two parallel passages, "remain in thy house," 2 Kings 14¹⁰ has שֵׁב, while 2 Chr. 25¹⁹ has שָׁבָה.

¹² The putting of the subj. first after כִּי (so Gen. 42³⁸) serves to emphasize the contrast between it and the emphatic הוּא of the next sentence—somewhat like μέν and δέ in Greek. But in the similar sentence Gen. 44²⁰ the clause וְאָחִיו מֵת (the normal order with the ptc.) is simply followed by the normal waw consec. with impf. וַיִּוָּתֵר הוּא לְבַדּוֹ and he alone is left (impf. Niph. of יתר—a Pe waw vb.).

¹³ So in Gen. 44²⁹ (for 3 s. m. suffix הוּ to pf. of Lamedh he vbs., see § 44. 2. 1). If we use the vb. קָרָא, with which קָרָה is sometimes confused (§ 38. 1. 5), we should naturally expect the form וּקְרָאוֹ (the similar words מְצָאוֹ and נְשָׂאוֹ are both found—formed exactly like קְטָלוֹ) ; but the analogy of קָרָה has been followed and has produced in Gen. 42³⁸ the curious form וּקְרָאָהוּ (ahû is strictly the original form, which has passed, through aû, into ô : § 19. 1).

A conditional sentence is sometimes formed, as here, by two perfects with waw consec., e.g. Gen. 44²² וְעָזַב אֶת־אָבִיו וָמֵת (and he will leave his father and he will die=) and if he leaves his father, he will die (for מֵת see § 40. 1, and for וְ see § 15. 1 d). When there is a string of pfs. with waw consec., it might seem to be difficult to say precisely where the apodosis begins, but, in point of fact, there is seldom any ambiguity. Perhaps the most interesting case is that of Jacob's vow in Gen. 28²⁰ᶠ· אִם־יִהְיֶה אֱלֹהִים עִמָּדִי וּשְׁמָרַנִי וְנָתַן־לִי לֶחֶם וְשַׁבְתִּי בְשָׁלוֹם וְהָיָה יְהוָה לִי לֵאלֹהִים וְהָאֶבֶן הַזֹּאת יִהְיֶה בֵּית אֱלֹהִים If God will be with me and keep me and give me bread and I return in peace, then shall Yahweh be my God and this stone shall be God's house. But the meaning might be, "and I return in peace and Yahweh be my God, then this stone," etc., though this would certainly involve a very unusual form of apodosis. With the present text, however, the former trranslation is probably correct. But it is only to this one clause that any doubt can attach in this context. For "if God will be with me, then he will keep me," etc., while grammatically possible, is excluded by the context.

§ 40.

A.

נָס 3 sing. masc. pf. Qal *or* sing. masc. ptc. Qal of
נוּס. *He fled* or (*one*) *fleeing.*

סָרָה 3 sing. fem. pf. Qal of סוּר. *She turned aside.*

סָרָה fem. sing. ptc. Qal of סוּר. (*One*) *turning aside.*

שָׁבָה fem. sing. ptc. Qal of שׁוּב. (*One*) *returning.*

וּבָאָה 3 sing. fem. pf. Qal of בּוֹא with waw consec.[1]
And she will come.

וְסָרוּ 3 pl. pf. Qal of סוּר with waw consec. *And they
will turn aside.*[1]

אָרוּם 1 sing. impf. Qal of רוּם. *I will be* (high, *i.e.*)
exalted.

תָּשׁוּבִי 2 sing. fem. impf. Qal of שׁוּב. *Thou* (f.) *shalt
return.*

תְּשׁוּבֶינָה 2 or 3 pl. fem. impf. Qal of שׁוּב. *Ye* (f.) *or
they* (f.) *shall return.*

יָרֹם 3 sing. masc. jussive Qal of רוּם. *Let him be
exalted.*

אָמוּתָה 1 sing. cohortative Qal of מוּת (§ 23. 1. 2). *Let
me die.*

וַיָּמָת (*way-yāmoth*, § 3. 1 *b*), 3 sing. masc. impf. Qal
of מוּת with waw consec. *And he died.*

לָצוּד inf. cstr. Qal of צוּד, with לְ. *To hunt.*

תִּכּוֹן 2 sing. masc. or 3 sing. fem. impf. Niph. of כּן.
Thou shalt or *she shall be established.*

הֲרִימוֹתָ 2 sing. masc. pf. Hiph. of רוּם. *Thou hast lifted
up.*

וְהֲשִׁבֹתִי (*scriptio defectiva* for וַהֲשִׁיבוֹתִי) 1 sing. pf. Hiph. of
שׁוּב with waw consec. *And I will turn* (or
bring) *back.*[2]

יָאִיר 3 sing. masc. impf. Hiph. of אוֹר. *He will give
light* (or *cause to shine*).

וְיָרֵם 3 sing. masc. jussive Hiph. of רוּם with simple
waw. (*In order*) *that he may lift up*: § 23.
3. 6; or, *and let him lift up, may he lift up.*

אַל־תָּשֵׁב 2 sing. masc. *or* 3 sing. fem. jussive Hiph. of שׁוּב, with prohibitive אַל. Cf. 1 Kings 2²⁰ אַל־תָּשֵׁב אֶת־פָּנַי *do not turn away my face*, i.e. *do not deny me.*[3]

הָבִיאָה 2 sing. masc. emphatic imperat. Hiph. of בּוֹא: § 23. 2. (Cause to come, *i.e.*) *bring* (cf. Gen. 27⁷, Amos 4¹, Prov. 23¹²).

נָשִׂימָה 1 pl. cohortative Hiph. of שׂוּם or שִׂים: § 23. 1. 2. *Let us put* or *place.*

יְכוֹנְנֶהָ 3 sing. masc. impf. Po'lel of כּוּן (יְכוֹנֵן) with 3 sing. fem. suffix. *He will establish her* (Ps 48⁹). For נּ,[4] see *Grammar*, p. 18, lines 5–8.

מוּבָא masc. sing. ptc. Hoph. of בּוֹא. Cf. 2 Kings 22⁴ הַכֶּסֶף הַמּוּבָא בֵּית יְהֹוָה *the money that was brought in to the house of Yahweh.* (Notice the accus. בית in answer to the question *whither?* after a verb of motion—*Syntax*, § 69. b.)

תְּמֹתֵת (תְּמוֹתֵת) 2 sing. masc. or 3 sing. fem. impf. Po'lel of מוּת. Cf. Ps. 34²² תְּמוֹתֵת רָשָׁע רָעָה *evil* (i.e. *misfortune*) *shall slay the wicked.*

---

[1] In the 3 sing. fem. and the 3 plur. the tone very frequently falls, even with the waw consec., on the *penult*: cf. Mic. 3⁶ וּבָאָה הַשֶּׁמֶשׁ עַל־הַנְּבִיאִים *and the sun shall go down upon the prophets*; 1 Kings 8⁴⁷ᵇ וְשָׁבוּ *and they shall turn.*

[2] It is important not to confuse יָשַׁב with שׁוּב. The corresponding part of ישׁב would be וְהוֹשַׁבְתִּי. In unpointed Hebrew the confusion is very easy in the Qal and the Hiph.: *e.g.* וישׁב may be as Qal, either וַיָּשָׁב (way-yāshobh) *and he returned*, or וַיֵּשֶׁב *and he dwelt*; as Hiph. וַיָּשֶׁב *and he restored*, or וַיֹּשֶׁב (*scr. def.* for וַיּוֹשֶׁב) *and he caused to dwell.*

[3] " Here the close connexion of אל to the jussive by means of *Maqqef* causes a retraction of the tone, just as in the case of the Impf. with ו *consec.*" (C. F. Burney, *Kings*, p. 20). But this retraction is not universal; cf. Gen. 26² אַל־תֵּרֵד

[4] According to Ginsburg only a few MS. have here נּ. Kittel reads יכוננה.

B.

1. In the sweat of thy face thou shalt eat bread till thou return[1] to the ground; for dust thou art, and unto dust shalt thou return.   2. And on my part, behold, I am about to bring[2] the flood, (that is), waters[3] upon the earth, to destroy all flesh from under[4] heaven.   3. Know ye for certain[5] that, if ye put me to death,[6] it[7] is innocent blood[8] that ye will be bringing upon yourselves.   4. But the dove found no resting-place for the sole of her foot, so she returned unto Noah to the ark; and he put forth his hand and took her and brought her in[9] unto him into the ark.   5. O Yahweh, my God, I pray thee, let the soul of this child return.[10]

6 הִנֵּה אָנֹכִי [11]מֵת וְהָיָה אֱלֹהִים עִמָּכֶם וְהֵשִׁיב אֶתְכֶם אֶל־אֶרֶץ אֲבוֹתֵיכֶם:

Behold, I am about to die; but God will be with you and bring you back to the land of your fathers.

7 אִם־[12]שָׁכֹחַ תִּשְׁכַּח אֶת־יְהוָֹה אֱלֹהֶיךָ וְהָלַכְתָּ אַחֲרֵי אֱלֹהִים אֲחֵרִים וַעֲבַדְתָּם [13]הַעִדֹתִי בְךָ הַיּוֹם כִּי [12]אָבֹד תֹּאבֵד:

If thou shalt at all forget Yahweh thy God and go after other gods and serve them, I (solemnly) testify against thee this day that thou shalt assuredly perish.

---

[1] Cstr. inf.   An alternative construction is עַד אֲשֶׁר with a finite vb.: cf. עַד אֲשֶׁר־תָּשׁוּב חֲמַת אָחִיךָ *till thy brother's rage shall turn away* (Gen. 27[44], which is immediately followed in [45] by the equivalent phrase עַד־שׁוּב אַף־אָחִיךָ מִמְּךָ, *till the turning of thy brother's anger away from thee.*

[2] Imminent future expressed by ptc. (Hiph. of בּוֹא), with הִנֵּה (§ 46. IV. 1. iii).

[3] Not "the flood *of* waters."   A construct could not have the article.

[4] Note the compound preposition.   Cf. Note 9 of Exercise 38 B.

[5] Inf. abs.   The jussive (which here, as usually, has the same form as the impf.) has here practically the force of an imperative ("ye are to know").   It is sometimes parallel to an imperative: cf. Ps. 43[1], which begins with שָׁפְטֵנִי, *judge me*, and ends with תְּפַלְּטֵנִי (*thou shalt*) *deliver me.*

[6] Pl. ptc. Hiph. (sing. מֵמִית) of מוּת.   The subj. usually precedes the ptc., but in clauses beginning with כִּי or, as here, אִם, the ptc. precedes

the subj.: cf. Gen. 27⁴⁶ אִם־לֹקֵחַ יַעֲקֹב אִשָּׁה מִבְּנוֹת־חֵת *if Jacob takes a wife of the daughters of Heth* (cf. Ps. 1⁶).

⁷ The second כִּי merely resumes the first. This resumptive כִּי is frequent after an intervening clause (as here) or phrase, as, *e.g.*, 1 Kings 20³¹ שָׁמַעְנוּ כִּי מַלְכֵי בֵּית יִשְׂרָאֵל כִּי־מַלְכֵי חֶסֶד הֵם *we have heard that the kings of the house of Israel are merciful kings.*

⁸ Notice the obj. put first, for emphasis. This is usually followed by vb. and subj.; but if the vb. be a ptc., the subj. usually precedes the ptc.: cf. Gen. 41⁹ אֶת־חֲטָאַי אֲנִי מַזְכִּיר *my faults* (from חטא) *I call to remembrance* (*Syntax*, § 111).

⁹ וַיָּבֵא—not, of course, וַיָּבֵא (like וַיֵּשֶׁב), as the last syllable, with its long vowel, is virtually open, and therefore remains long (§ 5. 3 a) and retains its accent. Impf. Hiph. of בוא.

¹⁰ *tå-shobh*—the jussive תָּשֹׁב, with the accent retracted before נָא, to avoid the collocation of two accented syllables (§ 10. 3 a).

¹¹ The ptc. may mean *dead*, or *about to die* (§ 46. IV. 1. iii).

¹² Note the force of the inf. abs. at the beginning and the end of this sentence.

¹³ *Scriptio defectiva* for הַעִידֹתִי. We should expect, by analogy, הָ ; but the Hiph. of עוד, as also of עוּר *to awake* (Hiph. *to rouse*), has always הָ.

C.

1 וַיָּנֻסוּ ¹דֶּרֶךְ הַמִּדְבָּר׃ 2 אַל־תָּסֻרוּ מֵאַחֲרֵי יְהוָה וַעֲבַדְתֶּם אֹתוֹ בְּכָל־לְבַבְכֶם׃ 3 קוּמִי אוֹרִי כִּי בָא אוֹרֵךְ׃ 4 וְלֹא לָקַח מִיָּדוֹ אֵת אֲשֶׁר־הֵבִיא׃ 5 שׁוֹב אָשׁוּב אֵלֶיךָ׃ 6 וַיָּקָם בַּבֹּקֶר ²וַיַּחֲבֹשׁ אֶת־³חֲמֹרוֹ וַיֵּלֶךְ עִם־⁴שָׂרֵי מוֹאָב׃ 7 וַיִּקְרָא לָאִישׁ וַיֹּאמֶר אֵלָיו ⁵הֲבֵאתָ עָלַי וְעַל־מַמְלַכְתִּי חֲטָאָה גְדוֹלָה׃ 8 וַתֹּאמֶר לוֹ אִשְׁתּוֹ ⁶לוּ חָפֵץ יְהוָה ⁷לַהֲמִיתֵנוּ לֹא לָקַח מִיָּדֵנוּ עוֹלָה׃ 9 ⁸וַתֵּצֵא הָאִשָּׁה ⁹לִקְרַאת שַׂר צְבָא הַמֶּלֶךְ וַתֹּאמֶר סוּרָה אֲדֹנִי ¹⁰סוּרָה אֵלַי אַל־תִּירָא ¹¹וַיָּסַר אֵלֶיהָ ¹²הָאֹהֱלָה׃

¹ דֶּרֶךְ, without a preposition, occasionally means, as here, *in the direction of*, practically = *towards*: cf. 1 Kings 8⁴⁴ וְהִתְפַּלְלוּ דֶּרֶךְ הָעִיר

"and they shall pray (Hithpa. of פלל: note absence of dagh. forte from first ל; § 7. 5) *towards* the city": 8⁴⁸ דֶּרֶךְ אַרְצָם "*towards* their land"; 18⁴³ הַבֵּט דֶּרֶךְ־יָּם "look (Hiph. imperat. of נבט) *towards* the sea."

[2] Impf. of חבשׁ very rarely has the first syllable closed (§ 34. 2 c).

[3] In Num. 22²¹ אָתֹון (אֲתֹנוֹ a she-ass).

[4] Not שָׂרִי. Root is שׂרר, hence שָׂרִי (=שָׂרְיִ) with unchangeable ָ (§ 43. 2).

[5] Or הֲבִיאֹתָ (§ 40. 6 b).

[6] So Jud. 13²³. לוּ (sometimes written לוּא) is here more appropriate than אִם. לוּ *if* (used mostly with the pf.), states a case which has not been, or is not likely to be, realized. Cf. the similar sentence in Jud. 8¹⁹ לוּ הַחֲיִתֶם אֹותָם לֹא הָרַגְתִּי אֶתְכֶם *if ye had spared* (pf. Hiph. of חָיָה, § 44) *them, I should not have killed you.* Note in 8¹⁹ and 13²³ the pf. in apodosis as well as in protasis. (But in apodosis the impf. is sometimes found: cf. Deut. 32²⁹ לוּ חָכְמוּ יַשְׂכִּילוּ זֹאת *if they had been wise*—as they are not—*they would understand this.*)

[7] Inf. cstr. Hiph. (הָמִית) of מוּת, with suffix.

[8] וַתֵּצֵא, not וַתֵּצֵא; see Note 9 of section B of this Exercise.

[9] The cstr. inf. (with ל) of קרא in the sense of *to meet* is regularly לִקְרַאת (of קרא *to call*, קֹרֵא): so לִקְרָאתִי *to meet me*, לִקְרַאתְכֶם *to meet you*, etc. לִקְרַאת never appears to be followed by אֵת before the accus.

[10] Cf. § 23. 2.

[11] Not וַיֶּסֶר (§ 40. 2 b).

[12] So Jud. 4¹⁸, cf. § 17. 3. אֶל־הָאֹהֶל would, of course, be possible (cf. Num. 19¹⁴), but הָאֹהֱלָה is the commoner phrase. Both phrases occur in Exod. 33⁸.

§ 41.

A.

1. Mine eyes are upon all their ways, they are not hidden from my face; neither is their iniquity concealed from mine eyes. 2. Ye shall not die,[1] for God knoweth that in the day that ye eat[2] of the tree, your eyes shall be opened.[3] 3. Your vineyards and olive-trees the locusts repeatedly devoured.[4] 4. The wealth[5] of the nations shall come[6] unto thee.[7] 5. Ye have delivered our lives from death. 6. I have no pleasure[8] in the death of him that dieth.

7

7 וַיִּשְׁמְעוּ אֶת־קוֹל יְהוָה מִתְהַלֵּךְ בְּתוֹךְ עֵץ הַגָּן ⁹לְרוּחַ הַיּוֹם ¹⁰וַיִּתְחַבֵּא הָאָדָם
וְאִשְׁתּוֹ מִפְּנָיו:

And they heard the voice of Yahweh as he walked in the
midst of the trees of the garden in the cool of the day,
and the man and his wife hid themselves from his
presence.

8 ¹¹וְלִמַּדְתֶּם אֹתָם אֶת־דְּבָרַי אֶת־בְּנֵיכֶם ¹²לְדַבֵּר ¹³בָּם בְּשִׁבְתְּךָ ¹⁴בְּבֵיתֶךָ ¹⁵וּבְלֶכְתְּךָ
בַדֶּרֶךְ ¹⁶וּבְשָׁכְבְּךָ וּבְקוּמֶךָ:

And ye shall teach my words to your children, speaking of
them when thou sittest in thy house, and when thou
walkest by the way, and when thou liest down, and
when thou risest up.

<hr>

[1] In Gen. 3⁴ the words are לֹא־מוֹת תְּמֻתוּן—*ye shall not surely die*—
the abs. inf. and the impf. with the older and fuller ending in ן which is
not uncommon, and which is also found with the 3rd pers. (§ 21. 1 b).
It usually marks emphasis, and commonly occurs at the end of sentences.
Note that it takes the tone (unlike תְּמֻתוּ), hence תְּ not תָּ. In negative
sentences the inf. abs. *precedes* the negative, *e.g.* Is. 30¹⁹ בָּכוֹ לֹא־תִבְכֶּה
thou shalt not weep at all (בָּכוֹ or בָּכֹה, abs. inf. § 44. 1 e), Ex. 5²³ הַצֵּל
לֹא־הִצַּלְתָּ *thou hast not delivered at all*. The irregular order in Gen. 3⁴
is usually explained by the fact that it is a negation of the threat in Gen.
2¹⁷ מוֹת תָּמוּת, i.e. *thou shalt not "assuredly die."* (Skinner, *Genesis*,
p. 74, dissents from this explanation, and remarks that " more probably
its effect is to concentrate the emphasis on the negative particle rather
than on the verbal idea.")

[2] In the day *of your eating*, inf. cstr., § 31. 3 c towards end.

[3] This might have been expressed by the simple תִּפָּקַחְנָה (Isa. 35⁵),
but the pf. with waw consec. is more idiomatic. See Note 2 of Exercise
31 C.

[4] This could, of course, equally well mean " will devour "; but in
Am. 4⁹ the reference is to the past, so that יֹאכַל is frequentative impf.
Note the obj. thrown first for emphasis.

[5] חַיִל has a very wide range of meaning—" strength, army; efficiency,
capacity, ability; wealth." The capacity may be physical, *e.g.* Jud. 3²⁹
אִישׁ חַיִל *a man of valour*; or intellectual and moral, *e.g.* Exod. 18²¹.²⁵
אַנְשֵׁי חַיִל *men of ability and worth*; Prov. 31¹⁰ אֵשֶׁת חַיִל *a woman of
worth* (rather than *a virtuous woman*).

[6] A collective noun may be followed (as here) or preceded by a plur.
vb. Both are illustrated in 2 Kings 25⁵ וַיִּרְדְּפוּ חֵיל־כַּשְׂדִּים אַחַר הַמֶּלֶךְ

and the army of the Chaldeans pursued after the king; וְכָל־חֵילוֹ נָפֹצוּ and all his *army was scattered* (pf. Niph. of פּוּץ, in Qal and Niph. *to be scattered*; in Hiph.—הֵפִיץ *to scatter*).

⁷ This may be dative—*for thine advantage* or *to* in the sense of *into* (or *unto*)—or there may be a blend of both ideas. In 1 Sam. 9¹² occurs בָּא לָעִיר *he has come into the city*; but the usual prepos. after בּוֹא is אֶל. לְ is sometimes used with vbs. of motion, such as שׁוּב, בּוֹא, הָלַךְ, but it is not so common as אֶל.

⁸ So Ezek. 18³². But in 33¹¹ occurs the strange אִם־אֶחְפֹּץ with the same meaning, only more emphatic. This form occurs chiefly after an oath, expressed or implied. The full form is found in 1 Sam. 3¹⁷ "God do so unto thee and more also, *if* (אִם) thou hide anything from me." But the formula of imprecation is very frequently omitted : *e.g.* 2 Sam. 11¹¹ אִם־אֶעֱשֶׂה אֶת־הַדָּבָר הַזֶּה " (may God bring all manner of evil upon me) *if* I do this thing "="*surely I will not* do this thing." By an easy and natural extension, this *emphatic negative* can be used even in a divine speech (as in Ezek. 33¹¹) where imprecation is out of the question. Similarly a very strong affirmation may be introduced by אִם לֹא ; cf. 1 Kings 20²⁵ אִם־לֹא נֶחֱזַק מֵהֶם " *surely* we shall be stronger than they "— (cursed be we) *if* we be *not* stronger. (For מִן to express comparative, see § 47. 1.) See § 49. 5 d, and *Syntax*, § 120.

It is possible, however, to explain this אִם as an interrogative particle (cf. 1 Kings 1²⁷, Amos 3⁶) following an oath ; and this explanation will commend itself to those who regard as inconceivable the connexion of the particle, in a divine oath, with an ultimate formula of imprecation. The Rev. Duncan Cameron, B.D., writes to me : "We have this" interrogative following an oath "in ordinary colloquial English—' By heaven, do you think I shall do that ? ' when the answer ' No ' is clearly expected. So in 2 Sam. 11¹¹, ' By my life and your life, shall I do this thing ? ' So 1 Kings 20²⁵, ' Are we not stronger than they ? ' "

⁹ See Note 9 of Exercise 26 A. In Gen. 3⁸ the preceding word גַּן has the disjunctive accent *ṭiphḥâ* (corresponding roughly to our comma ; *Grammar*, p. 231), which explains the choice of *ā* rather than *a*—בַּגָּן. It is to be noted, however, that the raising of a short vowel to the corresponding tone-long is rare with this accent and not to be imitated. See Note 8 of Exercise 43 B.

¹⁰ See Note 10 of Exercise 26 A.

¹¹ *To learn* (לָמַד Qal), followed by an accus. ; *to teach* (לִמַּד, Pi.), by two accus. (§ 38. 3 a).

¹² Inf. cstr. with לְ has something like the force of a gerund in the ablative—*dicendo*.

¹³ בְּ *about*, occasionally used with vbs. of *speaking*, *thinking*, etc.

But עַל is commoner : *e.g.* Jud. 9³ וַיְדַבְּרוּ אֲחֵי־אִמּוֹ עָלָיו *and his mother's brethren spoke of him.*

[14] For the original pointing of this word in this passage see Note 9 of Exercise 49 B.

[15] See § 39. 2. 2 (*d*) i.

[16] See § 31. 3 c.

B.

1 ¹הִנֵּה זָקַנְתִּי לֹא יָדַעְתִּי ²אֶת־יוֹם מוֹתִי : 2 בַּיָּמִים הָהֵם ³אֵין מֶלֶךְ בְּיִשְׂרָאֵל אִישׁ הַיָּשָׁר בְּעֵינָיו ⁴יַעֲשֶׂה : 3 ⁵וַיִּיקַץ נֹחַ מִיֵּינוֹ וַיֵּדַע אֵת אֲשֶׁר־עָשָׂה לוֹ בְּנוֹ ⁶הַקָּטָן : 4 וַיֹּאמֶר אֵלֶיהָ הַנָּבִיא וְאַתְּ קוּמִי לְכִי ⁷לְבֵיתֵךְ בְּבוֹא רַגְלַיִךְ הָעִירָה ⁸וּמֵת הַיָּלֶד : 5 וַיַּקְרֵב אֶת־אֵיל הָעוֹלָה : 6 וַיִּירְאוּ הָאֲנָשִׁים ⁹מְשׁוּב אֶל־בָּתֵּיהֶם :

¹ In Gen. 27² הִנֵּה־נָא behold, *I pray.* When a request follows such a sentence as this (as in Gen. 27³) נָא is sometimes added to הִנֵּה to crave favourable consideration of the fact to which attention is called by הִנֵּה, and נָא is often repeated with the request ; cf. here שָׂא־נָא כֵלֶיךָ *take* (imperat. of נשׂא), *I pray thee, thy weapons* (Gen. 27³). So Gen. 12¹¹.¹³ הִנֵּה־נָא יָדַעְתִּי כִּי אִשָּׁה יְפַת־מַרְאֶה אָתְּ : אִמְרִי־נָא אֲחֹתִי אָתְּ *Behold now, I know that thou art a beautiful woman* (fair in appearance) : *say, I pray thee, thou art my sister.*

² את is omitted in Gen. 27² ; but it is inserted in the similar sentence Deut. 16³ תִּזְכֹּר אֶת־יוֹם צֵאתְךָ *thou shalt remember the day of thy going out.* This shows how fluctuating the usage was ; but it is well to accustom oneself to add the את in prose composition.

³ The particle אַיִן is strictly a noun meaning *non-existence*, the negative of יֵשׁ *existence.* "Its natural place is therefore before the word which it denies, and in the *construct* state ; cf. Gen. 20¹¹ אֵין־יִרְאַת אֱלֹהִים בַּמָּקוֹם הַזֶּה *there is* (non-existence of=) *no fear of God in this place.* The word denied may stand for emphasis before אין, in which case the negative is properly in the *absolute* in apposition ; *e.g.* Gen. 2⁵ וְאָדָם אַיִן לַעֲבֹד *and man there was not* (*i.e.* there was no man) *to till*" (*Syntax,* § 127. *b*). Further, as the original character of אַיִן as a construct was forgotten, this form became habitual ; it is very frequently separated from its noun, and may even come after it : *e.g.* Gen. 40⁸

וּפֹתֵר אֵין אֹתוֹ *and an interpreter* (ptc.) *there is not of it* (there is no interpreter of it, none to interpret it).

If a vb. accompanies אֵין, it is in the participle; cf. preceding sentence; so 1 Sam. 26¹² וְאֵין רֹאֶה וְאֵין יוֹדֵעַ וְאֵין מֵקִיץ *and no man saw it or knew it, nor did any awake* (מֵקִיץ, ptc. Hiph.—pf. הֵקִיץ, used as Hiph. of יקץ, both = *to awake* in intransitive sense; *Grammar*, p. 152. 2. 7). For an example with suffix, cf. 1 Kings 21⁵ אֵינְךָ אֹכֵל לָחֶם *thou eatest no bread.*

⁴ Note the unusual order in both passages where this sentence occurs (Jud. 17⁶ 21²⁵)—sub. obj. vb. which has the effect of "bringing the subj. and the obj. into very close relation" (*Syntax*, § 111. c). Cf. Jer. 32⁴ וְעֵינָיו אֶת־עֵינָיו תִּרְאֶינָה *and his eyes shall see his eyes.*

⁵ This word appears 7 times thus—וַיִּיקֶץ (see *Grammar*, p. 152. 2. 7); but in Gen. 9²⁴, from which the sentence is taken, it appears as וַיִּקֶץ. The retraction of the accent is due, no doubt, to the desire to avoid the collocation of two accented syllables *qáç* and *nóªḥ*, but the change of _ to ָ is curious. It is not, however, without analogy: cf. יֶדְכֶם *your hand*, instead of יַדְכֶם; so מֶלֶךְ from the ground form *malk*. So וַיֹּאמֶר regularly, instead of וַיֹּאמַר (but once occurs וַתֹּאמֶר לוֹ *and she said to him*, Prov. 7¹³). All this illustrates the affinity of these vowels for one another: see, further, Note 1 of Exercise 44 B.

⁶ This could also mean *youngest*, if the context permitted. For comparative and superlative, see § 47. 1 and 2.

⁷ הָלַךְ most often followed by אֶל־, but sometimes, as here (1 Kings 14¹²), by לְ. See Note 7 of section A of this Exercise; also Note 1 of Exercise 48 B.

⁸ Waw consec. with the pf. comes to be practically equivalent to the simple impf. See Note 2 of Exercise 31 C.

At the *end* of a sentence (consequently in pause) וָמֵת would be used: cf. Gen. 44²² וְעָזַב אֶת־אָבִיו וָמֵת *and if he leave his father, he will die* (for the *if*, see Note 13 (2nd paragraph) of Exercise 39 C).

⁹ Or לָשׁוּב.

<h1 style="text-align:center">§ 42.</h1>

<h1 style="text-align:center">A.</h1>

בַּזּוֹנוּ 1 plur. pf. Qal of בזז (so Deut. 3¹). *We have plundered.* In the similar sentence, however, Deut. 2³⁵ בָּזַזְנוּ is found. So Jer. 4²⁸ זַמֹּתִי *I have purposed*; but Zech. 8¹⁴ᶠ· זָמַמְתִּי.

קַלּוּ 3 plur. pf. Qal of קלל. *They are light* (slight, abated, of the waters of the flood, Gen. 8[8, 11]); *they are swift* (of horses; Jer. 4[13], Hab. 1[8]).

וְחַגֹּתֶם 2 plur. masc. pf. Qal of חגג with waw consec. *And ye shall hold a festival* (Exod. 12[14]).

אָאֹר I sing. impf. Qal of ארר. *I will curse* (Gen. 12[3]).

וַיָּחָן (*way-yắḥon*) 3 sing. masc. impf. Qal of חנן, with waw consec. *And he was gracious* (impf. by itself יָחֹן, Deut. 28[50]). Note that חנן takes the *accus.* of the person favoured; 2 Kings 13[23] וַיָּחָן יְהֹוָה אֹתָם *and Yahweh was gracious to them*; Ps. 4[2] חָנֵּנִי *be gracious to me* (חֹן—not found alone—and I sing. suffix).

גֹּל 2 sing. masc. imperat. Qal of גלל. *Roll.* Cf. Ps. 37[5] גּוֹל עַל־יְהֹוָה דַּרְכֶּךָ *roll* (גּוֹל erroneous *scriptio plena*—as the vowel is not unchangeable; cf. חָנֵּנִי above—for גֹּל) *thy way upon Yahweh* (*i.e.* commit thy way to Y.).

תֵּרַע 2 sing. masc. or 3 sing. fem. impf. Qal. of רעע (§ 42. 3 b). Cf. Deut. 28[54, 56] תֵּרַע עֵינוֹ בְאָחִיו *his eye shall be evil against his brother* (*i.e.* he will regard him with *disfavour, grudge*).

בֹּזּוּ 2 plur. masc. imperat. Qal of בזז. Nah. 2[10] בֹּזּוּ כֶסֶף בֹּזּוּ זָהָב *plunder the silver, plunder the gold.*

לָקֹב cstr. inf. Qal of קבב, with לְ (§ 42. 2 a. *a*). *To curse.* Num. 24[10] לָקֹב אֹיְבַי קְרָאתִיךָ *I called thee to curse mine enemies* (cf. 23[11]).

וְנָקַל 3 sing. masc. pf. Niph. of קלל with waw consec. (Niph. *to show oneself swift* or *to appear trifling*). Cf. 2 Kings 3[18] וְנָקַל זֹאת בְּעֵינֵי יְהֹוָה *and this shall be* (but) *a light thing in the eyes of Yahweh* (note the 3 sing. *masc.* vb. with the *fem.* subj.—a common construction when the vb. precedes: *Syntax*, § 113. *b*).

וּנְמַקֹּתֶם 2 plur. masc. pf. Niph. of מקק with waw consec. (Ezek. 24[23]). *And ye shall waste away.*

יִמַּד 3 sing. masc. impf. Niph. of מדד. *It shall be*

measured: cf. Jer. 33²² לֹא יִמַּד חוֹל הַיָּם *the sand of the sea cannot be measured* (potential use of impf., § 46. II. 4).

הֲשִׁמּוֹתָ 2 sing. masc. pf. Hiph. of שָׁמֵם (Job 16⁷). *Thou hast desolated.*

הֵתַמּוּ 3 plur. pf. Hiph. of תמם. *They completed, finished, ended.* The *a* instead of *ē* under ת—often found before gutturals and ר, § 42. 2 (b) i—is occasionally found before other consonants. But the Septuagint here (2 Sam. 20¹⁸) εἰ ἐξέλιπον, presupposes הֲתַמּוּ, *whether* (§ 49. 2. 2 a) *they had come to an end*, Qal.

תִּדֹּם 2 sing. masc. or 3 sing. fem. impf. (Aramaizing form, § 42. 8, of the) Qal of דמם (Lam. 2¹⁸). *Thou shalt* or *she shall be silent.* Some regard this as a Niph. formed on the analogy of Ayin waw vbs.; but this seems needless, as the form יִדַּמּוּ (*they shall be brought to silence*), which is the regular Niph. form, occurs in Jer. 49²⁶ 50³⁰.

אֶקֹּב 1 sing. impf. (Aramaizing form of the) Qal of קבב. *I will curse.*

וַיִּתְּמוּ 3 plur. masc. impf. (Aramaizing form of the) Qal of תמם with waw consec. Deut. 34⁸ וַיִּתְּמוּ יְמֵי בְכִי "and the days of weeping *were ended.*" In Num. 14³⁵, and 4 times elsewhere, occurs the form יִתַּמּוּ, which looks like a Niph.; but as the Niph. of תמם is not elsewhere found, and the Qal (inf. cstr. תֹּם) occurs but two verses before (14³³), it seems better to treat this word also as an Aramaizing form of the Qal.

תָּתֵּם 2 sing. masc. impf. (Aramaizing form of the) Hiph. of תמם. *Thou shalt complete* or *make perfect.* Cf. Job 22³ דְּרָכֶיךָ תַתֵּם *thou makest thy ways perfect* or blameless.

B.

1. As for me, I will make all my goodness pass before thee,[1] and I will be gracious to whomsoever[2] I will be gracious, and I will have compassion[3] on whomsoever I will have compassion.[3]   2. Men began to multiply on the earth, and daughters were born[4] unto them.   3. And Jacob drew near unto Isaac his father, and he felt him.[5]   4. Upon the woman with whom I am seeking hospitality[6] thou hast brought evil, by slaying[7] her son.   5. And she said to them, Call[8] me not Naomi, call me Mara,[9] for the Almighty hath dealt very bitterly with me. As for me, I went away full,[10] and Yahweh hath brought me back[11] empty;[10] why do ye call me Naomi, seeing that Yahweh hath testified against me, and the Almighty hath wrought me evil?

6 [12]וַיּוֹרֶד אֶת־הָעָם אֶל־[13]הַמַּיִם וַיֹּאמֶר יְהֹוָה אֶל־גִּדְעוֹן כֹּל אֲשֶׁר־[14]יָלֹק בִּלְשׁוֹנוֹ

מִן־הַמַּיִם כַּאֲשֶׁר יָלֹק [15]הַכֶּלֶב [16]תַּצִּיג אוֹתוֹ [17]לְבָד:

And he brought the people down to the water; and Yahweh said to Gideon, Every one that laps of the water with his tongue as a dog laps, him shalt thou set by himself.[17]

[1] עַל־פְּנֵי is a little more definite and distinct than לִפְנֵי; cf. Gen. 32²² וַתַּעֲבֹר הַמִּנְחָה עַל־פָּנָיו "and the present passed on *in front of him*."

[2] חנן takes accus.; see Note on the parsing of וַיִּחַן in the previous section of this Exercise.

[3] See § 36. 1. 3 *a* towards end. רחם is found only in Pi. and Puʻal. The Pi. takes, like חנן, the accus., except in Ps. 103¹³, where it is (twice) followed by עַל.

[4] The Pu. (as here) and Niph. (נוֹלְדוּ) are found in this sense (*were born*). The Pi. is found only in inf. cstr. (once) and in ptc. (several times), מְיַלֶּדֶת *a woman who causes* (or *helps*) *to bring forth, a midwife*.

[5] Impf. Qal (יְמֻשׁ—not found alone) with 3 sing. m. suffix. The addition of the suffix compels the restoration of the lost שׁ of the root (hence שֵׁ), and the vowel of the closed syllable מֻשׁ, which is now unaccented (the accent falling on the *ē* of the suffix), becomes short, and u (rather than o) before the daghesh forte (§ 7. 7). Cf. with 1 s. suff. יְמֻשֵּׁנִי Gen. 27¹², יְסַבֵּנִי Ps. 49⁶.

[6] Hithpoʻlel.

[7] לְ with cstr. inf.=abl. of gerund (*interficiendo*).

[8] 2 pl. *fem.* jussive Qal of קרא. So אֱלֵיהֶן, *fem.*, because Naomi (strictly *No‘omi*, from נעם *to be pleasant*, נֹעַם *pleasantness*) is addressing women.

For the construction after קרא see Note 1 of Exercise 14 A. For dagh. forte in לְ after unaccented ā, see Note 28 of Exercise 33 B.

[9] מָרָה=מָרָא, fem. of מַר (cf. § 43. 2) *bitter*.

[10] *Full* and *empty* are placed first in their respective clauses for emphasis. רֵיקָם *emptily*, is an *adverb* (and therefore cannot be put in the fem.).

[11] הֱשִׁבַנִי 3 sing. masc. pf. Hiph. (הֵשִׁיב)—*scriptio defectiva*—of שׁוּב *to return*, with 1 sing. suffix. The 3 sing. Hiph. of such vbs. with suffix takes, as here, ַ rather than ָ. Cf. Gen. 11⁹ הֱפִיצָם *he scattered them*. So also 3 plur., cf. Jer. 26¹⁹ הֱמִתֻהוּ *they killed him*.

[12] Impf. Hiph. of ירד with waw consec., § 39. 2. 1 a.

[13] The real middle of the verse, considered as narrative; hence athnaḥ.

[14] Impf. (of לקק) very appropriate to express the frequentative idea involved in the phrase "every one that," "whosoever." So also with the next ילק: it is the *habit* of dogs so to lap.

[15] Notice the definite article in a comparison, where we should say *a*: see Note 2 of Exercise 14 B.

[16] 2 sing. masc. impf. Hiph. of (יצג not found) Hiph. pf. הִצִּיג; § 39. 3. See Note on מַצִּיג in Exercise 39 A.

[17] Lit. "in a state of separation."

C.

1 אָאֹר ¹מְקַלְלֶיךָ: 2 ²יָאֵר יְהוָה פָּנָיו ³אֵלֶיךָ ⁴וִיחֻנֶּךָּ:
3 ⁵בִּמְקוֹם אֲשֶׁר לָקְקוּ הַכְּלָבִים אֶת־דָּמוֹ יָלֹקּוּ אֶת־דָּמְךָ ⁶גַּם־
אָתָּה: 4 ⁷גֹּל עַל־יְהוָה דַּרְכֶּךָ וּבְטַח עָלָיו: 5 ⁸הָיָה מִסְפַּר
הַמְלַקְּקִים ⁹שְׁלֹשׁ מֵאוֹת ¹⁰וַיִּכְרַע כָּל־יֶתֶר הָעָם עַל־¹¹בִּרְכָּיו:

[1] Not מְקַלְלֶיךָ (§ 7. 5). So in sentence 5, מְלַקְּקִים.
[2] Jussive Hiph. of אוֹר (impf. Hiph. יָאִיר).
[3] So Num. 6²⁵. עָלֶיךָ would be equally possible (cf. Ps. 31¹⁷ הָאִירָה פָנֶיךָ עַל־עַבְדֶּךָ *cause thy face to shine upon thy servant*). The later books tend to use אל instead of על, and sometimes the two are interchanged, apparently without discrimination, in the same or parallel sentences: cf. Jud. 6³⁷ "let there be dryness on על the earth," but in ³⁹ " on אל the fleece." This interchange is probably often not original, but due to transcribers. See *BDB*, p. 41.

[4] Jussive (and impf.) יְחָן, with the 2 s. m. suffix and *nûn energicum* in pause. For ֲ, see Note 5 of section B of this Exercise. For וְ, see § 9. 1.

Without the *nûn energ.* this form appears twice (Gen. 43[29], Isa. 30[19]) as יְחָנְךָ *yoḥnᵉkhâ* (for יְחָנְךָ by throwing back the *o*). Note that, while the vowel before נ in יְחָנֶּךָ is *u*, it is, with this vb., much more frequently *o* (as commonly under gutturals, § 7. 7): cf. imper. with 1 s. suff. חָנֵּנִי Ps. 4[2], impf. with 1 pl. suff. יְחָנֵּנוּ Ps. 67[2].

[5] This sentence might have ended (after דמו) with שָׁם (§ 13. 2). Cf. Gen. 40[3] מְקוֹם אֲשֶׁר יוֹסֵף אָסוּר שָׁם *the place where Joseph was imprisoned* (ptc. pass. Qal of אסר *to bind*, or *imprison*, whether bound or not).

Note that a construct (as in both these sentences מְקוֹם) may precede a *clause* as well as a noun. "A clause may occasionally take the place of a genitive" (*Syntax*, § 25); cf. Isa. 29[1] קִרְיַת חָנָה דָוִד *thou* (voc.) *city* (cstr. of קִרְיָה) *where David encamped* (=of David's encamping).

[6] See Note 1 of Exercise 29 A.

[7] See Note on גל in Exercise 42 A, p. 102.

[8] וַיְהִי (so Jud. 7[6]) in continuous narrative: see § 45. 2. 3.

[9] See § 48. 1. 5.

[10] In Jud. 7[6] the order is וְכֹל יֶתֶר הָעָם כָּרְעוּ. This is either designed to call special attention to the rest of the people, or is perhaps better explained as a plupf. "they *had* bowed down" (see Note 2 of Exercise 15 A).
Note the plur. כרעו after the collective: when the vb. comes first it may be singular (וַיִּכְרַע), but it is frequently plur. (וַיִּכְרְעוּ). For the construction with collectives, see Note 2 of Exercise 29 B.

[11] Dual (*Grammar*, p. 101; also § 16. 5 a).

§ 43.

A.

1. And David came[1] to his house, and behold, the maiden was coming out to meet him with timbrels.   2. And in its shadow many nations used to dwell.[2]   3. They have set[3] their arrow upon the string.   4. And I gave them to the priest and his sons for an everlasting statute.   5. And the woman came to him and said, Behold, thy handmaid hath hearkened unto thy voice, and I have put[4] my life in

my hand. 6. Our end is near, our days are fulfilled.
7. Behold, the young woman⁵ is about to bear a son and
she shall call⁶ his name Immanuel.⁷ 8. And he came to
his house displeased,⁸ and he lay down upon his bed and
turned away his face, and ate⁹ no bread. 9. God thou
shalt not revile,¹⁰ and a ruler among thy people thou shalt
not curse.

10 אֵלֶּה הַחֻקִּים וְהַמִּשְׁפָּטִים אֲשֶׁר תִּשְׁמְרוּ בָּאָרֶץ אֲשֶׁר נָתַתִּי לָכֶם לְרִשְׁתָּהּ

כָּל־הַיָּמִים אֲשֶׁר־אַתֶּם חַיִּים עַל־הָאֲדָמָה כִּי עַמִּי אַתֶּם:

These are the statutes and the judgments which ye shall
observe in the land which I have given you to possess
it,¹¹ all the days that ye live¹² upon the earth, for ye
are my people.

¹ בּוֹא, primarily *go in, enter*, but often simply *come*. In sentence 8 the
meaning might be *entered*.

² Or "shall dwell." In Ezek. 31⁶ the true reading may be יֵשְׁבוּ
dwelt, as some MSS. and Versions actually read.

³ 3 plur. pf. Po'lel (כּוֹנְנוּ, § 40. 5) of כּן.

⁴ Note carefully וָאֶשִּׁים, not וָאָשֶׂם (impf. Qal of שִׂים). With waw
consec. and impf. "in the *first* pers. sing. alone the retraction of the
tone and the reducing of the long vowel in the final syllable are not
usual" (G.K. § 49 e). Thus, though we write וַיָּקָם, we should write
וָאָקוּם (or וָאָקֻם): so Hiph. וַיָּקֶם but וָאָקִים (or more generally וָאָקִם).
So in the I sing. impf. Hiph. of *all* vbs. the long *î* is almost always
retained ; *e.g.* Am. 2⁹ וָאַשְׁמִיד *and I destroyed* (while וַיַּשְׁמֵד, 2 Kings 10²⁸,
for the *third* person, is normal). In the last two words, retraction is, of
course, impossible, as the penult is not open (§ 23. 3. 4).

⁵ עלמה, a young, marriageable woman, not necessarily a virgin, the
proper word for which is בְּתוּלָה. For the παρθένος (virgin) of the Septuagint, the later translators, Aquila, Symmachus, and Theodotion, of
the 2nd century A.D., substituted the more correct νεᾶνις.

⁶ In Gen. 16¹¹ וְקָרָאת must mean "and *thou* (f.) shalt call." But
here (in Isa. 7¹⁴) the context shows that it must rather be regarded as a
rare Aramaizing form (from קָרָאת) of the *third* pers. sing. fem. (For
other Aramaizing forms see Note I of Exercise 37 A, and the last four
words of Exercise 42 A.)

⁷ Not "God with us"—as if a prophecy of the incarnation ; but a
sentence embodying a confession of faith—"with us *is* God." Cf.
I Sam. 10⁷ הָאֱלֹהִים עִמָּךְ "God *is* with thee."

⁸ זָעֵף, only in I Kings 20⁴³ 21⁴ (of Ahab)—out of humour, vexed ; in

both passages preceded by the almost equally rare סַר *sullen* ; cf.
1 Kings 21⁵ מַה־זֶּה רוּחֲךָ סָרָה *why then is thy spirit sullen?*

⁹ i.e. "*would* eat" in our idiom.

¹⁰ קלל in Pi., *to make light, slight, contemptible*, hence *to curse* ;
practically synonymous with ארר.

¹¹ Cstr. inf. Qal of ירשׁ with 3 s. f. suffix : § 39. 2. 2 (*d*) i.

¹² Pl. of חַי, *alive, living*, from root חיי (which appears in verb form
as חָיָה, § 44) ; hence dagh. forte in י.

B.

1 נַחֲמוּ עַמִּי דַּבְּרוּ ¹עַל־²לִבּוֹ וְקִרְאוּ אֵלָיו כִּי מָלֵא ³צְבָאוֹ :

2 רִיבוּ בְאִמְּכֶם רִיבוּ כִּי ⁴הִיא לֹא אִשְׁתִּי וְאָנֹכִי לֹא אִישָׁהּ :

3 עַל־הָרֵי יִשְׂרָאֵל ⁵תִּפֹּל אַתָּה וְכָל־הָעַמִּים אֲשֶׁר ⁶אִתָּךְ :

4 וַיִּשְׁלַח שַׂר הַצָּבָא מַלְאָכִים אֶל־הַמֶּלֶךְ לֵאמֹר ⁷כָּרְתָה
בְרִיתְךָ אִתִּי וְהִנֵּה יָדִי ⁸עִמָּךְ לְהָסֵב אֵלֶיךָ אֶת־כָּל־יִשְׂרָאֵל :

¹ This beautiful phrase, *to speak home to the heart of*, i.e. *kindly*,
occurs several times, always with the shorter form לֵב, except in 2 Chr.
32⁶ לֵבָב.

² *Its*, i.e. the people's, heart—masc. *sing.* suffix ; as in Isa. 6¹⁰ make
fat the heart of this people, וְאָזְנָיו הַכְבֵּד "and *its* ears make heavy."

³ If צָבָא is to be regarded as always masc. the מָלְאָה of Isa. 40²,
which could not then agree with it, should perhaps be pointed as a Pi.
מִלְּאָה *she* (i.e. Jerusalem) *has fulfilled her warfare.*

⁴ הִיא and אָנֹכִי at the beginning of each clause, contrasted : cf. μέν
. . . δέ.

⁵ In Ezek. 39⁴ incorrectly written with scriptio plena, תִּפּוֹל. See
Note 3 of Exercise 22 C.

⁶ Not here the fem. suffix (cf. אַתָּה, *m.* earlier), but the pausal form
of אִתָּךְ.

⁷ Emphatic imper. (*korᵉthâ*) of כרת : § 23. 2.

⁸ Pausal form of עִמְּךָ. For *athnaḥ* at this place in a verse, after two
principal clauses, and before a clause beginning with לְ and infinitive, cf.
Gen. 22¹⁰ (see W. Wickes, *Hebrew Prose Accents*, p. 34). In the translated
sentence, taken from 2 Sam. 3¹² (which is, however, a longer sentence
in the original—*athnaḥ* falling earlier), עמך, though only accompanied
by the lesser distinctive accent known as *Zaqeph qaṭon*ˊ, appears in its
pausal form—עָמָּךְ (*Grammar*, p. 230, 2 d). The pausal changes in the

vowel are regular with the great distinctive accents Silluq and Athnaḥ, but "there are often pausal changes with the lesser distinctives, especially *S^egolta*, *Zaqeph qaṭon*, *R^ebhi^{aᶜ}*, and even *Tiphḥa*," C.K. § 29 *i* : see *Grammar*, pp. 230 f., and Note 9 of Exercise 41 A. These, however, had better not be imitated in ordinary prose composition.

§ 44.

A.

1. Thus saith Yahweh to these bones, Behold, I will cause breath to enter[1] into you, and ye shall live.[2] 2. Command the priests that bear the ark of Yahweh that they come up[3] out of the Jordan. 3. I will not again smite[4] any more every living thing, as I have done. 4. The stone which the builders rejected is become the[5] head of the corner. 5. And it shall be that when I bring clouds[6] over the earth, then the bow shall be seen in the clouds, and the bow shall be in the clouds, and I will look upon it, to remember my covenant. 6. Lift up[7] now thine eyes and look ; for all the land which thou art looking upon, to thee will I give it; and I will make thy seed as the dust of the earth, so that[8] if a man can number the dust of the earth, thy seed also may be numbered. 7. And Pharaoh said, Depart from me,[9] take heed to thyself, see my face no more[10] ; for in the day thou seest my face thou shalt die. 8. O that I had water to drink ![11]

9 וַאֲנִי הִנְנִי מַמְטִיר עַל־הָאָרֶץ אַרְבָּעִים [12]יוֹם וְאַרְבָּעִים לַיְלָה וּמָחִיתִי אֶת־כָּל־אֲשֶׁר עָשִׂיתִי מֵעַל פְּנֵי הָאֲדָמָה׃

And I, behold, I will cause it to rain upon the earth forty days and forty nights, and I will blot out every thing that I have made from off the face of the ground.

10 נַעַר הָיִיתִי גַּם־זָקַנְתִּי וְלֹא רָאִיתִי צַדִּיק נֶעֱזָב וְזַרְעוֹ [13]מְבַקֶּשׁ־לָחֶם׃

I have been young and now am old :[14] yet have I not seen the righteous forsaken, nor his seed seeking bread.

---

[1] Hiph. ptc. of בּוֹא, I am about to cause to enter.

[2] Pf. with waw consec., natural after a ptc., which has the practical equivalence of an impf. (§ 23. 3. 5 b).

[3] Note the simple waw with jussive—a construction common after

an imperative (§ 23. 3. 6), lit. "and let them come up." It is "greatly used to express *design* or purpose ; or, according to our way of thought, sometimes effect" (*Syntax*, § 65)—and natural therefore after a vb. signifying "command" : cf. Ex. 27²⁰ תְּצַוֶּה אֶת־בְּנֵי יִשְׂרָאֵל וְיִקְחוּ שֶׁמֶן *thou shalt command the Israelites that they fetch oil* (lit. and let them fetch). But the inf. (with לְ) may also be used after צוה (Pi.) : *e.g.* Gen. 50² וַיְצַו יוֹסֵף אֶת־עֲבָדָיו לַחֲנֹט אֶת־אָבִיו "and Joseph commanded his servants *to embalm* his father."

⁴ Lit. "I will not add (1 s. impf. Hiph. of יסף) to the smiting" (inf. cstr. Hiph. of נכה) ; for the idiom, see § 39. 4.

⁵ For לְ after היה, see Note 4 of Exercise 22 B, and Note 10 of Exercise 33 B.

For the omission of the article before אבן and פנה, see Note 4 (2nd paragraph) of Exercise 22 B ; and note its absence before צדיק in sentence 10 (also poetry) of this Exercise.

⁶ עֲנָנִי inf. cstr. Pi. of ענן with 1 s. suff. According to Ginsburg, many MSS. read simply בְּעֲנָנִי. See Note 4 of Exercise 40 A. עָנָן is cloud-mass, *clouds*, as well as *cloud*.

⁷ Imperat. of נשא.

⁸ Hebrew has few conjunctions, and a few (like כִּי and אֲשֶׁר) are used in a wide range of meaning. אֲשֶׁר may be used (as here) to introduce a consecutive clause, and is=*so that*. So כִּי with a slightly different shade of meaning ; cf. Ex. 3¹¹ מִי אָנֹכִי כִּי אֵלֵךְ *who am I that I should go?* 2 Chr. 2⁵ (A.V. 6) מִי אֲנִי אֲשֶׁר אֶבְנֶה־לּוֹ בַיִת *who am I that I should build him a house?*

⁹ מֵעָלַי, a vivid phrase, *from upon me*, i.e. *from* being a burden *upon* me, a trouble to me. See Note 9 of Exercise 38 B.

¹⁰ Juss. Hiph. of יסף : "do not add to the seeing." For the retraction of the accent after אַל־, see Note 3 of Exercise 40 A.

The next clause is literally, "in the day *of thy seeing of* my face"—inf. cstr. Qal with suffix. Cf. sentence 2 of Exercise 41 A.

¹¹ A wish may be expressed in Hebrew by the jussive or cohortative : *e.g.* 1 Sam. 1²³ יָקֵם יְהוָה אֶת־דְּבָרוֹ *may Yahweh establish* (Hiph. of קום) *his word*. It may also be expressed interrogatively, as in the above sentence, by מִי—מִי *Who will give me water to drink?* Ps. 4⁷ מִי־יַרְאֵנוּ טוֹב *who will cause us to see* (i.e. show us, Hiph. of ראה with 1 pl. suff.) *good* (i.e. prosperity)?=O that we saw some prosperity. More idiomatic still is the use of מִי יִתֵּן *who will give?* Cf. Deut. 28⁶⁷ מִי־יִתֵּן עֶרֶב *would that it were evening* ; 2 Sam. 19¹ מִי־יִתֵּן מוּתִי אֲנִי תַחְתֶּיךָ *would that I had died in thy stead* (lit. who will grant my dying, mine, § 43. 6, instead of thee ; for תחת, see *Grammar*, p. 121, 1st two lines).

12 For the sing. after "forty," see § 48. 1 (6).
13 For מְבַקֵּשׁ instead of ״, see § 10. 3 a.
14 Lit. "also I have grown old," am old.

B.

1 הִנֵּה שִׁפְחָתֵךְ בְּיָדֵךְ עֲשִׂי־לָהּ הַטּוֹב בְּעֵינָיִךְ: 2 ¹וַיֶּחְדְּלוּ
לִבְנוֹת הָעִיר: 3 לֹא ²אוּכַל לַעֲשׂוֹת ³דָּבָר ⁴עַד־בֹּאֲךָ שָׁמָּה:
4 וַיִּרְבּוּ הַמַּיִם מְאֹד ⁵וַיְכֻסּוּ רָאשֵׁי הֶהָרִים: 5 ⁶צִוִּיתִיהָ
לְבִלְתִּי ⁷אֲכָל מִן־הָעֵץ אֲשֶׁר בְּתוֹךְ ⁸הַגָּן פֶּן־תְּמוּת: 6 כִּי־אַתָּה
יְהוָה צְבָאוֹת אֱלֹהֵי יִשְׂרָאֵל גָּלִיתָ אֶת־אֹזֶן עַבְדְּךָ לֵאמֹר בַּיִת
אֶבְנֶה־⁹לָּךְ: 7 וַיֹּאמֶר אֶל־בְּנֵי יִשְׂרָאֵל עֶרֶב ¹⁰וִידַעְתֶּם כִּי
¹¹יְהוָה הוֹצִיא אֶתְכֶם מֵאֶרֶץ מִצְרָיִם וּבֹקֶר וּרְאִיתֶם אֶת־
כְּבוֹדוֹ:

¹ The sing. is יֶחְדַּל, but the shifting of the tone forward frequently
changes the ‗ into ‗ (and also *vice versa*); the cohortative of אֶחְדַּל
is אֶחְדְּלָה, Job 16⁶. See Note 13 of Exercise 35 B.
² Impf. Qal (rather than Hoph.) of יכל (§ 39. 4).
³ דָּבָר is frequently used in the sense of *matter, affair*, and generally
as equivalent to our *thing: e.g.* Gen. 22¹⁶ עָשִׂיתָ אֶת־הַדָּבָר הַזֶּה *thou hast
done this thing.* So דָּבָר may be used for *anything*; cf. Gen. 18¹⁴
הֲיִפָּלֵא מֵיְהוָה דָּבָר *is anything too wonderful* (Niph.) *for Yahweh* (for מִן to
express comparison, *more wonderful than*, see § 47. 1): cf. Deut. 17⁸.
Consequently *nothing* may be rendered by לֹא . . . דָּבָר: cf. Deut. 2⁷
לֹא נוֹדַע דָּבָר *thou hast lacked nothing*; 2 Sam. 17¹⁹ לֹא חָסַרְתָּ דָּבָר
nothing was known (Niph.). *Anything* may also be מְאוּמָה: cf. Num.
22³⁸ הֲיָכֹל אוּכַל דַּבֵּר מְאוּמָה "have I any power at all (abs. inf. and impf.
Qal of יכל, *Grammar*, p. 152, 2. 5) to speak (notice absence of לְ after
יכל) *anything?*" מְאוּמָה is usually found in *negative* sentences, so
לֹא . . . מְאוּמָה is another way of expressing *nothing*, cf. Gen. 30³¹
לֹא־חָשַׁךְ מִמֶּנִּי לֹא־תִתֶּן־לִי מְאוּמָה *thou shalt give me nothing*; Gen. 39⁹
מְאוּמָה *he withheld nothing from me*; Gen. 22¹² אַל־תַּעַשׂ לוֹ מְאוּמָה *do
nothing to him.* (For תעש, see § 45. 1. 3.)
⁴ Or עַד אֲשֶׁר תָּבוֹא (or even pf. בָּאתָ until thou *shalt have come*—

fut. pf.—though the pf. is more rarely used of future time). See Note 1 of Exercise 40 B.

⁵ בסה is used only 3 times in Qal (twice in act. ptc. and once in pass. ptc.) and twice in Niph. The regular part is the Pi. of which the Pu. (as above) is passive. For omission of the dagh. forte in י, see § 7. 5.

⁶ Not צֵ, for the first syllable, ending in the strengthened consonant, is closed : § 8. 4 b.

⁷ So (not אֱכֹל) after לְבִלְתִּי, in Deut 12²³, and—quite naturally—in Gen. 3¹¹ אֱכָל־מִמֶּנּוּ, where the vowel is farther from the tone (§ 8. 2 b). Nearly always the inf. cstr. and imperat. of Pe Aleph vbs. take ֱ (§ 8. 2 b), but in a very few cases ֲ: cf. Num. 26¹⁰ בַּאֲכֹל הָאֵשׁ *when the fire devoured.*

⁸ For a similar division of a verse by *athnaḥ* (hence וָ, not וַ), leaving in the second half one word (or word-group), cf. Gen. 3³ which has twelve words (or word-groups) in the first half, and in the second only פֶּן־תְּמֻתוּן. Similarly, *athnaḥ* may stand alone at the beginning of a verse ; cf. Gen. 34³¹ וַיֹּאמְרוּ. See Note 7 of Exercise 39 B.

⁹ Pausal form. For *daghesh forte*, see Note 28 of Exercise 33 B.

¹⁰ See Note 2 of Exercise 31 C.

¹¹ יהוה precedes the vb., because it is emphatic—"that it is Yahweh who has brought you out." See Note 1 of Exercise 26 A.

§ 45.

A.

1. And she conceived;¹ and when² she saw that she had conceived, her mistress³ was despised⁴ in her eyes. 2. Walk before me and be⁵ perfect, and I will establish my covenant to be thy God.⁶ 3. And Noah removed⁷ the covering of the ark ; and he looked, and behold, the face of the ground was dry. 4. And Noah planted⁸ a vineyard, and he drank of the wine and was drunken ; and he uncovered himself⁹ within his tent. 5. And the king was diseased¹⁰ in his feet, yet¹¹ in his disease he sought not Yahweh. 6. Stretch forth thy hand and cause frogs¹² to come up.¹³ 7. And there was strife between the herdsmen¹⁴ of Abram's cattle and the herdsmen of Lot's cattle ; and they said to one another, Let there be¹⁵ no strife,

I pray thee, between me and thee. 8. And Yahweh
appeared [16] to Abram, and Abram built there an altar to
Yahweh who had appeared [17] to him. 9. Let the name of
Yahweh be [18] blessed.

10 וַיִּרְאוּ הַשֹּׁמְרִים אִישׁ יֹצֵא מִן־הָעִיר וַיֹּאמְרוּ לוֹ [19] הַרְאֵנוּ נָא אֶת־מְבוֹא
הָעִיר [20] וְעָשִׂינוּ עִמְּךָ חָסֶד : [21] וַיַּרְאֵם אֶת־מְבוֹא הָעִיר [22] וַיַּכּוּ אֶת־הָעִיר
לְפִי־חָרֶב וְאֶת־הָאִישׁ שִׁלֵּחוּ : וַיֵּלֶךְ הָאִישׁ אֶרֶץ הַחִתִּים וַיִּבֶן עִיר וַיִּקְרָא [23]
שְׁמָהּ לוּז הוּא שְׁמָהּ עַד הַיּוֹם הַזֶּה :

And the watchers saw a man coming out of the city, and
    they said to him, Show us, we pray thee, the entrance
    to the city, and we will deal with thee kindly. And
    he showed them the entrance to the city, and they
    smote the city with the edge of the sword; but the
    man they let go. And the man went to the land of
    the Hittites; and he built a city, and called the name
    of it Luz; that is its name to this day.

[1] תִּהְרֶה (after waw consec.) becomes תַּהַר, as יַעֲלֶה becomes יַעַל
(§ 45. 1. 3). This phrase וַתַּהַר occurs many times, and always in the
apocopated form. But "the *full* forms (without apocope of the ה ָ)
not infrequently occur after waw consec., especially in the 1st pers. and
in the later books : *e.g.* וָאֶרְאֶה *and I saw*, occurs more frequently than
וָאֵרָא. So וַיַּעֲשֶׂה *and he made*, occurs four times, but וַיַּעַשׂ over 200
times." G.K. § 75 *t*.

[2] Hebrew more simply, "*and* she saw, and . . . was despised."
Hebrew is very fond of this co-ordination of clauses by the multiplica-
tion of waws, where other languages subordinate one clause to another.
See *Grammar*, Introduction, pp. 2 f.

[3] גִּבְרָתָהּ ; see § 29. 3, col. 3.

[4] תֵּקַל impf. Qal of קלל (§ 42. 3 b ; p. 226, col. 3).

[5] וְהֵיה ; see § 45. 2. 3 *a*.

[6] Lit. "to be to thee for (a) God"—a very common construction.
Cf. Jer. 31[33] וְהָיִיתִי לָהֶם לֵאלֹהִים וְהֵמָּה יִהְיוּ־לִי לְעָם *and I will be their
God, and they shall be my people.* (See Note 4 of Exercise 22 B.)

[7] *Hiph.* impf. of סור (but *not* written וַיָּסֵר), just as the Qal is also
וַיָּסַר and not וַיִּסַר ; cf. § 40 2 b.

[8] Impf. Qal with waw consec., of נטע.

[9] Apocopated impf. Hithpa'el, with waw consec. of גלה.

[10] וַיָּחֶל from חלה ; cf. ותהר in Note 1 of this section. In 1 Kings

8

15²³ instead of the Chronicler's בְּרַגְלָיו we find אֶת־רַגְלָיו, the accusative of the part affected : cf. Ps. 3⁸ הִכִּיתָ אֶת־כָּל־אֹיְבַי לֶחִי "thou hast smitten (Hiph. of נכה) all mine enemies *upon the cheek*" (pausal form of לְחִי). In 2 Chr. 16¹² occurs the curious form וַיֶּחֱלֶא (unapocopated —see Note 1 of this section). This illustrates the tendency of Lamedh He vbs. to appear as Lamedh Aleph (for the reverse, see § 38. 1. 5). Here the Lamedh He vocalization is retained in the last syllable : sometimes the Lamedh Aleph vocalization is adopted, *e.g.* Gen. 49¹ וְאַגִּידָה לָכֶם אֵת אֲשֶׁר־יִקְרָא אֶתְכֶם *that I may tell you that which will befall you* (for יִקְרֶה).

¹¹ גַּם and וְגַם have sometimes, though rarely, an adversative force.

¹² Note the article in Hebrew : see Note 8 of Exercise 14 A.

¹³ Apoc. imperat. Hiph. of עלה.

¹⁴ Cstr. ptc. (active) Qal of רעה.

¹⁵ Jussive fem.

¹⁶ Apoc. impf. Niph. of ראה (§ 34. 3 a).

¹⁷ Niph. ptc. of ראה with article.

¹⁸ Jussive. This is the more accurate translation of Job 1²¹, not "blessed be the name of Y." The Satan has asserted that Job will *curse* Yahweh (1¹¹), and with great dramatic propriety the decisive word is reserved for the end—"the name of Y. be—*blessed*."

¹⁹ Hiph. imperat. (הַרְאֵה) of ראה with 1 pl. suffix. "Cause us to see."

²⁰ Note the accent on the penult וְעָשִׂינוּ. This is *not* to be explained by the principle laid down in § 44. 4, but is *regular* with the *first* person plur. with waw consec. (§ 23. 3. 4). For order, see Note 7 of Exercise 30 C.

²¹ Hiph. impf. with waw consec. and 3 pl. masc. suffix.

²² 3 pl. masc. Hiph. impf. of נכה with waw consec. נכה is not used in Qal, but in Hiph. and Hoph., *e.g.* וַיַּכּוּם *and they smote them,* הֻכּוּ *they were smitten,* וַיֻּכּוּ *and they were smitten.*

²³ פִי cstr. of פֶה *mouth* (*Grammar*, p. 153).

B.

1 וַיַּעַשׂ נֹחַ כְּכֹל אֲשֶׁר־צִוָּהוּ יְהֹוָה : 2 וַיְצַו אֶת־הַכֹּהֲנִים לֵאמֹר עֲלוּ מִן־הַיַּרְדֵּן וַיַּעֲלוּ : 3 ¹וַיֵּט אִישׁ הָאֱלֹהִים אֶת־יָדוֹ ²וַיַּעַל אֶת־הַצְפַרְדְעִים וַיַּרְא פַּרְעֹה אֶת־הַמַּכּוֹת וַיִּירָא ³יִרְאָה גְדוֹלָה : 4 וַיְהִי בִּהְיוֹתָם בַּשָּׂדֶה ⁴וַיָּקָם הָאִישׁ אֶל־רֵעֵהוּ וַיַּהַרְגֵהוּ : 5 יִקָּווּ הַמַּיִם אֶל־מָקוֹם אֶחָד ⁵וְתֵרָאֶה הַיַּבָּשָׁה

⁶וַיְהִי־כֵן: 6 וַיִּפְתַּח אֱלֹהִים אֶת־עֵינֶיהָ ⁷וַתֵּרֶא בְּאֵר מָיִם
וַתֵּלֶךְ וַתְּמַלֵּא אֶת־הַחֵמֶת מַיִם וַתַּשְׁקְ אֶת־הַנָּעַר: 7 וַיֹּאמֶר
שַׂר הַצָּבָא ⁸אֲשֶׁר־⁹יַכֶּה אֶת־קִרְיַת־סֵפֶר ¹⁰וּלְכָדָהּ ¹¹וְנָתַתִּי לוֹ
אֶת־¹²בִּתִּי לְאִשָּׁה: 8 הַט שָׁמֶיךָ ¹³וְתֵרַד:

¹ Apocopated impf. Qal of נטה. Full form יִפֶּה: when the ה is
dropped, the short *i* becomes the tone-long *ē* (§ 43. 1 a) ; cf. יֵחַ.
With maqqeph וַיֵּט־שָׁם אָהֳלֹה *and he* stretched (i.e. *pitched*) *his tent
there.* For this rare ending of s. m. suffix, see *Grammar*, p. 12, footnote
1 ; and for ה, see p. 67, paragr. 1. Hiph. apocop. וַיַּט "*and he turned*
(*i.e.* influenced) the hearts of all the men of Judah" (2 Sam. 19¹⁵).

² Hiph.—indistinguishable, except by context, from Qal (§ 45. 1. 4).

³ For this construction, cf. Jon. 1¹⁰. ¹⁶. See Note 21 of Exercise 39 B.

⁴ Impf. with waw consec.—the regular construction after ויהי. After
עַל, קוּם is very much commoner than אֶל־ to express hostility. These
prepositions are frequently interchanged, possibly even confused with
one another. See Note 3 of Exercise 42 C.

⁵ So Gen. 1⁹. As this must be regarded as a jussive, we should
have expected the shorter form תֵּרָא. But in Lamedh He vbs. "the
full form of the imperfect is frequently used with the meaning of the
jussive, especially *in* and immediately *before* the principal pause," as
here (G.K. § 109 a, Note 2). Cf. Jud. 6³⁹, at the beginning of a clause
יְהִי־נָא חֹרֶב *let there be dryness, I pray thee* ; but at the end, יְהִיֶה־טַּל *let
there be dew.* יהיה must here be regarded as jussive as much as יהי.

⁶ ויהי is written with *methegh* when followed by *maqqeph* : cf. Gen 1⁵·⁷.

⁷ We write וַיִּרְא, but never וַתֵּרָא or וָאֵרָא (§ 45. 1. 4).

⁸ = "he who." מִי is sometimes used in such connexions to express
whoever, whosoever (§ 13. 3) ; cf. Jud. 7³ מִי־יָרֵא יָשֹׁב *whosoever is
afraid, let him return* (jussive of שׁוּב). But probably the Hebrew
regarded מִי in such usage as a real interrogative (="*who is afraid?*
let him return").

⁹ The apocopated form יַךְ would, of course, be here impossible, as
the jussive idea is not present, nor is there a waw consec., as, *e.g.*, in
וַיַּךְ *and he smote.*

¹⁰ The proper sequence (pf. with waw consec.) after the impf. (יכה).

¹¹ Pf.—with waw consec.,—a very frequent construction in the
apodosis, instead of the simpler impf. אֶתֶּן־לוֹ. There is seldom any
possible confusion as to where the apodosis begins. See Note 13 (2nd
paragraph) of Exercise 39 C. ¹² *Grammar*, p. 153, בַּת.

[13] So Ps. 144⁵ *and mayest thou come down* (jussive). For juss. following imper. see Note 5 of Ex. 40 B. וְרֵד (cf. 1 Kings 18⁴⁴) would have been possible. וְיָרַדְתָּ, which would be theoretically possible (see Note 2 of Exercise 26 B), would be rather improbable, unless the sentence were continued farther ; as in Jer. 18² קוּם וְיָרַדְתָּ בֵּית הַיּוֹצֵר *rise and go down to the potter's house*. In any case it would not be so impressive in a poetical passage like this. Note in Jer. 18² the absence of a prep. before בֵית, which is in the accus. See Note 1 of Exercise 48 B, and Note on מוּבָא in Exercise 40 A, p. 94.

(In וְיָרַדְתָּ, if it were the last word, the accent would fall on the penult—not therefore וְיָרַדְתָּ—in accordance with the principle that when a perfect with waw consec. stands in pause, the tone is not thrown forward, as it otherwise would normally be, cf. § 23. 3. 4 : cf. Deut. 8¹⁰ וְאָכַלְתָּ וְשָׂבָעְתָּ *and thou shalt eat and be satisfied*.)

C.

1. And when David and his men came [1] to the city, behold, it was burned with fire ; and their wives and their sons and their daughters were taken captive.   2. And it came to pass, when [2] he saw her, that he rent his garments, and said, Alas, my daughter, thou hast bowed me down to the very ground.[3]   Yes, it is thou [4] that art the cause of my calamity ; [5] for, as for me, I have made a solemn promise [6] to Yahweh, and I cannot go back (upon it).   3. Children's children are the crown of old men, and the glory of children are their fathers.   4. Happy [7] are they that dwell in thy house.   5. And he took Pharaoh's daughter and brought her [8] into the city of David till [9] he had finished [10] building [11] his house.   6. And he slept [12] with his fathers, and he was buried in the city of his father.   7. And Moses arose and came to their rescue [13] and watered their flock : and when they came to their father, he said, Why have you come (so) quickly [14] to-day ?   8. Thou hast despised [15] me and hast taken the wife of Uriah to be thy wife.

9 וְעַתָּה לֵךְ וְאָנֹכִי אֶהְיֶה עִם־פִּיךָ [16]וְהוֹרֵיתִיךָ אֲשֶׁר תְּדַבֵּר:

And now go, and I, on my part, will be with thy mouth, and teach thee what thou shalt speak.

10 וַהֲקִימֹתִי אֶת־בְּרִיתִי [17]אִתָּךְ וּבָאתָ אֶל־הַתֵּבָה אַתָּה וּבָנֶיךָ וְאִשְׁתְּךָ וּנְשֵׁי־ בָנֶיךָ אִתָּךְ:

And I will establish my covenant with thee, and thou shalt enter into the ark, thou and thy sons and thy wife and thy sons' wives with thee.

[1] The vb. coming first, is sing., agreeing with the noun next it—*David*. But the plur. would have been quite possible.

[2] כְּ, like בְּ, though not so often, may be used with the cstr. inf.

[3] Abs. inf. Hiph.—"thou hast utterly bowed me down" in grief—or "struck me down."

[4] אַתְּ is added for emphasis.

[5] Lit. "among those that trouble me." This, however, is much too weak. (i) עכר is a very strong word—used of the effect produced upon Jacob by the treacherous barbarity of Simeon and Levi (Gen. 34³⁰) ; of the confusion produced by the conduct of Achan (Josh. 7²⁵), of Saul (1 Sam. 14²⁹), and of Ahab (1 Kings 18¹⁸, cf. ¹⁷). Further (ii) בְּ may mean *in the character of*; cf Exod. 18⁴ אֱלֹהֵי אָבִי בְּעֶזְרִי *the God of my father was my help* (lit. in the character, or capacity, of help, עֵזֶר). It is possible, therefore, that here (Jud. 11³⁵) we should read the sing. בְּעֹכְרִי *in the character of one who brings disaster upon me* (=one who brings, etc.). So perhaps (in the light of Exod. 18⁴) Ps 118⁷ יְהוָה לִי בְּעֹזְרָי " Yahweh is for me *among* them that help me," should be read as בְּעֹזְרִי or בְּעֶזְרִי.

[6] Lit. "opened my mouth wide."

[7] Lit. "O the happinesses of." Cf. Ps. 1¹ אַשְׁרֵי הָאִישׁ " *happy* (not *blessed*, which is בָּרוּךְ) *is the man*."

[8] Impf. Hiph. (יָבִיא) of בּוֹא with waw consec. and suffix.

[9] עַד אֲשֶׁר כִּלָּה would have been possible.

[10] כִּלָּה Pi. followed by an infin. cstr. more usually with than without לְ. So with vbs. meaning *to begin* הֵחֵל (Hiph. of חלל), *to cease* חָדַל, *to be able* יָכֹל, etc. (See G.K. § 114 *m*, and Note 6 of Exercise 22 B.)

[11] בְּנוֹת (cstr. inf. Qal of בנה) could not in this context be confused with the cstr. plur. of בַּת *daughter*.

[12] Lit. "lay"—*i.e.* in death or the grave.

[13] Lit. "helped, delivered, or saved."

[14] Lit. "hastened to come"—מִהַר (Pi.) followed by inf. here (Exod. 2¹⁸) *without* לְ; frequently with לְ, cf. Prov. 1¹⁶ וִימַהֲרוּ לִשְׁפָּךְ־דָּם *and they make haste to shed blood* (cf. Isa. 59⁷). Hebrew has often to express an English advb. by a vb. ; cf. § 39. 4.

[15] *Scriptio defectiva* for בְּזִיתִי בָּזִיתָ, from בזה, with 1 sing. suffix). In 2 Sam. 12¹⁰ the normal תָ (before 1 s. suf., § 31. 4 b) has become תָ because it is accompanied by *zaqeph qaṭon* : see Note 8 of Exercise 43 B.

[16] Hiph. of ירה.

[17] Pausal form of אַתְּךְ.

D.

1 כַּבֵּד אֶת־אָבִיךָ וְאֶת־אִמֶּךָ כַּאֲשֶׁר צִוְּךָ אֱלֹהֶיךָ׃ 2 וַתֹּאמַרְנָה
בְנוֹתָיו אִשָּׁה אֶל־אֲחוֹתָהּ ¹לֵאמֹר ²נַשְׁקֶה אֶת־אָבִינוּ יַיִן וַיֵּשְׁתְּ
וַיִּשְׁכָּר׃ 3 ³וַתֹּסֶף אִשְׁתּוֹ לָלֶדֶת בֵּן וַיִּגְדַּל וַיֶּאֱהַב ⁴אֶת־אָבִיו
וְאֶת־אִמּוֹ בְּכָל־לְבָבוֹ ⁵וַיֶּרֶב לְהֵיטִיב לְאֶחָיו וּלְאַחְיוֹתָיו׃
4 שָׁבוּ אֶת־נְשֵׁי אֹיְבֵיהֶם וַיָּבֹאוּ אֶת־בָּתֵּיהֶם וַיֵּלְכוּ ⁶לְדַרְכָּם
וְלֹא הֵמִיתוּ ⁷אִישׁ׃ 5 יָשְׁבָה בִתּוֹ ⁸בְּבֵית אָבִיהָ ⁹שְׁנָתָיִם׃
6 יוֹמַיִם לֹא ¹⁰יִפְתַּח אָבִיו אֶת־פִּיו׃ 7 ¹¹עֲזָבוּנִי אָבִי וְאִמִּי׃
8 יִהְיֶה שְׁמוֹ בְּפִי תָמִיד׃ 9 מָצָאתִי בְבֵיתְךָ כְּלֵי כֶסֶף
¹²וּכְלֵי זָהָב׃ 10 אַשְׁרֵי אֲנָשֶׁיךָ׃

[1] ותאמרנה Hebrew has no objection to a repetition like this— . . .
לאמר; cf. Jud. 15¹³ וַיֹּאמְרוּ לוֹ לֵאמֹר. But וַתְּדַבֵּרְנָה would have been
equally possible; cf. Jer. 44²⁵ ותדברנה בפיכם . . . לאמר (*with your
mouth*: notice the *masc.*—as the more familiar—suffix, even beside a
fem. vb.).

[2] Not נַשְׁקָה, though the idea to be expressed is cohortative. Lamedh
He vbs. "hardly ever receive the הָ‍ of the cohortative"—only twice in
all, according to the punctuation; Isa. 41²³, Ps. 119¹¹⁷; Driver, *Hebrew
Tenses*, § 47.

[3] See § 39. 4.

[4] Hebrew has no word for *parents*, corresponding to the New Testament γονεῖς (from γονεύς), cf. Luke 8⁵⁶, John 9²², etc. Delitzsch, in his
New Testament translation, renders the former passage by *her father
and mother* אָבִיהָ וְאִמָּהּ, but the latter by יֹלְדָיו (ptc. Qal of ילד: *his
parents*). The usual meaning of ילד is *to bear*: in the J document it
also means *to beget*—usually in genealogical lists (cf. Gen. 4¹⁸ and often
in ch. 10): with this meaning, however, the P document uses the Hiph.
הוֹלִיד. The justification of Delitzsch's translation may be found in
Zech. 13³, where twice occurs the phrase אָבִיו וְאִמּוֹ יֹלְדָיו *his father and
mother who begot him*.

[5] Apoc. impf. Hiph. with waw cons. (of רבה *to be*, or *become much,
many, great*). The Hiph. of רבה, followed by ל with an inf. cstr. = *to do
much in respect of*: e.g. 2 Kings 21⁶ הִרְבָּה לַעֲשׂוֹת הָרַע *he wrought much
evil* (lit. he did much in respect of working evil); Amos 4⁴ הַרְבּוּ לִפְשֹׁעַ
transgress greatly; 2 Sam. 18⁸ וַיֶּרֶב הַיַּעַר לֶאֱכֹל בָּעָם מֵאֲשֶׁר אָכְלָה הַחֶרֶב

and the forest devoured more among the *people than* those whom *the sword devoured* (lit. many away from, *i.e.* more than ; see § 47. 1 a).

The abs. inf. Hiph. הַרְבֵּה is also frequently used as an adverb= *greatly, exceedingly* ; *e.g.* 2 Kings 10¹⁸ יֵהוּא יַעַבְדֶנּוּ הַרְבֵּה *Jehu will serve him much* ; 2 Kings 21¹⁶ דָּם נָקִי שָׁפַךְ הַרְבֵּה מְאֹד *innocent blood he shed very much*. Here, therefore, we might write וַיֵּיטֶב . . . הַרְבֵּה (apoc. impf. Hiph. of יטב ; see *Grammar*, p. 152, 2 (2) טוֹב). Or, by means of the inf. abs. (§ 21. 2 b) וּלְאָחִיו . . . הֵיטֵב הֵיטִיב (cf. Gen. 32¹³, Jer. 7⁵).

⁶ לְ is the regular prep. in this phrase ; cf. Gen. 32² הָלַךְ לְדַרְכּוֹ *he went on his way*.

⁷ This is the order in 1 Sam. 30². The אִישׁ might, however, come first ; cf. 1 Sam. 27¹¹ וְאִישׁ וְאִשָּׁה לֹא־יְחַיֶּה דָוִד *and neither man nor woman did David save alive* (*i.e.* spare : impf. Pi. of חיה, § 26. 1 (*b*) ii).

⁸ Or without בְּ ; cf. Gen. 38¹¹ שְׁבִי בֵית־אָבִיךְ *remain* (*f.*) *in thy father's house*. This accus. to express rest is found chiefly with בַּיִת and פֶּתַח, and only when these words are in the *cstr.*

⁹ By a curious idiom יָמִים may be added (in apposition) to שָׁנֶתִים : *two years, days*, i.e. *two years' time*=*two full years* (cf. Gen. 41¹, Jer. 28³·¹¹). So חֹדֶשׁ יָמִים *a month* of *days*, i.e. *a month's time*=*a whole month* (*Syntax*, § 29 *d*).

¹⁰ The impf. suggests "did not *at any moment* open his mouth" (cf. the impf. יִחְיֶה in Note 7). This phrase occurs (with the impf.) in Ps. 38¹⁴, Prov. 24⁷, Isa. 53⁷. "He opened his mouth"—the simple fact—would be expressed by the pf. ; cf. Job 3¹ פָּתַח אִיּוֹב אֶת־פִּיהוּ *Job opened his mouth*.

¹¹ Or עֹזְבִי, agreeing with the gend. and numb. of the nearest noun (see Note 10, Exercise 26 A). In Ps. 27¹⁰, where the vb. comes at the end, the pl. עֲזָבוּנִי is natural.

¹² It would not be wrong to say simply וְזָהָב ; cf. Gen. 14¹⁹ קֹנֵה שָׁמַיִם וָאָרֶץ *creator* (cstr. ptc.) *of heaven and earth* ; 1 Sam. 23⁷ עִיר דְּלָתַיִם וּבְרִיחַ *a city of* (*i.e.* that has) *gates and bars*. But Hebrew prefers to repeat the construct (*Grammar*, p. 61, first four lines). In Jer. 8¹ אֶת־עַצְמוֹת *the bones of* (cstr. pl. of עֶצֶם) is actually repeated five times. See Note 4, Exercise 35 A.

§ 46.

A.

1. Yahweh is my shepherd,¹ I shall not want.² 2. A child³ has been born to us, a son has been given to us. 3. A prophet will I raise⁴ up unto them from the midst of their brethren, like unto thee.⁵ 4. Every man did⁶ that

which was right in his own eyes. 5. Thy servant was [7] shepherding his father's flock; and if a lion came [8] and took [9] a sheep out of the flock, I would go out after him, and smite [10] him, and rescue it from his mouth. 6. The poor [11] man had nothing [12] but [13] one little [14] ewe-lamb, which he had bought and kept alive, and it grew up together with him and his children; it would eat [15] of his morsel and drink of his cup and lie in his bosom, and it was like a daughter [16] to him. 7. Yahweh knoweth [17] the way of the righteous, but the way of the wicked shall perish. 8. And he looked, and behold, a well in the field, and behold, there were flocks of sheep lying [18] there by [19] it, for out of that well they used to water [18] the flocks.

9 זֹאת הַבְּרִית אֲשֶׁר אֶכְרֹת ²⁰אֶת־בֵּית יִשְׂרָאֵל אַחֲרֵי הַיָּמִים הָהֵם ²¹נָתַתִּי אֶת־
תּוֹרָתִי בְּקִרְבָּם וְעַל־לִבָּם ²²אֶכְתְּבֶנָּה ²³וְהָיִיתִי לָהֶם לֵאלֹהִים וְהֵמָּה
יִהְיוּ־לִי לְעָם:

This is the covenant that I will make with the house of Israel after those days: I will put my law in their inward parts, and on their hearts will I write it, and I will be their God,[24] and they shall be my people.

[1] רֹעֶה (ptc. of רעה)=shepherd: רֹעִי, lit. "is shepherding me," in LXX. ποιμαίνει με.

[2] Or "do not want" or "cannot want."

[3] ילד and בן placed first in their respective clauses for emphasis.

[4] The context (Deut. 18⁹⁻¹⁴) shows that the meaning is—not once for all, but from time to time, as occasion demands (Deut. 18¹⁵).

[5] See *Grammar*, p. 87, footnote 1.

[6] The impf. goes appropriately with the distributive idea involved in אִישׁ (§ 13. 4). See Note 14 of Exercise 42 B.

[7] For the addition of היה to the ptc. see Note 7 of Exercise 27 A.

[8] Lit. "and a lion would come (*or* used to come) and take." The pf. with waw consec. has the force of a *frequentative* impf., and the vbs. would be in the impf. (יָבֹא and יִשָּׂא) if they did not happen to be associated with *waw*. The meaning is that this was no isolated experience of David's, but that lions *repeatedly* came. All the following perfects with waw consec. are to be similarly understood. The article before ארי is generic: see Note 8 of Exercise 14 A.

Notice this manner of expressing a conditional sentence, by a series of co-ordinate vbs. with waw consec. "And a lion would come and I

would go out " = " and if a lion came, I would go out." See Note 13
(2nd paragraph) of Exercise 39 C.

⁹ נשא *to lift up*, and so often *to carry off*, *to take away*—hence also
to forgive sin.

¹⁰ For הכיתיו (pf. Hiph. of נכה with 3 s. m. suffix); הצלתי, from
נצל (Hiph.).

¹¹ רָשׁ is the ptc. of רוּשׁ or רִישׁ, not found in pf. *sing.*; but pl. רָשׁוּ
they are in want (Ps. 34¹¹). Here (2 Sam. 12³) it is spelt רָשׁ, but in
vv.¹· ⁴ רָאשׁ—the א indicating the naturally long *â*. This is rare
(*Grammar*, p. 10, footnote 2).

¹² Lit. "there was not anything" (cf. § 13. 4). For more usual ways
of expressing *nothing*, see Note 3 of Exercise 44 B.

¹³ כי אם *but, except*, after a negative : see Note 7 of Exercise 38 B.

¹⁴ קָטֹן is very common, but it is not inflected (except that *once*,
2 Chr. 21¹⁷, it appears in the construct—קְטֹן בָּנָיו *the youngest*—§ 47. 2 a
—*of his sons*). The fem. (as here), the plur., and the suffixes are
supplied by קָטָן, for declension of which see § 43. 4.

¹⁵ The impfs. suggest that that was its *habit*.

¹⁶ Not בַּת in pause : see Note 1 of Exercise 33 C. בַּת is ultimately
בַּנְתְּ (from בֵּן), hence the retention of the ‿ even in pause.

¹⁷ ידע is often (as here) *know*, in the sense of *care for* : cf. Prov. 12¹⁰
יוֹדֵעַ צַדִּיק נֶפֶשׁ בְּהֶמְתּוֹ "a righteous man *careth for* the life of his beast."
The ptc. suggests that the care of Yahweh is *continual*. The subj.
normally comes before the ptc., but after כִּי (which introduces this
sentence in Ps. 1⁶) the adj., or (as here) the ptc. usually comes first ; cf.
Gen. 3⁵, and see Note 2 of Exercise 16 A.

¹⁸ A capital illustration of the difference between the ptc. and the
impf. Cf. Isa. 6² שְׂרָפִים עֹמְדִים *seraphim were standing*, but each
יְכַסֶּה פָנָיו *would cover, used to cover, his face*.

¹⁹ For עַל of location beside water, see Note 3 of Exercise 16 A.

²⁰ The prep., not the sign of the accus.

²¹ This would be prophetic pf., § 46. I. 2 (3) ; but probably we
should read with many MSS. the smoother וְנָתַתִּי *and I will give*.

²² אֶכְתְּבֶנָּה ; so Jer. 31³³ for the more normal תָּ. This brings out
distinctly, as simple sheʷwa could not do, the quality of the original
vowel *ō* in אֶכְתֹּב. Composite sheʷwas are rarely written to other consonants than gutturals, § 3. 3 b. Cf. Ezek. 35⁶ also דָּם יִרְדְּפֶךָ *blood
shall pursue thee* (yirdᵒphékhâ). See Note 3 of Exercise 33 C.

²³ Accent on penult וְהָיִיתִי, not וְהָיִיתִי (§ 44. 4).

²⁴ Lit. "to them for (a) God" ; for לְ after היה see Note 4 of Exercise
22 B, and Note 10 of Exercise 33 B.

B.

1 כַּאֲשֶׁר יְעַנּוּ ²אֹיְבֵיהֶם כֵּן יִרְבּוּ: 2 יַקַּח אֶת־הָאֹהֶל
3 וְנָטָה ⁴מִחוּץ לַמַּחֲנֶה: 3 לֹא־יֵעָשֶׂה כֵן בְּאַרְצֵנוּ: 4 ⁵אַבֵּד
יְאַבֵּד יְהוָה אֶת־מַעֲשֵׂה יָדֶיךָ: 5 ⁶כַּאֲשֶׁר אָבַדְתִּי אָבָדְתִּי
6 אָז ⁷יָשִׁיר מֹשֶׁה וּבְנֵי יִשְׂרָאֵל אֶת־הַשִּׁירָה הַזֹּאת
לֵאלֹהֵיהֶם: 7 כָּל־אִישׁ אֲשֶׁר ⁹יְחַזֵּק אֶת־לִבּוֹ וְעָבַר אֶת־
תּוֹרָתִי ¹⁰יוּמָת: 8 הָאָרֶץ ¹¹עֹמֶדֶת לְעוֹלָם: 9 וְעַצְּתִיךָ
¹²יֵאָסֵף כָּל־עַמֶּךָ: 10 מָצְאוּ נְעָרוֹת יֹצְאוֹת לִשְׁאֹב מָיִם:
11 אֶת־כָּל־זֹאת ¹³נָתַתִּי לְךָ אִם־¹⁴תִּקֹּד ¹⁵וְתִשְׁתַּחֲוֶה לִי:
12 ¹⁶יוֹדֵעַ צַדִּיק נֶפֶשׁ ¹⁷בְּהֶמְתּוֹ: 13 ¹⁸סוֹמֵךְ יְהוָה ¹⁹לְכָל־
הַנֹּפְלִים: 14 עוֹד הוּא מְדַבֵּר ²⁰וְאֶחָד מֵעֲבָדָיו בָּא וַיֹּאמֶר
²¹נִדְמִינוּ ²²כֻּלָּנוּ:

¹ *As . . . so*—the nearest Hebrew equivalent to *the more . . . the more*. The *series* of oppressions and increases implied by *the more*, is adequately indicated by the impf. (Pi. of עגה, *to be bowed down, afflicted*, with 3 pl. m. suff.).

² Hebrew prose hardly ever speaks of "the enemy" הָאֹיֵב—it prefers the more concrete "their (our, etc.) enemies." In poetry, אֹיֵב (without the article) is frequently used much as we say "the enemy" : cf. Ex. 15⁹ אָמַר אוֹיֵב *the enemy said* (cf. Ps. 74¹⁸ 106¹⁰). In sentence 5 of Exercise 48 A, instead of הָאֹיֵב appears in the original (2 Sam. 23¹⁶) פְּלִשְׁתִּים.

³ As it happens, נטה in the Qal (pf. and impf.) never seems to occur with a pronom. suffix (which would here be נָטָהוּ). The original (Exod. 33⁷) here reads וְנָטָה־לוֹ "and pitched (it) for himself." לוֹ is not supported by LXX., which reads simply ἔπηξεν.

⁴ Lit. "(from) without, with reference to" the camp—a common use of מִן . . . לְ ; see Note 1 of Exercise 36 C.

⁵ אבד is used both in Pi. and Hiph. for *destroy*. In the Pi. the impf. is more frequently used than the pf.: in the Hiph., while the pf. is frequently found, the impf. occurs only once—in the interesting form אֹבִידָה *I will destroy*, Jer. 46⁸ (one of the few illustrations of a Pe Aleph vb. taking its impf. in *ǒ* in a conjugation other than the Qal).

⁶ כַּאֲשֶׁר (*as*, or *when*) is used here (Esth. 4¹⁶) and in the similar expression of resignation in Gen. 43¹⁴ כַּאֲשֶׁר שָׁכֹלְתִּי שָׁכָלְתִּי *if I am bereaved, I am bereaved*. (For שָׁכֹלְתִּי, see Note 2 of Exercise 22 C.)

⁷ Sing. rather than plur., to agree with the *adjacent* noun ; but the *next* vb. (after *both* subjects have been mentioned) is וַיֹּאמְרוּ (Exod. 15¹). See Note 10 of Exercise 26 A.

⁸ Or—to express *whosoever*—אִישׁ may stand alone, without כֹּל (*a man who*) ; or אֲשֶׁר alone would be possible (*he who*). See Note 7 of Exercise 45 B.

⁹ *To harden* the heart (usually with the shorter form לֵב in this phrase) is represented by the Pi. of חָזַק (in the Elohist and the Priestly documents), by the Hiph. of כבד (in the Jahwist), and by the Hiph. of קשׁה (once, in the Priestly document, Exod. 7³). Therefore יַכְבִּיד or יַקְשֶׁה might have been used here. The *Pi.* of כבד is also used for *harden* in 1 Sam. 6⁶ (see sentence 2 in the Hebrew into English of § 26), but its usual meaning is *to honour* or *glorify*.

¹⁰ וָמֵת (waw consec. with pf.)—*then he shall die*—would also be possible : cf. Exod. 30³⁸ אִישׁ אֲשֶׁר־יַעֲשֶׂה כָמֹוהָ וְנִכְרַת *whosoever makes* (incense) *like it* (*Grammar*, p. 87, footnote 1) *shall be cut off* (= יִכָּרֵת) ; 1 Kings 1⁵² אִם־רָעָה תִמָּצֵא־בֹו וָמֵת *if wickedness be found in him* (*then*) *he shall die*. But with the word מוּת, the simple impf. (usually in the Hoph. and frequently strengthened by the abs. inf. Qal = *he shall surely be put to death*) appears to be preferred to waw consec. with the pf. Two contiguous verses in Lev. illustrate this preference : Lev. 24¹⁵ אִישׁ אִישׁ כִּי־יְקַלֵּל אֱלֹהָיו וְנָשָׂא חֶטְאֹו *every one who* (lit. when he) *curses his God shall bear his sin* ; but 24¹⁷ אִישׁ כִּי יַכֶּה כָל־נֶפֶשׁ אָדָם מֹות יוּמָת *whosoever smites a man mortally shall surely be put to death*.

¹¹ Ptc. denoting continuous duration. In Eccl. 1⁴ לְעֹולָם עֹמָדֶת *for ever standeth*.

¹² In 2 Sam. 17¹¹ this jussive (impf.) is strengthened by a preceding abs. inf. הֵאָסֹף. Here the abs. inf. is, as we might expect, in the Niph. But sometimes, even with a finite vb. in another conjugation than the Qal, the abs. inf. of the *Qal* is used, as "the simplest and most general representative of the verbal idea" (G.K. § 113 *w* ; cf. מֹות יוּמָת at the end of Note 10 of this section). There are two forms of the abs. inf. Niph.—נִקְטֹל is used with the pf. (cf. 1 Sam. 20⁶ נִשְׁאֹל נִשְׁאַל, *he earnestly asked* for himself) ; and הִקָּטֹל with the impf.

¹³ The pf. implies, "it is already as good as yours." It differs from the impf. much as our "I give" differs from "I will give" (אֶתֵּן).

¹⁴ Or תִּפֹּל אַרְצָה (cf. 2 Sam. 1², Job 1²⁰) ; but קדד and the Hithpa'lel

of שָׁחָה (§ 44. 3) are very frequently found together. The impf. form of קדד in use is the Aramaizing form יִקַּד, § 42. 8.

[15] Simple waw with impf. is better here than waw consec. with pf. (וְהִשְׁתַּחֲוִיתָ) as the words are practically synonymous (§ 23. 3. 7); (cf. Deut. 9[14] הֶרֶף מִמֶּנִּי וְאַשְׁמִידֵם וְאֶמְחֶה שְׁמָם "let me alone [apoc. Hiph. imper. of רפה]—in Jud. 11[37] [הַרְפֵּה] that I may destroy them and blot out their name," rather than וְמָחִיתִי). לְפָנַי would also be possible (cf. Deut. 26[10]), but after שָׁחָה the simple לְ is much commoner.

[16] For ידע, see Note 17 in section A of this Exercise. The ptc. may precede its subj. (though this order is unusual) when "a certain stress falls naturally on the idea conveyed by the verbal form": cf. Gen. 18[17] הַמְכַסֶּה אֲנִי מֵאַבְרָהָם אֲשֶׁר אֲנִי עֹשֶׂה "shall (§ 49. 2. 2 b) I hide from Abraham that which I am about to do?" Driver, Hebrew Tenses, § 135. 4.

[17] Grammar, p. 154, lines 2 and 3.

[18] So Ps. 145[14]. For place of ptc. see Note 16. It may be accounted for, however, simply by the fact that Ps. 145 is an alphabetic psalm, and at this point a line beginning with ס is needed.

[19] So Ps. 145[14]. But סמך elsewhere takes accus.; cf. Ps. 3[6] יִסְמְכֵנִי he daily (impf.) sustains me; Ps. 37[24] יְהֹוָה סוֹמֵךְ יָדוֹ Yahweh upholds his hand. The parallel word in Ps. 145[14] זוֹקֵף (ptc. he raises up) also takes לְ before its obj.; but in Ps. 146[8], before the very same obj., it takes no לְ. The construction with לְ may have been influenced by Aramaic usage, which frequently introduces the obj. by לְ. If the לְ be regarded as a pure Hebrew construction, it may be explained as "Y. is a supporter for or to all who fall."

[20] The phrase "one of" may be rendered in three ways: (i) as above, אֶחָד abs. followed by מִן; (ii) אַחַד cstr. (§ 48. 1. 7) followed by מִן; and (iii) אַחַד cstr., followed immediately by a noun in the abs. without מִן, e.g. Gen. 22[2] אַחַד הֶהָרִים one of the mountains (cf. Gen. 21[15]). Within the compass of a few verses we find examples of both (i) and (ii) in the same phrase—2 Kings 7[13] אֶחָד מֵעֲבָדָיו (cf. 2 Sam. 2[21]), and 2 Kings 6[12] אַחַד מֵעֲבָדָיו (cf. 2 Sam. 1[15]). Cf. Deut. 19[5] אַחַת הֶעָרִים and 4[42] אַחַת מִן־הֶעָרִים one of the cities.

[21] See Grammar, p. 228 (footnote 1).

[22] Not כֻּלָּנוּ. Lit. "the totality of us." כֹּל is strictly a noun (=the whole, totality), and can take pronominal suffixes.

§ 47.

A.

1. Take away[1] my life, for I am not better than my fathers. 2. What is sweeter than honey? and what[2] is stronger than a lion? 3. Yahweh loves the gates of Zion more than all the dwelling-places of Jacob. 4. The day of death is better than the day of one's birth.[3] 5. There was no man of the Israelites goodlier than he: from his shoulders and upward he was taller than any[4] of the people. 6. O thou[5] fairest among women! 7. Behold, obedience is better than sacrifice, and to hearken than the fat of rams. 8. As thy sword has bereaved women, so shall thy mother be the most bereaved[6] of women. 9. And death shall be chosen rather than life by[7] all that are left of this evil family.

10 וְעַתָּה יְהֹוָה קַח־נָא אֶת־נַפְשִׁי מִמֶּנִּי כִּי טוֹב מוֹתִי מֵחַיָּ֑י:

And now, O Yahweh, take away my life, I pray thee, from me; for it is better for me to die than to live.[8]

11 אֶעֱשֶׂה אוֹתְךָ לְגוֹי־עָצוּם [9]וָרָב מִמֶּֽנּוּ:

I will make of thee a nation more powerful and numerous than it.[10]

[1] קַח Imp. Qal of לָקַח (§ 33. 3 b).

[2] The pointing of מַה before gutturals is rather more intricate than is suggested by § 13. 3 (see G.K. § 37). Suffice it here to say that before ח and ע, and even when these consonants have not qameç, it is frequently pointed (as here before עַ) as מֶה. Cf. 1 Sam. 20[1] מֶה עָשִׂיתִי מֶה־עֲוֹנִי וּמֶה־חַטָּאתִי *what have I done? what is mine iniquity? and what is my sin?* (But Gen. 31[36] מַה חַטָּאתִי.)

[3] Cstr. inf. Niph. of יָלד, with suffix (§ 39. 2. 1 c)—the day *of one's being born.* Here, in accordance with the Septuagint, where the vb. has no suffix (ὑπὲρ ἡμέραν γεννήσεως), הִוָּלֶדֶת has been proposed (cf. Ezek. 16[4])—the Hoph. inf. cstr. of יָלד. This curious form appears in a more natural form (in the same phrase—*birthday*) in Ezek. 16[5] and Gen. 40[20] as הֻלֶּדֶת—for הֻלֶּדֶת or, in its more strictly normal form, הֻלֶּדֶת (§ 39. 2. 1 f). The strengthened ל might be regarded as a case of an assimilated *yôdh* (§ 39. 3).

[4] Not, of course, than *all*: see sentence 7 (with Note) of Hebrew into English of Exercise 36.

[5] "The person addressed is naturally definite to the mind, and the so-called vocative often has the article: cf. 1 Kings 18[26] הַבַּעַל עֲנֵנוּ 'O Baal, hear us.' Jud. 6[12] יְהוָה עִמְּךָ גִּבּוֹר הֶחָיִל 'Yahweh is with thee, O man of valour'"—the article in the second illustration naturally with the noun that is in the absolute (Grammar, p. 60, Rule 1 b). See Syntax, § 21 f.

[6] Lit. "more bereaved than (other) women"—i.e. bereaved above women. Cf. Jud. 5[24] תְּבֹרַךְ מִנָּשִׁים יָעֵל most blessed of women shall Jael be—Jael shall be blessed (Pu'al) more than (other) women.

[7] The agent after a passive is usually expressed by לְ (§ 25. 5) ; cf. Gen. 14[19] בָּרוּךְ לְאֵל blessed by God. "מִן is usual of cause or means, not personal ; cf. Gen. 9[11] יִכָּרֵת מִמֵּי הַמַּבּוּל 'shall be cut off by the waters of the flood.' בְ (through, of instrum.) is also used of persons : cf. Gen. 9[6] בָּאָדָם דָּמוֹ יִשָּׁפֵךְ 'through man shall his blood be shed.'" Syntax, § 81.

[8] Lit. "my death is better than my life."

[9] Cf. § 15. 1 d. רַב, great, usually in point of numbers, i.e. many, numerous.

[10] i.e. the stiff-necked people (עַם—hence the sing. suffix) mentioned in the preceding verse (Deut. 9[13]).

B.

1 [1]וַיְהִי הַנָּחָשׁ עָרוּם [2]מִכֹּל חַיַּת הַשָּׂדֶה אֲשֶׁר עָשָׂה אֱלֹהִים:
2 הָרַג צַדִּיקִם מִמֶּנּוּ: 3 חָכָם אַתָּה מִדָּנִאֵל: 4 [3]טוֹב הַכֶּלֶב
הַחַי מִן־הָאֲרִי הַמֵּת: 5 וַיְהִי הָאִישׁ הַהוּא גָּדוֹל מִכָּל־בְּנֵי־
קֶדֶם: 6 וַיֶּאֱהַב אֶת־יוֹסֵף מִכָּל־בָּנָיו כִּי־בֶן־זְקֻנִים הוּא לוֹ:
7 וַיִּשָּׂא [4]אֶת־עֵינָיו וַיַּרְא אֶת־אָחִיו בֶּן־אִמּוֹ וַיֹּאמֶר הֲזֶה
אֲחִיכֶם הַקָּטֹן אֲשֶׁר אֲמַרְתֶּם אֵלָי: 8 וְלוֹ [5]שְׁתֵּי בָנוֹת וַתְּהִי
הַקְּטַנָּה יָפָה מִן־הַגְּדוֹלָה: 9 גְּדוֹלֵי הָעִיר: 10 לֹא נִשְׁאַר־לוֹ
כִּי אִם [6]קָטֹן בָּנָיו: 11 וַיְהִי רְכוּשָׁם [7]רַב מִשֶּׁבֶת יַחְדָּו וְלֹא
יָכְלָה הָאָרֶץ [8]לָשֵׂאת אֹתָם:

[1] In Gen. 3[1] this appears as וְהַנָּחָשׁ הָיָה, which is "the usual order of words when a new subject is introduced" (Skinner's Genesis, p. 73). There is nothing, of course, in the sentence, apart from its context, to indicate that the subject is new : hence the customary ויהי in the above translation.

[2] Than *any*, rather than *all* : see Note 4 in section A of this Exercise.

[3] In Eccl. 9⁴ this appears as לְכֶלֶב חַי הוּא טוֹב מִן־הָאַרְיֵה הַמֵּת which may be explained as, "with regard to a living dog, it is better," etc. (though some scholars understand the לְ, on the analogy of the Arabic *la*, as an emphasizing particle=*surely* : see G.K. § 143 *e*). אַרְיֵה is another form of אֲרִי. In the above translation the article is used with both nouns, in accordance with a familiar idiom (see Note 8 of Exercise 14 A) ; in Eccl. it is only used with the latter noun.

[4] In this phrase, אֶת־ (cf. Gen. 13¹⁰ 22⁴, ¹³ 33⁵) is often omitted even in prose (cf. Gen. 18² 24⁶³ 43²⁹).

[5] Cstr., cf. § 48. 1. 5. The absolute would, however, also be possible : cf. 2 Kings 2²⁴ שְׁתַּיִם דֻּבִּים *two she-bears* (from דֹּב, cf. § 43. 1 a—here fem.), 1 Kings 10¹⁹ שְׁנַיִם אֲרָיוֹת *two lions* (pl. of אֲרִי).

[6] This construct of the otherwise indeclinable קָטֹן occurs only once (see Note 14 of Exercise 46 A). On the other hand, as it happens, the constr. sing. of the declinable קָטָן does not occur at all, but we may infer its existence from forms which do occur ; *e.g.* Jon. 3⁵, Jer. 6¹³ קְטַנָּם *the least of them*, and *plur.* cstr. in 1 Sam. 9²¹, Prov. 30²⁴ קְטַנֵּי.

[7] The normal רַב is here (Gen. 36⁷) raised to רָב, because it is accompanied by the accent *ṭiphḥâ* (רָב) which marks a pause preliminary to one of the two great pauses—here athnaḥ—יַחְדָּו (*Grammar*, p. 231 f).

[8] Always לָשֵׂאת, not לִשְׂאֵת (still less לִנְשֹׂא) : see *Grammar*, p. 151, 1 (1) נָשָׂא. The pronominal object to לָשֵׂאת is never added in the form of a pronom. suffix : the pronoun is written separately ; cf. Gen. 45²⁷ (46⁵) *the wagons which Joseph had sent* לָשֵׂאת אֹתוֹ *to carry him*.

§ 48.

A.

1. And he said to his father, My two sons[1] thou mayest[2] slay, if I bring him[3] not to thee. 2. And he took a present for his brother—two hundred she-goats,[4] and twenty rams, and thirty milch[5] camels and their colts.[6] 3. And it came to pass in the six hundred and first year of[7] his life, in the second month, on the twenty-seventh day of[7] the month, the earth was dry. 4. In the thirty-seventh year, in the twelfth month, on the twenty-seventh

(day) of[7] the month, the king of Babylon lifted[8] up the head of the king of Judah out of the prison-house. 5. And the three mighty men[9] broke through the enemy's host, and drew water, and brought it to him, but he refused[10] to drink it.[11] 6. A day in thy courts is better than a thousand. 7. And five of you shall chase[12] a hundred, and a hundred of you shall chase ten thousand. 8. And he said to them, Come out, the three of you;[13] and they came out, the three of them.[13]

9 ¹⁴וַיְחִי אַחֲרֵי־¹⁵זֹאת מֵאָה וְאַרְבָּעִים שָׁנָה ¹⁶וַיַּרְא אֶת־בָּנָיו וְאֶת־בְּנֵי בָנָיו
אַרְבָּעָה ¹⁷דֹּרוֹת:

And after this he lived a hundred and forty years, and he saw his sons and his sons' sons—four generations.

10 ¹⁸וַיִּמְלָךְ־שָׁם שֶׁבַע שָׁנִים וְשִׁשָּׁה חֳדָשִׁים וּשְׁלֹשִׁים וְשָׁלֹשׁ שָׁנָה מָלַךְ
בִּירוּשָׁלָ͏ִם:

And he reigned there seven years and six months, and thirty-three years he reigned in Jerusalem.

[1] Not "two of my sons" ; see Note 4 of Exercise 18 C.

[2] Hiph. of מוּת. This is the concessive or permissive use of the impf. (§ 46. II. 4)—not quite so strong as the imper. slay (הָמֵת or הָמִיתָה) which is the rendering of A.V. and R.V. The impf., of course, is also used where may implies indefiniteness : cf. Exod. 5¹¹ קְחוּ לָכֶם תֶּבֶן מֵאֲשֶׁר תִּמְצָאוּ "get you straw wherever (lit. from what) you may (or can) find it."

[3] Impf. Hiph. of בּוֹא with 3 s. m. suff. and nûn energ. (Gen. 42³⁷). The pf. (=fut. pf.) would also have been possible here—הֲבִיאֹתִיו ; see the similar sentence in Gen. 43⁹, and cf. Note 1 of Exercise 40 B.

[4] Note that in this enumeration the noun comes first, as in an inventory ; but very frequently the numeral precedes.

[5] Hiph. ptc. fem. pl. of ינק (Grammar, p. 223, col. 4): giving suck (lit. causing to suck). The sing. takes the form מֵינֶקֶת, not מֵינִיקָה (=nurse) ; see § 29. 3 b.

[6] Note the use of the masc. pronom. suffix referring to a fem. subject. This irregularity is occasionally found ; e.g. Is. 3¹⁶ the women of Zion בְּרַגְלֵיהֶם תְּעַכַּסְנָה make a tinkling with their feet (where the pronom. suffix is masc., though the vb. is fem.). See Grammar, p. 154, footnote 2, with accompanying sentence. See also end of Note 1 of Exercise 45 D.

[7] ל is customarily used in dates before the second substantive (e.g. month, year, life, reign, captivity, etc.) : e.g. 2 Kings 25²⁷ (sentence 4 of

this Exercise) " in the 37th year *of* the captivity of Jehoiachin " לְגָלֻוֹת
יְהוֹיָכִין (qāmeç in גלות unchangeable), " on the 27th day *of* the month "
לַחֹדֶשׁ. When the word שָׁנָה appears, it is sometimes in the absolute, sometimes in the construct, and sometimes the MSS. vary. *E.g.* 1 Kings 16¹⁰
בִּשְׁנַת עֶשְׂרִים וָשֶׁבַע לְאָסָא *in the 27th year of Asa*, 2 Kings 17⁶
הַתְּשִׁיעִית לְהוֹשֵׁעַ *in the 9th year of Hoshea'* (some MSS. here read בְּשָׁנָה).
So 2 Kings 25¹ בִּשְׁנַת הַתְּשִׁיעִית לְמָלְכוֹ *in the 9th year of his reign* (cstr.
inf. of מלך with suffix) ; but Jer. 52⁴, in practically the same sentence,
בַּשָּׁנָה. The construct, where it occurs, is to be explained on the analogy
of נְהַר פְּרָת *the river Euphrates*, בְּתוּלַת יִשְׂרָאֵל *the virgin Israel* (not *of*
Israel), Am. 5², where the absolute is a nearer definite of the construct.

⁸ *i.e.* lifted to gladness and honour. In Gen. 40 there is a play on
the double sense of this phrase : in 40¹³ the butler's head is lifted up,
i.e. he is restored to his office ; in 40²⁰ the baker's head is lifted up (by
hanging, v.²² ; or lifted " from off him," by decapitation, v.¹⁹).

⁹ Not " three of the mighty men." See Note 1 of this section.

¹⁰ לֹא אבה, like its Septuagint equivalent οὐκ ἠθέλησεν, is more than
" he was not willing."

¹¹ Plur. suffix, agreeing with מִים.

¹² וְרָדְפוּ well illustrates the use of pf. with waw consec. ; it is exactly
= the impf. ירדפו at the end of the verse.

¹³ שְׁלִשָׁת takes suffixes on the exact analogy of קְטֹרֶת (cf. בְּקֹר),
Grammar, pp. 101 f.

¹⁴ From חָיָה *to live*, not to be confused with הָיָה *to be* (*Grammar,*
p. 148, line 3).

¹⁵ For fem. (=τοῦτο), cf. § 16. 4. 7.

¹⁶ In Job 42¹⁶ this is pointed וַיִּרְאֶה (=וַיִּרְאֶה). But the consonantal
text, which is without the ה, should doubtless be pointed וַיֵּרֶא. See
Note 1 of Exercise 45 A.

¹⁷ רוּחוֹת, despite its fem. termination, is *masc.*, because the *sing.* is
masc., § 16. 4. 6 (last two lines) ; hence אַרְבָּעָה is in the *fem.*, § 48. 1. 3 a.

¹⁸ So, rather than שָׁם וַיִּמְלֹךְ (§ 10. 3 a).

B.

1 הָלְכוּ עִמּוֹ חֲמֵשֶׁת אֶחָיו וּשְׁלֹשׁ אַחְיוֹתָיו ¹בֵּית אֲבִיהֶם :
2 ²שִׁשִּׁים וְאַרְבַּע שָׁנָה מָלְכָה הַמַּלְכָּה וַתָּמָת ³בַּת־שְׁמֹנִים
וּשְׁתַּיִם שָׁנָה וְלָהּ אַרְבָּעָה בָנִים וְחָמֵשׁ בָּנוֹת וְאִישָׁהּ מֵת

⁴ בְּאַרְבָּעִים וּשְׁתַּיִם שָׁנָה ⁵לְחַיֶּיהָ ⁶וּבִשְׁנַת עֶשְׂרִים וְאַרְבַּע שָׁנָה
⁷לְמָלְכָהּ: 3 וַיִּוָּלְדוּ לוֹ שְׁלֹשָׁה בָנִים ⁸וָשֶׁבַע בָּנוֹת וַיְהִי
⁹מִקְנֵהוּ שֶׁבַע ¹⁰אֲלָפִים צֹאן וְאַרְבַּעַת אֲלָפִים גְּמַלִּים וּשְׁבַע
מֵאוֹת ¹¹חֲמוֹרִים: 4 יְמֵי שְׁנֵי חַיֵּי ¹²אַרְבַּע שָׁנִים וְשִׁבְעִים
שָׁנָה: 5 בְּאַרְצוֹ ¹³הָיוּ ¹⁴מֵאָה עֶשְׂרִים וָשֶׁבַע עָרִים וּבְאַחַת
¹⁵הֶעָרִים ¹⁶הָאֵלֶּה שְׁתֵּים־עֶשְׂרֵה ¹⁷רִבְבוֹת אָדָם: 6 טוֹב
הַחֲצִי מִן־הַכֹּל: 7 וַיֹּאמְרוּ אִישׁ אֶל־¹⁸אָחִיו נִשָּׁבְעָה ¹⁹שָׁנִינוּ
בְּשֵׁם אֱלֹהֵינוּ וַיִּשָּׁבְעוּ שְׁנֵיהֶם:

---

¹ ל is found after הלך, בוא, and שׁוב; *e.g.* 1 Sam. 10²⁶ הָלַךְ לְבֵיתוֹ
he went to his house; but אל is commoner (see sentence 6 of Exercise
49 A). Often, however, as in the above sentence, the simple accus. is
used (*i.e.* without any prepos.): *e.g.* 2 Sam. 13⁸ וַתֵּלֶךְ בֵּית אָחִיהָ *and she
went to her brother's house*, 2 Sam. 4⁷ וַיָּבֹאוּ הַבַּיִת *and they went into
the house*. The *He locale* is also common (though very rarely as a
construct, § 17. 3; cf. Gen. 44¹⁴ וַיָּבֹא בֵּיתָה יוֹסֵף *and he went into the
house of Joseph*), *e.g.* Gen. 24³² וַיָּבֹא הַבַּיְתָה *and he went into the house*,
2 Sam. 17¹⁷ לָבוֹא הָעִירָה *to come into the city*, Gen. 44¹³ וַיָּשֻׁבוּ הָעִירָה
and they returned to the city.

² In the Book of Kings, the years of the reign precede the vb., and
the tens precede the units.

³ Note that "so many years old" is rendered by "*son*" or "*daughter*
of so many years." Cf. Deut. 34⁷ מֹשֶׁה בֶּן־מֵאָה וְעֶשְׂרִים שָׁנָה בְּמֹתוֹ *Moses
was one hundred and twenty years old when he died*: 2 Kings 15²
בֶּן־שֵׁשׁ עֶשְׂרֵה שָׁנָה הָיָה בְמָלְכוֹ *he was sixteen years old when he began to
reign* (cstr. inf.). Gen. 17¹⁷ שָׂרָה בַּת־תִּשְׁעִים שָׁנָה *Sarah that is ninety
years old*. In 2 Kings 15² occurs חֲמִשִּׁים וּשְׁתַּיִם שָׁנָה, *fifty-two years*;
so 2 Kings 10¹⁴ אַרְבָּעִים וּשְׁנַיִם אִישׁ *forty-two men*. It is interesting to
note, however, that with the same number in 2 Kings 2²⁴ the construct
of *two* is used, ארבעים וּשְׁנֵי יְלָדִים *forty-two lads*. See Note 5 of Ex. 47 B.

⁴ Cf. Neh. 6¹⁵ חֲמִשִּׁים וּשְׁנַיִם יוֹם *fifty-two days*.

⁵ For ל here and with מָלְכוֹ, see Note 7 in section A of this Exercise.

⁶ For this construction, with the repetition of the word *year*, see
2 Kings 15¹· ⁸· ¹⁷.

⁷ Cstr. inf. of מלך with suffix. מַלְכוּת is a late word for *reign*, found

chiefly in Chron., Esther, and Dan., and therefore here avoided. For לְמַלְכוּ, see 2 Kings 24[12] 25[1].

[8] For וְ in the pre-tone (cf. 2 Kings 15[1]), see § 15. 1 d; so וְתֵשַׁע; but וְשֶׁבַע and וְתֵשַׁע are also found.

[9] The general word for *cattle*. רְכֻשׁוֹ might also have been used: רְכֻשׁ *property*, often including cattle.

[10] In Job 1[3] the construct אַלְפֵי is used; but this is much rarer than the absolute. The sing. is also used, cf. Isa. 37[36] מֵאָה וּשְׁמֹנִים וַחֲמִשָּׁה אֶלֶף *185,000*—also when it is followed by a substantive; cf. 2 Sam. 24[9] חֲמֵשׁ־מֵאוֹת אֶלֶף אִישׁ *500,000 men*.

[11] Or אֲתֹנוֹת if *she-asses*.

[12] For the repetition of שָׁנָה, cf. Gen. 12[4] בֶּן־חָמֵשׁ שָׁנִים וְשִׁבְעִים שָׁנָה *seventy-five years old*.

[13] Cf. the sentence in Gen. 47[9a], where the vb. is omitted. In the similar sentence Gen. 47[28b], the vb. appears (וַיְהִי), and 47[9b]—a little dissimilar—also adds הָיוּ.

[14] This same number, one hundred and twenty-seven, appears in Esth. 1[1] 8[9] (a late book) in the order *seven and twenty and a hundred* (מֵאָה): cf. the similar order in Gen. 47[28], Exod. 6[16. 18] (P), where *hundred* is in the constr. מְאַת. In the lists in Ezra 2 and Neh. 7 the order is usually as above, with the *hundred*(s) first, and with no *waw* before the *tens*.

[15] So Deut. 19[5. 11]; also 2 Sam. 2[1] אַחַת עָרֵי יְהוּדָה *one of the cities of Judah*. In Deut. 4[42], however, אַחַת מִן־הֶעָרִים, cf. Gen. 2[21] אַחַת מִצַּלְעֹתָיו *one of his ribs*. See Note 20 of Exercise 46 B.

[16] הָאֵלֶּה rather than הָהֵם; cf. Deut. 4[42] 19[5. 11], 1 Kings 9[13].

[17] For this, in Jonah 4[11] the later Aramaizing form רִבּוֹ appears. The number might also have been written מֵאָה וְעֶשְׂרִים אֶלֶף (cf. Isa. 37[36], quoted in Note 10).

[18] Or רֵעֵהוּ (§ 45. 4).

[19] Not שָׁנֵינוּ, although the שׁ is pretonic, because the absolute is שָׁנִים.

§ 49.

A.

1. Whither shall I go from thy spirit? 2. Whence[1] shall my help come? 3. And he wept;[2] and thus he said,

as he went,[3] O that I[4] had died instead of thee,[5] my son.
4. Far be it from me,[6] O Yahweh,[7] that I should do[8] this
thing:[9] (shall I drink)[10] the blood of the men who went at
the risk of their lives?   5. Entreat[11] Yahweh your God that
he may remove[12] this death[13] from me.[14]   6. Thou shalt
assuredly go[15] to my father's house and take a wife for my
son.   7. Surely I will not take of anything that is thine.
8. Which is better for you—(is it) that seventy men rule[16]
over you or that one man rule over you?

9 וַיִּשָּׁבַע לָהּ שָׁאוּל בַּיהוָה לֵאמֹר[17] חַי־יְהוָה אִם־[18]יִקְּרֵךְ[19] עָוֺן[20] בַּדָּבָר הַזֶּה:
[24]וַתֵּרֶא הָאִשָּׁה אֶת־[25]שְׁמוּאֵל וַתִּזְעַק בְּקוֹל גָּדוֹל וַיֹּאמֶר לָהּ הַמֶּלֶךְ אַל־ [23]הַעֲלִי־לִי:
וַתֹּאמֶר הָאִשָּׁה אֶת־מִי[21] אַעֲלֶה־[22]לָּךְ וַיֹּאמֶר אֶת־שְׁמוּאֵל
[26]תִּירְאִי כִּי מָה רָאִית וַתֹּאמֶר הָאִשָּׁה[27] אֱלֹהִים רָאִיתִי עֹלִים מִן־הָאָרֶץ:

And Saul swore to her by Yahweh, saying, As Yahweh
    liveth, there shall no punishment befall thee for this
    thing.   Then the woman said, Whom shall I bring
    up for thee?   And he said, Bring me up Samuel.
    And when the woman saw Samuel, she cried with a
    loud voice.   But the king said to her, Be not afraid;
    for what didst thou see?   And the woman said, I
    saw a god coming up out of the earth.

[1] This אַיִן, which has no connexion with the negative אַיִן meaning
(there) is not, no (Grammar, p. 136, footnote 1), is never found alone, but
always in the combination מֵאַיִן whence? (interrog.). The word for
where? (interrog.) is אַיֵּה. This is the lengthened form of אִי (cf. הִנֵּה
from הֵן), which, however, is never found by itself, but only with pronom.
suffixes, e.g. אַיּוֹ where is he? אַיָּם where are they? The form אֵי is
found four times (e.g. Gen. 4[9] אֵי אָחִיךָ where is thy brother?); in
every other case it is accompanied by the enclitic זֶה where, then? (even
in indirect quotations, e.g. 1 Sam. 9[18] הַגִּידָה־נָּא לִי אֵי־זֶה בֵּית הָרֹאֶה tell
me, I pray thee, where the seer's house is), or by מִזֶּה, e.g. Job 2[2] אֵי מִזֶּה
תָּבֹא whence comest thou? Jon. 1[8] אֵי־מִזֶּה עַם אָתָּה whence, as regards
people, art thou? i.e. of what people art thou?

[2] וַיֵּבְךְּ; see § 45. 1. (1). c.

[3] לְכִתּוֹ, not לְכתוֹ (§ 39. 2. 2. (d) i)—inf. cstr. of הלך with 3 s. m. suffix.

[4] "Observe in what follows the feeling which David throws into the
expression of his sorrow by the addition of the pronoun אָנִי," Driver,

Notes on the Hebrew Text of the Books of Samuel (2 Sam. 19¹). For
the addition of the pronoun to emphasize a pronominal suffix, see
Note 1 of Exercise 29 A.

⁵ For suffixes to תַּחַת, see *Grammar*, p. 121, first two lines.

⁶ Note the dagh. forte in the לְ after חלילה (see Note 28 of Exercise
33 B).

⁷ General usage (cf. 1 Sam. 26¹¹) and the parallel passage in 1 Chron.
11¹⁹ מֵאֱלֹהַי combine to suggest that the true reading here is מֵיהוָה,
which is found in some MSS.

⁸ *Yahweh forbid it me.* The act deprecated is expressed by מִן
followed by the inf. cstr.

⁹ Fem. ; cf. § 16. 4. 7.

¹⁰ The omission of the vb. is strange and difficult ; the Chronicler
supplies it (1 Chr. 11¹⁹ אֶשְׁתֶּה), but his sentence is awkward. Perhaps
the original reading was זֶה דָם or הוּא דָם *it is the blood* of the men, etc.

¹¹ The impf. Qal (יֶעְתַּר), the Niph. (נֶעְתַּר) and the Hiph. (אַעְתִּיר, 1 s.
impf.) of עתר always have the first syllable closed (§ 34. 2 c). This vb. is
followed by לְ or אֶל.

¹² Simple waw with *jussive* Hiph. of סוּר—§ 23. 3. 6. Cf. sentence 2
of Exercise 44 A and Note.

¹³ *i.e.* this deadly plague (of locusts, Exod. 10¹⁷).

¹⁴ Hebrew more expressively "from *upon* me"—this *crushing*
deadly plague. Cf. Note 9 of Exercise 38 B.

¹⁵ אִם and אִם לֹא often used in oaths, or as here (cf. Gen. 24³⁸) in
adjurations. See Note 8 of Exercise 41 A.

¹⁶ הַמְשֹׁל is not, of course, the Hiph. (which it could not be), but the
inf. cstr. Qal of מָשַׁל with the interrog. ה. Note the order in both these
clauses—the בכם immediately after the vb., and the subj. of the inf.
cstr. after that. See Note 5 of Exercise 36 C.

¹⁷ Note the phrase חַי־יְהוָה וְחֵי נַפְשֶׁךָ (1 Sam. 20³ 25²⁶) *as Yahweh
liveth and as thy soul* (*i.e.* thou) *liveth.* "It is evidently only a rabbinical
refinement which makes the pronunciation חַי distinctive of an oath by
God (or of God by himself)." G.K., p. 270, footnote 1.

¹⁸ 3 s. m. impf. Qal (יִקְרֶה) of קָרָה, with 2 s. *fem.* suffix (referring to
the witch, 1 Sam. 28¹⁰). The daghesh forte, which seems surprising, is
the *dagh. f. dirimens* (§ 7. 6), a device to secure the more audible
enunciation of the sheʷa. It is used occasionally with לְ, מ, נ, ר, ק (as
here), and the sibilants: cf. עִנְּבֵי (for עִנְבֵי cstr. pl. of עֵנָב *grape*),
קַשְּׁתוֹתָם Ps 37¹⁵ (*their bows* from קֶשֶׁת *a bow*: note the ending ם ,,
Grammar, p. 69, vi.), הַצְּפִינוֹ Exod. 2³ (for הַצְפִינוֹ *to hide him,* Hiph. of
צפן).

¹⁹ עָוֺן (as sometimes also חֵטְא) may mean *punishment,* as well as
iniquity, guilt.

[20] Besides meaning *word*, דָּבָר not seldom means *matter* (here "in this matter"), *affair*, *thing*. See Note 3 of Exercise 44 B.

[21] 1 s. impf. Hiph. of עלה (pf. הֶעֱלָה): the Qal would be אֶעֱלֶה.

[22] Note the dagh. forte (see. Note 28 of Exercise 33 B).

[23] Imperat. sing. fem. ; masc. (הַעֲלֵה =) הַעַל, always found in this form (§ 45. 1. 3).

[24] Cf. § 45. 1. (4). See Note 6 of Exercise 45 B.

[25] Perhaps the true reading here (so 1 Sam. 28¹²) is שָׁאוּל, which is found in four Greek MSS. "When she *looked at Saul*." So W. O. E. Oesterley, *Immortality and the Unseen World*, pp. 68 f.

[26] 2 s. f. jussive of יָרֵא (§ 39. 2. 2 *a*).

[27] Notice the order—the emphatic אֱלֹהִים put first: it was a god that I saw. וַתְּחַסְּרֵהוּ מְעַט a superhuman being or beings: cf. Ps. 8⁶ אֱלֹהִים *and thou* (Yahweh) *didst make him to lack* (Pi. of חִסֵּר) *little of the* superhuman or *divine beings* (not *God*, which makes no sense, as God [Yahweh] is being addressed). In the Samuel passage the word is applied to the shade of Samuel: this would seem to imply that at this time the dead, or at least the great dead, like Samuel, were regarded as superhuman or divine (and perhaps worshipped?).

B.

1 וַיֹּאמֶר אֵלֶיהָ בִּתִּי הֲתֵלְכִי עִם־הָאִישׁ הַזֶּה אִם תֵּשְׁבִי ¹עִמָּדִי וַתֹּאמֶר אֶהְיֶה אָבִי לֹא ²אוּכַל לָשֶׁבֶת עִמָּךְ : 2 אָנָּא אֶבְרַח ³מִפָּנֶיךָ : 3 הַאַתָּה בְּנִי אִם־לֹא : 4 מִי־יִתֵּן מוּתֵנוּ בְיַד־יְהוָֹה ⁴בְּאֶרֶץ בָּבֶל בְּשִׁבְתֵּנוּ ⁵וּבְכִינוּ עַל־מֵימֶיהָ : 5 נִשְׁבַּעְתִּי בְאַפִּי אִם־⁶תָבֹאוּן אֶל־מְנוּחָתִי : 6 לֹא־יָמוּשׁ סֵפֶר הַתּוֹרָה הַזֶּה מִפִּיךָ וְהָגִיתָ בּוֹ יוֹמָם וָלַיְלָה לְמַעַן תִּשְׁמֹר לַעֲשׂוֹת כְּכָל־הַכָּתוּב בּוֹ ⁷וְדִבַּרְתָּ ⁸בּוֹ לְבָנֶיךָ אַחֲרֶיךָ בְּשִׁבְתְּךָ ⁹בְּבֵיתֶךָ ¹⁰וּבְלֶכְתְּךָ בַדֶּרֶךְ : 7 ¹¹לֹא יִיעַף אֱלֹהִים וְלֹא יִיגָע אִם תַּאֲמִינוּ בוֹ אֵיךְ תֹּאמְרוּ נִסְתְּרָה דַרְכִּי מֵאֱלֹהָי : כִּי ¹²זָכַר כִּי עָפָר אֲנַחְנוּ ¹³וְלֹחַ הוּא ¹⁴נֹתֵן ¹⁵לַיָּגֵעַ ¹⁶אֲשֶׁר יִבְטַח בּוֹ :

<hr/>

[1] On עִמִּי or אִתִּי (*Grammar*, p. 142, footnote 1). Both אֵת and עִם are used with יָשַׁב ; cf. Gen. 29¹⁹ שְׁבָה עִמָּדִי , 1 Sam 22²³ שְׁבָה אִתִּי *abide with me* (שְׁבָה emphatic form of imper. שֵׁב, § 23. 2).

[2] Impf. Qal of יָבֹל (*Grammar*, p. 152. 2. 5). יבֹל is usually followed by לְ (see Note 6 of Exercise 22 B, Note 10 of Exercise 45 C ; but see Num. 22³⁸ quoted in Note 3 of Exercise 44 B).

[3] In Ps. 139⁷ the last two words are transposed, doubtless simply for the sake of varying the more customary order of the first clause אָנָא אֵלֵךְ מֵרוּחֶךָ.

[4] The absolute בָּאָרֶץ might seem more natural, as a pure apposition. But Hebrew prefers to say "the land *of* Egypt, Canaan," etc. ; *i.e.* the construct may sometimes express apposition with the following word : cf. 1 Sam. 28⁷ אֵשֶׁת בַּעֲלַת־אוֹב *a woman, possessor of a soothsaying spirit* (see Note 7 of Exercise 48 A).

[5] "The construction of the infinitive with a preposition is almost always continued in the further course of the narrative by means of the *finite verb, i.e.* by an independent sentence, not by a co-ordinate infinitive" (G.K. § 114 *r*). The tense of the second vb. takes the sequence which it would take if the first vb. were finite : *e.g.* Gen. 39¹⁸ *and it came to pass* כַּהֲרִימִי קוֹלִי וָאֶקְרָא *as I lifted up my voice and cried* (exactly= כַּאֲשֶׁר הֲרִימֹתִי קוֹלִי ואקרא : Hiph. of רום); so 2 Kings 18³² עַד־אֲשֶׁר אָבוֹא =) עַד־בֹּאִי וְלָקַחְתִּי אֶתְכֶם *until I (shall) come and take you* (וְלָקַחְתִּי), Am. 1¹¹ עַל־רָדְפוֹ אָחִיו וְשִׁחֵת רַחֲמָיו (on account of his pursuing, *i.e.*) *because he pursued his brother and destroyed his compassion* (the waw consec. with the pf.—Pi'el—implies a preceding *impf.* in the *frequentative* sense ; cf. § 46. III., יִרְדֹּף *repeatedly* pursued). The latter construction has been followed in the translated sentence—"when we *used to* sit and weep" כִּי נֵשֵׁב וּבָכִינוּ (or כַּאֲשֶׁר). If the sitting and weeping referred to a single occasion, we should write בְּשִׁבְתֵּנוּ וַנֵּבְכֶּה.

[6] The form ן with the so-called *nûn paragogicum* (cf. Ps. 95¹¹ יְבֹאוּן) is occasionally found. "It usually expresses marked emphasis," and it bears the tone; hence not יָבֹאן (though, of course, we write יְבֹאוּ). It is found with the 2nd and 3rd plu. masc. ; also, but seldom, with the 2nd sing. fem. (ין). In pause the preceding vowel is lengthened, *e.g.* Exod. 15¹⁴ יִרְגָּזוּן *they tremble*.

[7] Waw consec. with pf. after the preceding impf. following לְמַעַן.

[8] For בְּ in the sense of *about, concerning*, after דִבֵּר (Pi.), cf. Deut. 3²⁶ 6⁷ 11¹⁹, 1 Sam. 19³. More commonly the object *about* which one speaks is indicated by עַל. See Note 13 of Exercise 41 A.

[9] In Deut. 6⁷ 11¹⁹ this is written as בְּבֵיתֶךָ. The accent over the last consonant is the *pashṭâ*, a so-called *post-positive* accent, *i.e.* one placed over or under the last consonant of a word (as the *pre-positive* accents are placed over or under the first). Occasionally (as here) a pausal change occurs in connexion with this accent, like the change chiefly

associated with *sillûq* and *athnâḥ* (G.K. § 29 *i*). "If the word in question has the tone on the penultima, *pashṭâ* is placed over it also: *e.g.* Gen. I² תֹּהוּ " (G.K., p. 60, footnote 1).

[10] See Note 3 in section A of this Exercise.

[11] *Never* is suggested by the impf.—not *at any time.*

[12] In Ps. 103¹⁴ this appears as זָכוּר, which may be regarded as the pass. ptc. Qal (*he bethinketh him*, or *is reminded*); or with Gesenius-Kautzsch (§ 50 *f*) as another form of word (not to be confused with the pass. ptc.), sometimes found with intransitive vbs., to denote an inherent quality; cf. עָצוּם *strong*; Ps. 112⁷ בָּטוּחַ *trustful.* The Septuagint, however, took it as imperat. μνήσθητι (=זְכֹר) *remember.* In view of the יָדַע in the first clause, Briggs proposes to read the simple pf. זָכַר *he remembers.*

[13] For this order (object first) with the ptc., cf. Jud. 9³⁶ אֵת צֵל הֶהָרִים אַתָּה רֹאֶה כָּאֲנָשִׁים *the shadow of the mountains thou seest as men* ; cf. Gen. 16⁸, Isa. 1⁷.

[14] *Evermore* is suggested by the ptc. ; cf. Ps 1⁶ כִּי־יוֹדֵעַ יְהוָה דֶּרֶךְ צַדִּיקִים *for Yahweh careth evermore for the way of the righteous.*

[15] With such words (cf. דַּל *weak*, עָנִי *afflicted*, *poor*) the sing. (so Isa. 40²⁹) and the plur. are both found—the sing. perhaps more frequently : cf. the recurring phrase *the sojourner, the fatherless, and the widow* (Deut. 14²⁹, etc.).

[16] אֲשֶׁר might be omitted. In prose, after an indeterminate substantive, and in poetry also after a determinate substantive, אֲשֶׁר is not seldom omitted. *E.g.* Gen. 15¹³ בְּאֶרֶץ לֹא לָהֶם *in a land* (*which*) *is not theirs;* Ps. 34⁹ אַשְׁרֵי הַגֶּבֶר יֶחֱסֶה־בּוֹ (O the happinesses of=) *happy is the man* (*that*) *takes refuge in him.* This omission is equally possible whether the English relative which would introduce such a clause be subj. or obj. In the illustrations given, it is subj., in Isa. 42¹⁶ it is obj.— בְּדֶרֶךְ לֹא יָדְעוּ *in a way* (*which*) *they know not.* (Note here the pausal effect of the accent *zaqeph qaṭon* ; see Note 22 of Exercise 34 A, and Note 8 of Exercise 43 B.) Sometimes the retrospective pronoun is expressed, *e.g.* as pronom. suffix to vb., cf. Deut. 32¹⁷ אֱלֹהִים לֹא יְדָעוּם *gods* (*whom*) *they knew not.* For other illustrations of omission of אֲשֶׁר see sentence 7 of Exercise 19 B, sentence 13 of Exercise 20 A, and sentence 6 of Exercise 38 B.

INDEX OF SUBJECTS.

(The first number represents the number of the Exercise, the letter in the middle represents the section of the Exercise, and the last number represents the number of the Note.)

INDEX OF HEBREW WORDS AND FORMS.

(The first number represents the number of the Exercise, the letter in the middle represents the section of the Exercise, and the last number represents the number of the Note.)

140

INDEX OF PASSAGES.

(The first number represents the number of the Exercise, the letter in the middle represents the section of the Exercise, and the last number represents the number of the Note.)

be retu   r before